PUBLIC POLICY
An Evolutionary Approach

PUBLIC POLICY
An Evolutionary Approach

JAMES P. LESTER
Colorado State University

JOSEPH STEWART, JR.
University of Texas at Dallas

WEST PUBLISHING COMPANY

Minneapolis/St. Paul   New York   Los Angeles   San Francisco

Text Design: © Lois Stanfield, LightSource Images
Copyeditor: Kathy Pruno
Composition: Carlisle Communications, Inc.
Index: Gerald Thomas
Photo Credit: **1, 59, 153,** and **233** AP/Wide World Photos

WEST'S COMMITMENT TO THE ENVIRONMENT

In 1906, West Publishing Company began recycling materials left over from the production of books. This began a tradition of efficient and responsible use of resources. Today, 100% of our legal bound volumes are printed on acid-free, recycled paper consisting of 50% new paper pulp and 50% paper that has undergone a de-inking process. We also use vegetable-based inks to print all of our books. West recycles nearly 27, 700,000 pounds of scrap paper annually—the equivalent of 229,300 trees. Since the 1960s, West has devised ways to capture and recycle waste inks, solvents, oils, and vapors created in the printing process. We also recycle plastics of all kinds, wood, glass, corrugated cardboard, and batteries, and have eliminated the use of polystyrene book packaging. We at West are proud of the longevity and the scope of our commitment to the environment.

West pocket parts and advance sheets are printed on recyclable paper and can be collected and recycled with newspapers. Staples do not have to be removed. Bound volumes can be recycled after removing the cover.

Production, Prepress, Printing and Binding by West Publishing Company

TEXT IS PRINTED ON 10% POST CONSUMER RECYCLED PAPER

Printed with **Printwise** ∞
Environmentally Advanced Water Washable Ink

British Library Cataloguing-in-Publication Data. A catalogue record for this book is available from the British Library.

Copyright © 1996 by **West Publishing Company**
610 Opperman Drive
P.O. Box 64526
St. Paul, MN 55164-0526

LIBRARY OF CONGRESS CATALOGING-IN-PUBLICATION DATA
Lester, James P., 1944–
        Public policy: an evolutionary approach / James P. Lester, Joseph
Stewart, Jr.
                p. cm
        Includes bibliographical references and index.
        ISBN 0-314-06750-7 (soft: alk. paper)
        1. Policy sciences. 2. Policy sciences—United States.
    I. Stewart, Joseph, 1951– . II. Title.
    H97.L473 1996
    320'.6—dc20   95-51040
                                                                   CIP

To William Howard Lester
and Paula F. Sutherland

ABOUT THE AUTHORS

James P. Lester is Professor of Political Science at Colorado State University. He received his Ph.D. from the George Washington University in 1980 and has also taught at Texas A&M University, the University of Kentucky, the University of Oklahoma, and Denver University. He is the author or coauthor of over sixty publications in the areas of public policy and environmental studies. His most recent book is *Environmental Politics and Policy: Theories and Evidence,* Second Edition (Duke University Press, 1995).

Joseph Stewart, Jr., is Professor of Government and Politics at the University of Texas at Dallas. He received his Ph.D. from the University of Houston in 1977 and has also taught at the University of New Orleans and West Virginia University. He is the author or coauthor of over forty publications in the areas of public policy and American politics. His most recent book (with Paula McClain) is *Can We All Get Along? Racial and Ethnic Minorities in American Politics* (WestviewPress, 1995).

CONTENTS

PREFACE

For several reasons, this is a particularly exciting time to study public policy. Moreover, it is likely to continue to be so for the foreseeable future. First, public policy studies have become one of the fastest growing subfields in political science. In less than twenty-five years, we have seen enormous growth in student interest in this area, in the course offerings at both undergraduate and graduate levels, in the graduate programs and policy institutes, and in the research conducted in this subfield. Second, the existing literature on policy studies has witnessed enormous intellectual growth over the past two decades, and many new conceptual developments have occurred. Finally, the nature of American public policy increasingly requires policy analysis as a guide to policy design and redesign. Governments at all levels (i.e., federal, state, and local) will continue to need advice from policy analysts in the years to come as policy debates continue to proliferate in such areas as welfare reform, environmental problems, crime policy, and educational reforms.

Yet, even though many areas of the policy cycle have witnessed significant intellectual growth as far as understanding the determinants of each phase, the major problem for students of public policy (and perhaps the major challenge for teachers) is that a sense of *history* is missing in most contemporary policy analysis texts. So little of this evolutionary development has been accumulated in a single textbook that students may not fully appreciate the amount of intellectual growth that has taken place over the last twenty-five years. In addition, to appreciate more fully the extent of policy evolution, it is necessary to examine substantive policy across time. Most recently, a number of scholars have suggested that we may gain a substantially better understanding of the contours of public policy by examining public policy changes over a period of at least a decade. By doing so, we begin to appreciate how systematic patterns have developed over time and across several areas of policy.

This book offers a unique approach to introducing students to policy studies by using a diachronic or evolutionary approach so that the student may fully appreciate the dynamic developments that have taken place in our understanding of both the policy process and several substantive areas of public policy. In fact, one of the clearest trends to emerge in the entire discipline of political science over the past twenty-five years is the need for historical or longitudinal versus contemporary or cross-sectional analysis. Therefore, we explicitly adopt the position that we can more fully appreciate and understand public policy developments by viewing them from an historical or evolutionary perspective. This simply means that we propose to use an historical (or longitudinal) approach in a conceptual, rather than a statistical, sense.

In developing this theme, the book is organized by four sections. The first section of the book introduces the student to the subfield of policy studies and notes several tensions in the field. It also discusses alternative approaches to policy analysis, what we mean by "models" and means of evaluating models. The second section of the book is devoted to an understanding of the evolution of research and thinking about various aspects of the policy cycle, noting the evolution of our conceptual understanding from the origin of the concept of each stage to the present time. The third section of the book explores the evolution of our thinking in four substantive areas of public policy, including education, welfare, crime, and the environment. This section provides an analysis of public policy from an historical perspective and thus complements our approach in the other two sections by drawing together the various trends identified earlier. The final section provides an explanation about the tendency for policy analyses to be utilized (or not to be utilized) by decision-makers and draws conclusions from the other three sections with regard to the evolution of public policy and policy studies.

A number of individuals have helped to make this book a reality. First, we owe an enormous intellectual debt to numerous scholars who, over the past two decades, have contributed greatly to our own intellectual development. Among these are (alphabetically): James Anderson, Charles Bullock, Richard Cole, Peter DeLeon, William Dunn, Malcolm Goggin, David Hedge, Richard Hofferbert, Hank Jenkins-Smith, Helen Ingram, Michael Kraft, Dean Mann, Daniel Mazmanian, Henry Nau, Walter Rosenbaum, Paul Sabatier, Harvey Tucker, Richard Waterman, and David Webber, among others. By their prolific writings, and often their willingness to provide constructive comments on our work, they have contributed in a very direct way to whatever success this book enjoys. We are very grateful for their help.

Second, several external reviewers offered their constructive criticisms and advice, including Les Alm, Brian Cook, Charles Davis, Bernie Kolasa, John Piskulich, Andrew Skalaban, and James Wunsch. We adopted many of their suggestions, and the book is much improved as a consequence. We extend our sincere thanks to all of them for their helpful advice.

We are also grateful for the encouragement and assistance we received from West Publishing Company. Several individuals, including Steve Schonebaum, Jana Otto Hiller, and Carrie Kish, provided a great deal of help which made this book much better than it otherwise might have been.

Finally, we are indebted to our families for creating an environment within which we were able to work. This book is dedicated to special members of our families who have stood by us in difficult times in years past. Of course, we are also appreciative of the support and encouragement we have received over the years from our students in public policy studies. It is our hope that this book will further enhance their perspectives and understanding about American public policy. Lastly, we will, of course, blame all errors and omissions contained in the following book on each other, or, as a residual category, on Paul Sabatier.

James P. Lester and Joseph Stewart, Jr.

PART ONE

THE CONTEXT OF PUBLIC POLICY STUDIES

THE NATURE OF PUBLIC POLICY

"The farther backward we can look, the better we can see ahead."
SIR WINSTON CHURCHILL

Every day national, state, and local newspapers carry stories that raise important public policy issues. How should public schools be financed? Is affirmative action fair? Are current welfare programs encouraging, reducing, or having no impact on poverty in the United States? What is the impact of capital punishment on crime? Are current environmental initiatives adequate, not enough, or too much to protect the environment? These are but a few of the public policy issues that have provoked exciting debates at national, state, and local levels. As society becomes increasingly interdependent and mobile because of changes in transportation and communication, people will need to be even more knowledgeable about public policy issues.

For example, at the national level, the ascendency of the Republicans in Congress has reopened debates about why poverty exists, how it should be measured, and what "welfare" is. Although welfare has always been a contentious issue, fundamental issues are now being readdressed, pitting liberals against conservatives, and raising questions about the rationale for programs that subsidize the poor.

At the state level, educational debates have emerged over how to make education more meaningful to a diverse population of blacks, Hispanics, and other minorities that increasingly comprise the population. For example, at the secondary level, this issue has pitted the "back-to-basics" group against the "globalists." The elementary grades are now concerned with the merits (and demerits) of restructuring their educational systems to meet the needs of a diverse population of various ethnic groups. At the college level, we have seen increased incidents of campus intolerance, as courses on cultural diversity have pitted the proponents of a "politically correct" way of speaking about racial and gender issues against the National Association of Scholars (NAS). The latter group believes that the banner of "cultural diversity" is being used by some whose paramount interest actually lies in attacking and denigrating Western culture and its institutions. This debate has spawned an "academic resistance" movement that opposes the new doctrine of multiculturalism. The struggle between these two groups is affecting the nature of public policy for higher education in the 1990s.[1]

At the local level, the "new federalism" of the 1980s and 1990s has made the policy debates even more important as jurisdictions struggle to decide which programs should be cut and which should be retained. Should taxes be raised to cover the costs of environmental and other programs that experienced cutbacks under President Reagan's "new federalism" and the decentralization of social programs? Should funds be shifted from low priority areas to those of higher priority? Should programs be cut? If so, which ones?

The above discussion clearly shows that public policy is more important now than ever before for a variety of reasons. First, from a purely **scientific** perspective, a better understanding of the causes and consequences of public policy would allow us to make policy recommendations that might improve the performance of national, state, and local governments in an era in which the public is demanding "better" government. For example, we could use the information generated by social science to suggest remedies that could alleviate many of the problems posed by educational inadequacies, poverty, crime, or pollution.

From a **political** perspective, this information would allow us to identify which states or cities are more successful or are lagging behind in their efforts to alleviate public policy problems. Such information would allow voters to reelect representatives who fight for the public interest or to throw out incompetent legislators. Indeed, some argue that policy analysts should not attempt to be "value free," but should help to ensure that governments adopt favored policies to attain the "right" goals.[2] In short, they advocate the use of "policy advocacy" and argue that policy analysts should use their work to advocate "correct" policies and gather evidence to support such objectives.

Finally, from a **practical** perspective, these kinds of issues are the ones that you will be called on to decide as a citizen. Thus, it is extremely important that one understand the nature of the policy process so that one may influence public policy if one so desires. During the next century, the public will be increasingly involved in the public policy process. One must, therefore, be prepared to deal with and understand contemporary issues to be a responsible citizen in an age of participatory democracy.[3]

WHAT DO WE MEAN BY PUBLIC POLICY AND POLICY ANALYSIS?

Various authors have offered definitions of what is meant by the term *public policy.* Thomas R. Dye, for example, defines public policy as "what governments do, why they do it, and what difference it makes."[4] Harold Lasswell, on the other hand, defines public policy as "a projected program of goals, values, and practices."[5] David Easton sees it as "the impacts of government activity," whereas Austin Ranney sees public policy as "a selected line of action or a declaration of intent."[6] Finally, James Anderson defines the term as "a purposive course of action followed by an actor or set of actors in dealing with a problem or matter of concern."[7] What all these various definitions have in common is that we are talking about a **process** or a **series** or **pattern** of **governmental activities** or **decisions** that are designed to remedy some public problem, either real or imagined. The special characteristic of public policies is that they are formulated, implemented, and evaluated by **authorities** in a political system, for example, legislators, judges, executives, and administrators. Public policies are always subject to change on the basis of new (or better) information about their effects. In the chapters to follow, we describe in greater detail the roles of each of these actors in each stage of the policy process. Private policy, on the other hand, refers to actions taken by individuals or businesses to deal with problems for themselves.

Likewise, there are several definitions of *policy analysis.* Essentially, Thomas Dye defines policy analysis as the description and explanation of the causes and consequences of government activity. His view is that public policy analysis should exhibit a primary concern with **explanation** rather than **prescription**.[8] That is, policy analysts should attempt to develop and test general propositions about the causes and consequences of public policy and to accumulate reliable research findings of general relevance. Grover Starling, on the other hand, thinks that policy analysis should be an interdisciplinary effort to facilitate the reaching of sound policy decisions.[9] Others, such as Garry Brewer and Peter DeLeon, see policy analysis as an attempt to provide suggestions to decision makers.[10] Clearly, a difference of opinion exists about the purposes of policy analysis, ranging from the scientific to the practical. Social scientists—political scientists, sociologists, and economists—who analyze policy often discover that the basic logic embodied in the original legislation is flawed or based on an incomplete understanding of a particular policy problem. At other times, administrators who are charged with policy evaluation or legislators engaged in oversight find that the policy simply does not work. Thus, the policy needs to be changed or terminated. In the United States, either designing new legislation to deal with a public problem or "fixing" previously designed policies that did not work as planned is a constant activity. In the last section of this book, we discuss how a changing understanding of a public policy problem leads to efforts to develop better (or more comprehensive) policies. In the meantime, it is important to understand what we mean by the policy process, or the policy cycle.

WHAT IS THE POLICY CYCLE?

Public policymaking is often viewed as a "conveyor belt" in which issues are first recognized as a problem, alternative courses of action are considered, and policies are adopted, implemented by agency personnel, evaluated, and finally terminated or changed on the basis of their success (actual or perceived) or lack thereof. Clearly this oversimplifies a complex process. Differentiating the consideration of alternatives from their adoption is not always easy. When vague pieces of legislation are adopted, we often do not know what the policy really is until the implementers promulgate rules and regulations. Despite this oversimplification, the policy cycle or "stages heuristic" is a political process through which most public policies pass over the course of their lifetime.[11] Although the reality of the policy process is very complex, thinking of it as a series of discrete stages such as those depicted in Figure 1-1 gives us a framework for classifying the many activities that occur in public policymaking and helps us understand it.

Over the past twenty-five years, substantial progress has been made in acquiring a better understanding of the policy cycle. For example, the first stage of the policy cycle—agenda setting—has been a subject of much recent research.[12] An agenda is, according to John Kingdon, "the list of subjects or problems to which government officials . . . are paying some serious attention at any given time."[13] For example, the list of items to be seriously considered at a public meeting of a city council or a legislature is a public agenda. Some problems never make it to

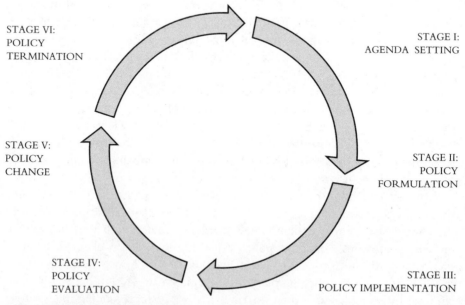

A PROBLEM FOR GOVERNMENT

STAGE VI:
POLICY
TERMINATION

STAGE I:
AGENDA SETTING

STAGE V:
POLICY
CHANGE

STAGE II:
POLICY
FORMULATION

STAGE IV:
POLICY
EVALUATION

STAGE III:
POLICY IMPLEMENTATION

FIGURE 1–1   The Policy Cycle

the public agenda, whereas others are immediately acted on or at least considered at a later date. On some occasions, action items are deliberately kept off the public agenda by those who seek to delay or block responsive action to a public problem.[14] At first, agenda setting was described as "a set of political controversies that will be viewed as falling within the range of legitimate concerns meriting the attention of the polity," and it included both "systemic agendas" and "institutional agendas."[15] More recently, John Kingdon describes agenda setting as the result of three streams, including the **problem stream**, the **policy stream**, and the **political stream**.[16] The problem stream is essentially concerned with how the public problem is defined, including how it comes to the public's attention in the first place. The policy stream is concerned with the technical feasibility of a proposed solution to the problem and the public's acceptance of it, among other things, whereas the political stream has to do with the national mood, public opinion, electoral politics, and all the factors that make the proposed solution a likely reality or not.[17]

The second stage of the policy cycle is **policy formulation,** usually defined as the passage of legislation designed to remedy some past problem or prevent some future public policy problem. For example, after discovering that abandoned toxic waste dumps had to be cleaned up even though the original owners of the facility were nowhere to be found, the U.S. Congress passed the Comprehensive Environmental Response, Compensation, and Liability Act of 1980 (CERCLA). Because it was the first area of research on the policy cycle, the policy formulation stage has been the most heavily researched phase and has resulted in numerous conceptual frameworks that help us understand this part of the cycle.[18]

Originally, policy formulation was explained in terms of an elitist or pluralist model.[19] More recently, however, policy formulation is viewed as the result of a multitude of forces that affect policy outputs, such as historical/geographic conditions, socioeconomic conditions, mass political behavior (including public opinion, interest groups, and political parties), governmental institutions (including legislatures, courts, and the bureaucracy), as well as elite perceptions and behavior.[20] For example, historical or geographical conditions set the context for what may or may not happen in policy formulation, whereas socioeconomic conditions limit (or provide opportunities for) policy outputs. Mass political behavior may affect elite decisions or government institutions independently from socioeconomic conditions. Finally, governmental institutions and elite responses exert a substantial influence on policy outputs.[21]

Policy implementation is the third stage in the policy cycle. It has most often been described as "what happens after a bill becomes a law."[22] Simply enacting legislation is no guarantee that action will be taken to put the law into effect or that the problem will be solved. Law must be translated into specific guidelines so that the federal, state, or local bureaucracy can see to it that the intent of the legislation is achieved at the point where the policy is to be delivered. According to various scholars, implementation may be described as a process, an output, or an outcome.[23] By an *implementation process*, we mean a series of governmental decisions and actions directed toward putting an already decided mandate into effect. The term *implementation outputs* refers to the means by which programmatic goals are pursued (expenditures by a state toward some problem, for example), whereas *implementation outcomes* are the changes in the larger societal problem that the program is intended to rectify (e.g., have crime rates been reduced?).[24]

Implementation may well be the most important part of the policy cycle, yet it is often overlooked by those who simply assume that policies will implement themselves. Clearly, they do not. For example, Congress passed the Hazardous and Solid Waste Amendments of 1984, which mandated that all small firms generating at least 100 kilograms of hazardous waste a month safely dispose of this waste. Yet there was no real mechanism (other than voluntary compliance) that this would, in fact, be carried out. Since that time, Congress has been paying much more attention to the implementation process when it formulates policy.

Policy evaluation is concerned with what happens as a result of the public policy, that is, what happens after a policy is implemented. It is concerned with the actual impacts of legislation or the extent to which the policy actually achieves its intended results. For example, the evaluation question might be: "Does increasing the level of per pupil educational expenditures bring about an increase in student performance or learning?"[25] Or, we might be concerned with an evaluation of the multiple impacts, if any, of the 55-mile-per-hour speed limit. Does it save lives by reducing highway fatalities? Does it reduce property damage and conserve fuel? These are the kinds of questions that policy evaluation studies seek to answer.

Prior to the 1960s, policy evaluation research did not exist. The War on Poverty and the Great Society programs of the late 1960s played a major role in the development of policy analysis and evaluation research. Early evaluation studies were concerned with costs and benefits, whereas more recent evaluations are concerned with equity and efficiency.[26]

Policy change is the newest conceptual development in the policy cycle. Largely developed by Paul Sabatier and his colleagues in the mid-1980s,[27] policy change absorbs several stages of the policy cycle, including policy formulation, policy implementation, policy evaluation, and policy termination. As an analytical concept, policy change means the point at which a policy is evaluated and redesigned so that the entire policy process begins anew. According to Sabatier, we must examine public policy over a period of a decade or more so that we can begin to appreciate the evolution of policy through time. The basic unit of analysis is the policy subsystem composed of competing advocacy coalitions, or the interaction of actors from many different institutions and levels of government interested in a policy area.[28] There have been very few applications of Sabatier's model of policy change in empirical settings, although there are likely to be many such studies in the future.[29] Chapter 9 describes policy change in greater detail.

Policy termination is a means of ending outdated or inadequate policies. Some programs are found to be unworkable and thus need to be abolished, whereas other programs are often scaled back due to a shortage of resources or for purely nonrational or symbolic reasons. Essentially, policy termination is the end point of the policy cycle. It can mean many things, such as agency termination, policy redirection, project elimination, partial elimination, or fiscal retrenchment.[30] There are several types of termination, including functional termination of a policy area, organizational termination, policy termination, and program termination. Terminations may occur with a "big bang," meaning a sudden authoritative decision, or a "long whimper," meaning a long-term decline in resources necessary to run a program.[31] At the present time, research on policy termination is relatively scarce. Scholars in this area are developing the concept and building up a body of case study materials that will help them eventually to develop an analytical framework for more systematic study of policy termination.

TYPES OF PUBLIC POLICIES

Many types of public policies exist. For example, some policies seek to distribute or cannot prevent distributing benefits to everyone, such as highway policies. Other policies seek to redistribute benefits from the haves to the have-nots. Such policies as welfare for the poor would fit this category. Finally, some policies seek to regulate behavior, such as crime policy or environmental protection policies. Theodore Lowi termed these policies **distributive, redistributive,** and **regulatory** policies.[32]

Policies also can be "liberal" or "conservative." Lowi and others argue that it is possible to define these two types of policies. **Liberal** policies are those in which the government is used extensively to bring about social change, usually in the direction of insuring greater levels of social equality.[33] **Conservative** policies, on the other hand, generally oppose the use of government to bring about social change, but may approve government action to preserve the status quo or to promote favored interests. In addition, liberals tend to favor a concentration of power in higher levels of government, whereas conservatives tend to favor decentralization of power and authority. This difference has colored much of the debate on new federalism since the 1970s and is due to the belief by liberals that an effective constituency exists at the national level and that regulatory and distributive capacities are stronger at the national level than at the state and local levels. Conservatives, on the other hand, believe that public policy problems should be solved at the level of government that is nearest to them; hence, they tend to favor state and local (or even neighborhood) governmental involvement, rather than national involvement, unless decentralization promotes uncertainties in markets. They fear the centralization of power in the national government that has developed over the past two hundred years in the United States.

There are also "substantive" and "procedural" policies. **Substantive** policies are concerned with governmental actions to deal with substantive problems, such as highway construction, environmental protection, or payment of welfare benefits. An example would be the National Environmental Protection Act (NEPA) of 1969, which sought to deal with pollution of the air, land, and water. **Procedural** policies, on the other hand, are those that relate to how something is going to be done or who is going to take action.[34] An example would be the Administrative Procedures Act of 1946, which describes the rule-making procedures to be used by agencies.

Policies also can be "material" and "symbolic," depending on the kind of benefits they allocate.[35] **Material** policies either provide concrete resources or substantive power to their beneficiaries, or impose real disadvantages on those adversely affected. For example, welfare payments, housing subsidies, and tax credits are material. **Symbolic** policies, on the other hand, appeal more to cherished values than to tangible benefits. Some examples of these policies are national holidays that honor patriots or policies concerning the flag or religion in schools.

Finally, public policies can embody "collective" versus "private" goods. **Collective** goods are those benefits that cannot be given to some but denied to others. Some examples would be national defense and public safety. **Private** goods are those goods that may be divided into units and for which consumers can be charged. For example, food is, for the most part, a private good in the United States. We have been engaged in a national debate for some time over whether to convert many of those goods historically treated as collective goods to private goods. Services such as trash collection and home security are sometimes purchased by consumers from private companies. This is called **privatization** of services, and it is based on a feeling that the private sector can do a better and less expensive job than the government. We have also debated the costs and benefits of **nationalization** of medical care, which would convert a private good to a public or collective good. This debate between privatization and nationalization of goods and services will likely continue well into the next century. It is thus important to understand the debate and the issues. We explore some of these issues in greater detail in Chapters 10 through 13 when we discuss alternative perspectives in education, welfare, crime, and the environment. For now, we will review some of the characteristics of the American political system which, in turn, affect the kinds of policies we promote and seek to push through the bureaucracy.

CHARACTERISTICS OF THE AMERICAN POLITICAL SYSTEM

The American political system has several characteristics that exert strong effects on public policy. Among these characteristics are federalism, separation of powers, political culture, pluralism, public opinion and ideology, and historical constraints. We discuss each of these factors in turn.

Federalism

Federalism, or intergovernmental relations, refers to the existence of three independent levels of government (i.e., the federal, state, and local) and the relationships among them. There are both **vertical federalism** (relations among different levels, that is, federal-state-local) and **horizontal federalism** (relations between similar units, that is, state-state or local-local). Federalism today is very different from what it was in 1787 or even from what it was in 1960. Intergovernmental relationships are constantly evolving as different presidential administrations have very different visions of the "proper" relationship among the three levels of government. For example, before 1937, **dual federalism** was the dominant view of the relationship between the state and federal governments. From this perspective, each level of government had its own separate authority and areas of responsibility. The analogy often used was that of a layer cake. In this period, the U.S. Supreme Court interpreted the Constitution as requiring a hands-off relationship between the federal and state governments. In effect, each level of government had its own responsibilities and was at least somewhat independent of the others. The belief was that separate functional responsibilities for each level of government were in the best interests of all.

From 1937 to 1960, federalism evolved into what could be best described as **cooperative**, in which the powers of these two levels of government were intermingled. There were occasions when the federal government intervened into state and local affairs. The three levels of government were no longer separate, as in the layers of a layer cake, but mixed together as in a marble cake. The separation between the states and the national governments was seen as artificial. Before 1960, the typical federal assistance program did not involve an expressly stated national purpose, but rather the federal role was limited to providing federal technical assistance rather than control.

From 1960 to 1972, another vision of federalism evolved into what was called **creative federalism**. In this version, the federal role was believed to be necessary for the state and local governments to achieve its social objectives; in other words, state and local governments were perceived to be major constraints on responsible action to achieve national goals, particularly to improve the plight of the poor. Creative federalism provided the basis for the implementation of national goals defined by Congress and carried out by the states. By way of grants-in-aid, control over programs resided with the federal government and Congress rather than the states. For example, the War on Poverty was a federal program directed from Washington, D.C., and carried out by the states, rather than the reverse. Essentially, power was shifted toward the national government and the states provided an implementing role. The period of creative federalism has been criticized extensively by a number of policy analysts who argue that the social programs of that era actually exacerbated rather than alleviated such problems as poverty.[36]

Finally, since 1972, we have had a **new federalism**, in which states and cities were given much more authority than in the 1960s. This period began with President Nixon's shift of power and authority from the national government back to state and local governments. Essentially, he believed that the locus of authority should reside with those closest to the problems. The 1972 State and

Local Fiscal Assistance Act (or General Revenue Sharing Act) provided the mechanism for "restoring" the balance among federal, state, and local governments that was seen as having been lost under creative federalism. The key difference between this version of federalism and the previous one was that the states and cities were given control over the resources that Washington provided (through revenue-sharing funds) so that they could decide which projects and programs would be funded and which would not be funded. In the 1980s, this version of new federalism was extended by President Reagan, who continued the decentralization of power and authority, but cut much of the federal support for these programs. Thus, under Reagan's version of new federalism, the states and cities had to make a choice among (1) cutting programs; (2) reprogramming funds from areas of low priorities to those with higher priorities; or (3) raising taxes to cover the costs of programs now under their control.

Given the changing nature of federalism, one may see how different visions of federalism affect the kinds of public policies that are formulated or implemented at the state and local levels. In addition, separation of powers also affects public policymaking in our intergovernmental system.

Separation of Powers

A second characteristic of American government and politics that affects public policy is **separation of powers**. This refers to the Founding Fathers' establishment of a system of checks and balances among the executive, legislative, and judicial branches. The president and members of Congress are elected separately, for terms of differing lengths, and have powers that are independent of each other. The Founding Fathers, exemplified by James Madison in **Federalist 10**, were fearful of a concentration of power in any one branch. One of his best-known quotes from **Federalist 51** is that "if men were angels, no government would be necessary." Clearly he held a constrained view of human nature and thus assumed that the abuse of power had to be controlled. By spreading power over the three branches, each branch was kept in its "proper" place.

Over time, however, there has been a tendency to concentrate power in the executive branch relative to the legislative and judicial branches. This has occurred within both the national and the state governments. The recent efforts toward "new federalism" can thus be seen as an attempt to redisperse some of the powers that have accumulated in the national executive branch over the past two hundred years.

Political Culture

In addition to being affected by federalism and separation of powers, public policy is also affected by citizens' attitudes, beliefs, and expectations about what governments should do, who should participate, and what rules should govern the political game.[37] These attitudes, beliefs, and expectations are known as **political**

culture, a term defined by Lucien Pye, as the "set of attitudes, beliefs, and sentiments that give order and meaning to the political process."[38] Political culture is a mind-set or a way of perceiving and interpreting politics. Daniel Elazar has identified three political cultures in America that exist side by side and have an effect on political behavior.[39] These three cultures are the moralistic, the individualistic, and the traditionalistic cultures. The **moralistic** culture emphasizes a "commonwealth" conception of politics in which politics is seen as a "search for the good society," or an effort to exercise power for the betterment of the commonwealth. It views politics as a healthy enterprise in which those who govern strive to promote the public good in terms of honesty, unselfishness, and a commitment to the public welfare. States that exhibit this culture are characterized by an issue-oriented public, high levels of participation, a respect for bureaucracy and government growth, a rejection of party ties and patronage, and little corruption. Some examples include the New England states, California, Washington, and Oregon.

The **individualistic** culture, on the other hand, conceives of politics as a "marketplace" or a "business" (albeit a "dirty" one). In this mind-set, government is initiated for strictly utilitarian ends to handle only those functions demanded by the people it is created to serve; that is, government should be limited only to those functions that the people want it to perform. Government is a source of favors, rather that a source of pursuit of the common good. States where this culture is dominant are characterized by very little issue concern, limited participation, an ambivalence about the place of bureaucracy in the political order, and corruption in government. Examples include Illinois, Indiana, and several other midwestern states that were settled by English and German immigrants.

Finally, the **traditionalistic** culture emphasizes an "elitist" conception of politics and views the function of government as limited to the preservation of the status quo. Where this culture is dominant, there is likely to be a *noblesse oblige* attitude toward government in which there is a positive view of government, but its role is limited to the preservation of the status quo. In states where this culture predominates, the public views issues as of little importance, and there is a lack of citizen participation, an antibureaucratic attitude, a view of political parties only as a source of favors (patronage), and what is thought of as a "conservative" position in the kinds of policies that are adopted. These states are largely those of the Deep South where the landed gentry settled and established sugar and cotton plantations.

These three political cultures were transferred to America in the various waves of immigration to this country in the last two centuries. These three cultures originated in Northern and Western Europe and were carried to this country by the Yankee Puritans, the English, the Germans, the French, and the Scandinavians. They persist to this day and affect the kinds of policies that are likely to be adopted in various states. In effect, they provide a set of contextual inducements or constraints on public policies in the states. For example, liberal policies might fare better in moralistic cultures, whereas conservative policies would fare better in traditionalistic states.

Recent waves of new immigrants, such as those from Africa, Latin America, and Asia, seek to have their cultures brought into the mainstream of American life through the educational system at all levels as well as in the workplace. This has given rise to the current debates within elementary schools over restructuring the curriculum to better serve the needs of new ethnic and cultural minorities among the U.S. population. It is also reflected in the call for globalism in the high schools and cultural diversity among our colleges and universities. In addition, affirmative action is an attempt to provide a more inclusive workforce composed of these immigrant groups. Both of these policies have recently come under much scrutiny and criticism.[40]

Pluralism

Similarly, **pluralism** affects the making and implementation of public policies. The pluralism theory of government contends that power is group based. Adherents to this theory claim that because American government has multiple points of access, each group possesses an equal opportunity when competing with other groups for power and resources. According to the pluralist model, several inherent characteristics of the American political system give the role of interest groups special importance. First, because contemporary government is very complex, individuals must join interest groups as a way of participating in politics. Power thus becomes defined as an attribute of individuals in their relationships with each other in the process of decision making. Second, these power relationships are highly fluid, meaning that they are formed for a particular decision and after the decision is made they disappear, to be replaced by a different set of power relationships when the next decision is made. Third, there is no permanent distinction between elites and masses. That is, individuals who participate in decision making at one time are not necessarily the ones who participate at another time. Individuals move in and out of the ranks of decision makers simply by becoming active or inactive in politics. Fourth, multiple centers of power exist within a community; no single interest group totally dominates all decisions or is dominated by another interest group. Finally, there is considerable competition among various interests so that the policy outcome is a result of bargaining and negotiation among competing groups.[41]

The pluralist model is not without criticism. Critics argue that it creates a "leaderless society" in which all values are treated as equivalent interests, without an a priori hierarchy or ranking of values. Instead, pluralist structures are reactive and do not engage in rational planning or long-range planning. In addition, some argue that pluralist politics is inherently incapable of achieving justice; when one group wins, another loses. Finally, pluralism, it is argued, is inherently corrupt because formal procedures have been replaced by informal bargaining in which the product is more likely to be a product of interest groups' strength, rather than a principled and reasoned outcome.[42]

Ideology and Public Opinion

Even though most groups and individual citizens lack a consistent ideological position, the majority of Americans are classified as "moderates" or "middle-of-the-road" in the ideological spectrum.[43] Historically, Americans have always held this position on the ideological spectrum. Figure 1-2 indicates the percentages of the American public that fall into different categories.

Although it is very difficult to link these ideological positions to specific groups, some generalizations can be made about liberals and conservatives in society. For example, liberals tend to favor redistributive policies, government services, progressive taxes, strong government, and maximum citizen participation. Conservatives, on the other hand, tend to favor distributive policies, minimal government services (unless such services benefit their interests), regressive taxes, weak government, and limited citizen participation.

Thomas Sowell labels these ideological positions "visions," or competing perspectives, which he identifies as "constrained" and "unconstrained."[44] The

We hear a lot of talk these days about liberals and conservatives. Here are the results of a questionnaire using a seven-point scale on which the political views that people might hold are arranged from extremely liberal to extremely conservative.

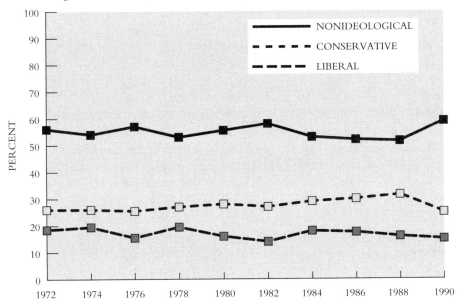

FIGURE 1–2   Ideology Over Time

Note: Those on the liberal side of the scale were combined into a single liberal category; those on the conservative side into a single conservative category; and persons in the middle, as well as those who haven't thought about it, were labeled as nonideological.

Source: Burns/Peltason/Cronin/Magleby, *Government by the People*, 15/e, ©1993, p. 207. Reprinted by permission of Prentice Hall, Upper Saddle River, New Jersey.

constrained vision is a picture of egocentric human beings with moral limitations. The fundamental social and moral challenge, therefore, is to make the best of possibilities that exist within that constraint, rather than to dissipate energies in a vain attempt to change human nature. By this logic, policy should be based on incentives, rather than dispositions, to obtain the desired behavior.[45] The prospect of rewards and the fear of punishment provide the incentives to obtain desirable behavior. Fundamentally, then, this results in a constrained view of human nature and leads to less ambitious policy positions if we assume that the primary constraints come from within the individual rather than being imposed from the environment outside the individual.

The **unconstrained vision,** on the other hand, provides a view of human nature in which understanding and human dispositions are capable of intentionally creating social benefits.[46] From this perspective, humans are capable of directly feeling other people's needs as more important than their own and, therefore, of acting impartially, even when their interests or those of their family are involved.[47] This view of human nature is often associated with the liberal view that human nature is no constraint; rather constraints are imposed by the environment outside the individual. In the substantive chapters of this book (Chapters 10 through 13), we identify how these visions affect public policy formation and evaluation.

History

Some historians and policy analysts argue that American public policy is best described by a "political cycle" in which conservative periods alternate with liberal periods.[48] Professor Arthur Schlesinger, for example, argues that a thirty-year conservative cycle is coming to an end in the 1990s, to be replaced by a liberal resurgence in the next century. Specifically, he argues that the rhythms of American politics dictate a fairly regular cyclical alternation between conservatism and liberalism in our national moods, or "swings back and forth between eras when the national commitment is to private interest as the best means of meeting our problems and eras when the national commitment is to public purpose."[49] He argues that this thirty-year cycle corresponds to the span of a generation as people's political attitudes are formed by the ideals dominant in the years during which they attain political consciousness, which is roughly between their seventeenth and twenty-fifth birthdays. Given this hypothesis, he predicts that the 1990s will usher in a new era of political liberalism in which government will be seen as an instrument of public welfare rather than a threat to people's liberties. This will be followed in the 2020s by a period of national conservatism when the mood of idealism and reform will have run its course and the public will turn once more to the view that, left to the unfettered market and the ethos of greed, our problems will solve themselves. Each swing of the cycle, he argues, "corrects the excesses of the other so that the republic survives."[50]

In addition, in examining U.S. public policies over a period of one hundred years or more, Amenta and Skocpol argue that a pattern of "zigzags" best describes American public policy since the late nineteenth century.[51] Specifically, they argue that American public policy may be divided into four different periods. In the late nineteenth century, the United States was a leader in activist (liberal) public policies, whereas in the second phase (1900 to 1930), liberalism was replaced by a conservative period in which these initial policies were undermined. In the next period, 1930 to 1950, U.S. public policy was progressive again. The most recent period is one of a conservative reaction to the previous era of liberalism. Their argument is a bit like Schlesinger's in that they believe that history has a strong effect on public policy or that we cannot fully understand public policy without examining it over a period of many years, from at least a decade to a hundred years or more. Indeed, that is the guiding theme of this book—that time affects the evolution of our understanding of public policy in a profound way.

THE PLAN OF THE BOOK

In this brief introduction, we have discussed what we mean by public policy and the policy cycle, identified various types of public policy, and discussed the nature of American politics itself. Understanding of the policy cycle has grown tremendously over the past twenty-five years, with empirical tests of various frameworks. Similarly, understanding of the contours of American public policy has increased over time as scholars seek a better perspective on the history of American public policy. Finally, American politics and policy is in transition, with new developments in federalism, public opinion, political parties, and fundamental values that shape public policy.

The thesis of this book is that by observing the changes in the past, we may obtain a better understanding of the present, and perhaps a glimpse of what to expect in the future. In the chapters that follow, three questions are used to structure the individual chapters. First, where have we been in terms of our conceptual understanding of each phase of the policy cycle or, in the case of the substantive chapters, how has policy evolved over time? Second, what is our present understanding of each phase of the cycle? In the case of the substantive chapters, what is the predominant "vision" within each policy area? Where are we in our conceptual understanding of various aspects of the policy cycle or substantive policy prescriptions? Third, where are we going in terms of our conceptual understanding or, in the case of the substantive chapters, where are we likely to go over the next twenty years? In some substantive areas, it may be useful to describe alternative visions for public policy. This concern with the various prescriptions for the future allows us to discuss and evaluate the normative implications of alternative policy choices. This reflects an emerging trend in the policy studies subfield.

In the first section of the book, Chapter 2 discusses the evolution of American public policy and the evolution of policy studies, including trends over time in the growth of the subfield, tensions inherent to policy studies, and current issues of concern. Chapter 3 discusses several approaches to policy studies ranging from the purely scientific to the political (or advocacy) use of policy studies. It also identifies two competing visions of public policy choices that are discussed in greater detail in the substantive chapters in Part III. Chapter 4 describes what we mean by a model and presents several criteria for evaluating models before we discuss several alternative models in the next few chapters.

In the next two sections of the book, we examine the evolution of our understanding of the policy cycle and our understanding of the substance of American public policy in four areas. In Chapters 5 through 9, an evolutionary perspective is presented for each phase of the policy cycle, noting how our understanding has advanced from initial concept development to the present agenda for future research. Chapters 10 through 13 discuss several substantive areas of public policy—education, welfare, crime, and the environment. We also use an evolutionary approach in these chapters, so that the student can fully appreciate how much policy history can aid our understanding and help to predict the future in each of these substantive areas.

Finally, the last section of the book discusses the utilization of policy analysis by decision makers, and in the concluding chapter, we offer some observations and conclusions based on the previous chapters about trends in American public policy from the past three decades. We also venture some predictions for the next few years. These conclusions and predictions are based on the idea that the past, under normal conditions, provides much insight into the future.

NOTES

1. Carolyn J. Mooney, "Academic Group Fighting the 'Politically Correct Left' Gains Momentum," *The Chronicle of Higher Education* 37 (December 12, 1990), p. A1.
2. James Anderson, *Public Policymaking: An Introduction* (Boston: Houghton Mifflin, 1990), p. 24.
3. See Benjamin R. Barber, *Strong Democracy: Participatory Politics for a New Age* (Berkeley: University of California Press, 1984), and Jane J. Mansbridge, *Beyond Adversary Democracy* (Chicago: University of Chicago Press, 1983).
4. Thomas R. Dye, *Understanding Public Policy,* 7th ed. (New York: Prentice Hall, 1992), pp. 2–4.
5. Grover Starling, *The Politics and Economics of Public Policy* (Homewood, IL: Dorsey Press, 1979), p. 4.
6. David Easton, *A Systems Analysis of Political Life* (New York: Wiley, 1965), p. 212.
7. Anderson, *Public Policymaking*, p. 5.
8. Dye, *Understanding Public Policy*, p. 4.
9. Starling, *The Politics and Economics of Public Policy*, p.11.
10. Garry D. Brewer and Peter DeLeon, *The Foundations of Policy Analysis* (Homewood, IL: Dorsey Press, 1983), p. 3.
11. Deborah Stone, to the contrary, rejects this "production" model of policymaking, "whereby policy is assembled in stages, as if on a conveyor belt." See her book entitled, *Policy Paradox and Political Reason* (Glenview, IL: Scott, Foresman, 1988), p. viii. In addition, Paul A. Sabatier and Hank Jenkins-Smith think that the "stages heuristic" has out-

lived its usefulness in teaching and research. See Paul A. Sabatier and Hank Jenkins-Smith, eds., *Policy Change and Learning: An Advocacy Coalition Approach* (Boulder, CO: WestviewPress, 1993). We obviously do not agree with either perspective of the critics of the policy cycle approach. Instead, we believe that the stages heuristic has great value both for teaching about public policymaking and for research on the policy process.

12. See Roger W. Cobb and Charles D. Elder, "The Politics of Agenda-Building," *Journal of Politics* 33 (1971), pp. 892–915; Roger W. Cobb and Charles D. Elder, *Participation in American Politics: The Dynamics of Agenda-Building* (Baltimore: The Johns Hopkins University Press, 1972); John W. Kingdon, *Agendas, Alternatives, and Public Policies*, 2d ed. (New York: HarperCollins, 1995); and Barbara Nelson, *Making an Issue of Child Abuse* (Chicago: University of Chicago Press, 1984).

13. Kingdon, *Agendas, Alternatives, and Public Policies*, p. 3.

14. See Peter Bachrach and Morton Baratz, "The Two Faces of Power," *American Political Science Review* 57 (December 1962), pp. 947–952.

15. Roger W. Cobb and Charles D. Elder, *Participation in American Politics: The Dynamics of Agenda-Building* (Baltimore: The Johns Hopkins University Press, 1972), pp. 14–15.

16. Kingdon, *Agendas, Alternatives, and Public Policies*, pp. 90–164.

17. See also Frank R. Baumgartner and Bryan D. Jones, *Agendas and Instability in American Politics* (Chicago: University of Illinois Press, 1993).

18. See Thomas R. Dye, *Understanding Public Policy*, 6th ed. (Englewood Cliffs, NJ: Prentice Hall, 1987), pp. 20–44.

19. See Thomas R. Dye and Harmon Zeigler, *The Irony of Democracy*, 5th ed. (Monterey, CA: Brooks Cole, 1981), and Floyd Hunter, *Community Power Structure* (Chapel Hill: University of North Carolina Press, 1953); see also Robert A. Dahl, *Who Governs?* (New Haven, CT: Yale University Press, 1961).

20. Richard I. Hofferbert, "Elite Influence in State Policy Formation: A Model for Comparative Inquiry," *Polity* 2 (Spring 1970), pp. 316–344.

21. Hofferbert, "Elite Influence in State Policy Formation," pp. 326–330.

22. See Eugene Bardach, *The Implementation Game: What Happens After a Bill Becomes a Law* (Cambridge, MA: MIT Press, 1977).

23. See Malcolm Goggin, Ann O'M. Bowman, James P. Lester, and Laurence O'Toole, *Implementation Theory and Practice: Toward a Third Generation* (New York: HarperCollins, 1990).

24. Ibid., p. 34.

25. See the report on student performance by Professor James Coleman in 1965–66 reported in Christopher Jencks, *Inequality: A Reassessment of the Effects of Family and Schooling in America* (New York: Basic Books, 1972).

26. Robert H. Haveman, "Policy Analysis and Evaluation Research After Twenty Years," *Policy Studies Journal* 16 (Winter 1987), pp. 191–218.

27. Paul A. Sabatier, "Knowledge, Policy-Oriented Learning, and Policy Change: An Advocacy Coalition Framework," *Knowledge: Creation, Diffusion, Utilization* 3 (June 1987) pp. 649–692.

28. Ibid., pp. 652–653.

29. See James P. Lester and Michael S. Hamilton, "Intergovernmental Relations and Marine Policy Change," in *Ocean Resources and U.S. Intergovernmental Relations*, ed. Maynard Silva (Boulder, CO: WestviewPress, 1986); and Richard Barke, "Hazardous Waste and the Politics of Policy Change," in *Dimensions of Hazardous Waste Politics and Policy*, ed. Charles Davis and James P. Lester (Westport, CT: Greenwood Press, 1988).

30. See Eugene Bardach, "Policy Termination as a Political Process," *Policy Sciences* 7 (June 1976), pp. 123–131; Peter DeLeon, "Policy Evaluation and Program Termination," *Policy Studies Review* (1983); and Robert Behn, "How to Terminate a Public Policy: A Dozen Hints for the Would-Be Terminator," *Policy Analysis* 4 (Summer 1978), pp. 393–413.

31. Bardach, "Policy Termination as a Political Process," pp. 123–131.

32. Theodore J. Lowi, "American Business, Public Policy, Case Studies, and Political Theory," *World Politics* 16 (July 1964), pp. 677–715.

33. Ibid.; also Anderson, *Public Policymaking*, p. 18.

34. Anderson, *Public Policymaking*, p. 10.

35. Ibid., p. 15.

36. See, for example, John Donovan, *The Politics of Poverty* (New York: Pegasus, 1967); Daniel P. Moynihan, *Maximum Feasible Misunderstanding* (New York: Macmillan, 1970); and Charles Murray, *Losing Ground: American Social Policy, 1950–1980* (New York: Basic Books, 1986).

37. John J. Harrigan, *Politics and Policies in State and Communities* (New York: HarperCollins, 1991), pp. 23–27.

38. Lucien Pye, "Political Culture," in *International Encyclopedia of the Social Sciences*, Vol. 12 (New York: Macmillan, 1968), p. 218.

39. Daniel J. Elazar, *American Federalism: A View from the States* (New York: Thomas Crowell, 1972).

40. See Linda Greenhouse, "By 5–4, Justices Cast Doubts on U.S. Programs That Give Preferences Based on Race," *New York Times*, 13 (June) 1995, p. A1.

41. Dye and Zeigler, *The Irony of Democracy*, pp. 10–11.

42. Theodore J. Lowi, *The End of Liberalism* (New York: Norton, 1969).

43. Harrigan, *Politics and Policies in States and Communities*, p. 6.

44. Thomas Sowell, *A Conflict of Visions* (New York: William Morrow, 1987).

45. Ibid., pp. 19–23.

46. Ibid., pp. 23–25.

47. Ibid.

48. See Arthur M. Schlesinger Jr., "America's Political Cycle Turns Again," *Wall Street Journal*, 10 December, 1987, p. 28.

49. Ibid.

50. Ibid.

51. See Edwin Amenta and Theda Skocpol, "Taking Exception: Explaining the Distinctiveness of American Public Policies in the Last Century," in *The Comparative History of Public Policy* ed. F. G. Castles (New York: Oxford University Press, 1989), p. 293.

CHAPTER TWO

THE EVOLUTION OF PUBLIC POLICY AND POLICY STUDIES

"Perhaps we can consider 1985 as being a year of graduation or commencement in the sense of policy studies now having truly arrived."

STUART NAGEL

One of the clearest trends to emerge in political science during the past twenty-five years is the use of historical or longitudinal versus cross-sectional analysis.[1] Public policy scholars increasingly argue that we can more fully appreciate and understand public policy developments by viewing them from the perspective of a decade or more.[2] For example, the initiation of a new education, antipoverty, anticrime, or antipollution program is unlikely to produce real, immediate results. However, when viewed from a longer-term perspective, impacts may become more clear. Furthermore, American public policy follows a pattern, with policy in any given area at any point in time being a predictable reaction to perceived problems with previous policies. This pattern may be repeated as the public mood and values change. Thus, the longer the perspective an analyst can take, the more likely he or she is to gain insight about the evolution of that particular public policy.[3]

Similarly, knowledge of the policy cycle continues to evolve on the basis of many new conceptual developments that have taken place over the past twenty-five years or so. Some areas of the policy cycle (e.g., policy formulation) have been more carefully researched for a longer time than others (e.g., agenda setting or policy change); yet all areas of the policy cycle have witnessed significant intellectual development in understanding the determinants of each phase of the cycle. However, a major problem for students is that a sense of history is missing in most contemporary policy texts. So little of this evolutionary development has been accumulated in a single textbook that students may not fully appreciate the amount of intellectual growth that has taken place over the past twenty-five years. For example, we have developed a number of theoretical explanations of what drives policymaking—elitism, pluralism, subgovernments, issue networks, and advocacy coalitions. Yet, too often students fail to understand how early conceptual developments paved the way for later ones.

This book adopts a diachronic or **evolutionary** theme as an organizing framework. In this way, students may fully appreciate the developments in our understanding of both the policy cycle and several substantive areas of public policy. Much of the newest research in public policy is diachronic in approach and comparative in method; that recognition is the basis for the book's theme— time and public policy studies. Thus, the historical or longitudinal approach is used in a *conceptual* rather than a statistical sense.

THE EVOLUTION OF AMERICAN PUBLIC POLICY

Our understanding of the policy cycle evolves over time as scholars contribute new conceptual developments and our knowledge base is extended. Similarly, our understanding of the substance of American public policy increases over time as we acquire a more extensive knowledge base about changes taking place in the near term (e.g., thirty years) and the long term (e.g., one hundred years or more).

The Near-Term View: American Values in Transition

If we observe American society over the past thirty to forty years, we observe a number of political transformations and value changes that affect the nature and direction of American public policy. For example, a growing distrust of the national government has led, in a very direct way, to the tendency toward decentralization or "new federalism," which began with the Nixon administration and was greatly accelerated under the Reagan administration. The new federalism advanced by President Reagan mandated a greatly expanded role for state and local governments. Proponents of this approach argued that it was time for the states and cities to reduce their dependency on Washington and to turn inward for solutions to their social and economic problems.[4] The concepts of **decentralization** and **defunding** were the key policy objectives of President Reagan's new federalism. Central to his approach was the premise that, "unlike a generation ago, a variety of structural changes, such as government reform, reapportionment, and reduced regional income disparities, have strengthened state and local capacity to perform as a full partner in the intergovernmental system."[5]

A distrust of the two dominant political parties is also growing, as the American public associates the Republicans with wealth and greed and the Democrats with incompetence.[6] Indeed, representative democracy in America has been increasingly criticized as scholars lament the failure of our political institutions or our elected officials. They suggest that our domestic political institutions are incapable of dealing effectively with many contemporary public policy problems.[7] For example, Charles Stoddard argues that America has "one of the clumsiest systems of popular government in the Western world."[8] By this he means that the growing paralysis of our federal system is due to built-in weaknesses that emphasize custodianship at the expense of forward-looking leadership.[9] Essentially, he argues that "pluralistic theory, reasonable in an era of dispersed power, deserves reconsideration in a period when corporate interests wield great power."[10] His conclusion is consistent with recent actions in California, where many citizens believe that it is now necessary to go directly to the voters through the initiative and referendum process because the California legislature is perceived to be so beholden to conservative special interests that legislative remedies for environmental pollution are impossible.[11] Similarly, voters in California also believe that legislators are beholden to liberal special interests as evidenced by the California proposition on affirmative action. Moreover, Oklahoma and several other states have recently decided to limit state legislators to twelve years in office.[12] These recent initiatives suggest a growing frustration among the public over traditional American politics.

As we examine public policy over the past thirty to forty years, it is increasingly clear that America is in the midst of significant and far-reaching value changes about how we should govern ourselves as well as more fundamental changes in social values.[13] Drawing on a recent poll by Daniel Yankelovich and other recent writings, Table 2-1 suggests the nature of some of these social value changes. These changes in how we view our domestic political institutions as well as more fundamental social value changes will, quite obviously, affect the direction of American public policy over the next decade or more. A longer-term perspective, on the other hand, suggests that many of these changes are recurring phenomena.

The Long-Term View: Some Recurring Patterns in American Public Policy

If we observe American public policy over a longer time frame of perhaps a hundred years or more, we find a number of recurring patterns. Some observers argue that American public policy resembles a "zigzag" pattern in which we pursue conservative policies for a time and then liberal policies (as a reaction) before eventually returning to conservative policies. More specifically, some argue that American public policy has evolved through four discrete periods.

The first period, during the late nineteenth century, was characterized by high levels of spending that largely benefited Northern white males, especially those

24

THE CONTEXT OF PUBLIC POLICY STUDIES

TABLE 2–1   Changes in American Values, 1950–1990
The Great American 40-Year Value Shift

1950s	1990s	Consequences/Results
Saving	Spending	Federal debt; Trade deficit
Delayed gratification	Instant gratification	Narcissism
Ozzie and Harriet	Latchkey kids	71% high-school graduation rate
Certainty	Ambivalence	Marriage counseling
Investing	Leveraging	Low rate of productivity growth; Michael Milken
Unionization	Bankruptcy	Middle-class decline
Lifetime employer	Outplacement	Look out for #1; Alienation
Neighborhood	Lifestyle	Community failure; Single-issue politics; Age segregation; Ethnic conflict; Gentrification
Middle class	Underclass	Drugs; Gangs; Teenage grannies; Colombia
Export	Import	Acura; Infinity; Lexus; FAX; VCRs
Containment	Economic security	Trade sanctions; Managed trade
Deterrence	Terrorism	Metal detectors
Upward mobility	Downward mobility	The homeless: Shrinking middle class
Duty	Divorce	Despair
"We"	"Me"	"Them"
Sexual repression	Affairs	Celibacy
Equity	Renting/leasing	Balloon payments
Organized religion	Cults: TV preachers	Authoritarianism
Heroes	Cover girls	Cynicism
Internationalism	Isolationism	Personality politics: "Psychiatrization" of foreign leaders (Mikhail and Raisa Gorbachev as role models)
Public troubles	Private issues	Greed; Fear; Pessimism
Money	More money	Even more money
"Do what you're told"	"Do what you want"	"You do it"
Young	Middle age	Old
Public virtue	Personal well-being	Decline of polity; Voter alienation
Civil rights	Affirmative action	Quotas and "Politically Correct" thinking
Press conference	Photo opportunity	*People* magazine
Achievement	Fame	Political polls
Manufacturing	Service	Mitsubishi buys Rockefeller Center; Sony buys Colombia Pictures
Value-added	Mastercard	Five-year car loans; Repossessions
Problems	Pathologies	Analysis paralysis
Hope	Happiness	Preference by L'oreal
Bomb shelters	Crack houses	Drug Czar William Bennett
Organization Man	Murphy Brown	Androgyny
NATO; Godless communists	Commie capitalists	Trading blocs; New alliances
Psychoanalysis/neurosis	Support groups/serial killers	Big book sales
Cheeseburger, fries, shake	Cheeseburger, fries, shake	American cultural hegemony
USA	Japan	"Japanaphobia"
Regulation	Deregulation	Re-regulation
Cash	Credit	Cash

Source: Richard D. Lamm and Richard A. Caldwell, *Hard Choices* (Denver, CO: The University of Denver, Center for Public Policy, 1991), p. 65. The table was authored by Richard A. Caldwell. Reprinted by permission of the Center for Public Policy, University of Denver.

who had served the North in the Civil War (1861–1865).[14] The Civil War pension system distributed benefits in a political way in that one's political affiliation to the Republican Party was a major criterion for acquiring the pension. This form of political patronage later led to a backlash against the "radical Republicans" in the Deep South.[15] Then, during the Progressive Era of 1900 to 1930, there was an attempt to eliminate this patronage and corruption of the previous era by Civil Service reforms, the adoption of the merit system, child labor laws, women's hours legislation, and various health and safety laws. At this time, the Democrats became known as the "reform party" due to their opposition to the previous policies of the radical Republicans. In addition, the Democrats began to establish a sort of social democracy, which spilled over into the next era from 1930 to 1950.

During the New Deal period (1930–1950), the Democrats led the support for social insurance programs and welfare programs, fueled to a large extent by the Great Depression. Some have argued that the major recipients of benefits during this period were the veterans of World War II and the retired veterans of wage-earning employment and their survivors. Finally, in the postwar period of 1950 to 1980, the Republicans reacted to the free-spending policies of the Democrats and argued against the welfare policies of the previous era.[16] Indeed, the Great Society programs of the 1960s are often viewed as failures and as a major determinant of the current welfare state.[17] Thus, when viewed from a long-term perspective, the current transformation taking place in American public policy (especially a rejection of centralization of power and authority in the federal government and a distrust of existing political institutions) can be seen as a "constrained vision" reacting to the previous more "unconstrained vision" of human nature.[18] This is a recurring phenomenon in American politics that has been going on for the last hundred years or more.

THE EVOLUTION OF POLICY STUDIES

Policy studies have clearly come of age. Since the late 1960s, the policy studies subfield has developed into a well-organized body of work with courses, curricula, schools of public policy, organizations, journals, textbooks, conferences, panels, summer institutes, awards, funding sources, research institutes, job opportunities, and other indicators.[19] During these thirty years, we have seen enormous growth in the subfield through courses offered, papers presented at national or regional meetings, graduates from public policy schools, and dissertations. For example, an examination of papers presented at the annual meeting of the American Political Science Association (APSA) illustrates the tremendous growth in policy studies over the past thirty years. In 1967, only four papers dealing with public policy were presented at the Annual Meeting of the APSA.[20] By 1990, there were over two hundred papers delivered on the topic of public policy at the national APSA meeting.

Other evidence of growth of this subfield is exhibited by membership in the Policy Studies Organization (PSO). In 1990, there were 1,174 individual members of the organization and 1,047 library members. In fact, the last few years has seen more increases in membership than at any time since the beginning of the Policy Studies Organization in the 1970s.[21] PSO membership is also becoming more interdisciplinary and international, and more people in various branches and levels of government are joining the organization. Clearly, in quantitative terms, policy analysis has had a major impact on political science, at least as indicated by papers given at national meetings, by membership levels, by doctoral dissertations, and by books published.

Trends in policy studies have been described in a number of studies. These studies examined articles on public policy in major policy journals from 1975 to 1986. They suggest a number of conclusions: (1) most of the articles are descriptive and rhetorical rather than empirical and quantitative; (2) most of the articles produced policy recommendations or proposals, regardless of the methods used in the analysis; (3) multidisciplinary research in policy studies is increasing; (4) most of the articles on policy research focused on a single aspect of the policy process (usually policy formulation) and used the case study approach; and (5) very little of this research has focused on policy evaluation and outcome analysis, which is the most useful area for decision makers.[22]

A key question that arises, therefore, is the impact of all this activity on public policy. Has this activity actually resulted in influences on governmental decision making? That is the subject of Chapter 14 of this book. In that chapter, we discuss the utilization of the knowledge generated by this activity and evaluate whether it has affected public policy as well as the determinants of this use (or nonuse).

Some Tensions in the Subfield

Many evaluative comments on the subfield have been made by social scientists and others. According to Stuart Nagel, those comments include the following: (1) policy studies is a fad that will eventually wither away; (2) policy studies are too practical or too theoretical; (3) policy studies are too multidisciplinary or too narrowly focused on political science; (4) policy studies are too quantitative or too nonscientific in method; (5) policy studies are too little used or overutilized; and finally, (6) policy studies are too liberal or too conservative.[23] Each of these arguments is examined in turn.

Nagel argues that public policy reflects a long-term philosophical tradition in the social sciences that has existed since Plato's *Republic*. Although the field is clearly not a fad, it has changed considerably such that modern practitioners in the 1990s emphasize the idea of synthesizing the essentially normative philosophy (associated with Plato through Marx) and the scientific method (associated with Harold Lasswell and others).[24] Since the 1970s, there have been a number of more specific trends in policy studies, such as the evaluation of alternative policies and the incorporation of new methods (both qualitative and quantitative) to achieve greater utilization of policy analysis by decision makers. More specifically, in the 1960s a great deal of emphasis was placed on public policy formulation, whereas the 1970s emphasized public policy implementation. In the 1980s, the emphasis shifted to policy optimization studies or policy analyses that sought to answer the question, What effects are we trying to achieve (i.e., what are the goals of public policy)? For example, which policy among those being considered is best able to reduce environmental pollution? Which type of welfare policy will best reduce the level of poverty? Given the growth of policy studies over the past thirty years, it would be difficult to argue convincingly that it will eventually wither away from lack of interest.

On the second point discussed above, one may argue that policy studies are *both* practical and theoretical. Some policy analysts lean toward the theoretical (scientific) side insofar as they avoid making policy recommendations that might improve policy performance. Rather, they are primarily interested in pursuing **pure science** as opposed to **applied science**. That is, they are more interested in scientific understanding than in improving policy performance. Others are more interested in the practical side of policy analysis, meaning that they are interested in providing information on the basis of their analysis to inform decision makers as to how to improve system performance. Yet, still others are interested in both the development of policy theory *and* the improvement of governmental performance and effectiveness. In fact, good theory is practical, so it is difficult to separate the two from one another. As William Glazer once said, "If the study of theory and fact do not fertilize each other, both will be barren."[25]

Sometimes, this dichotomy between the role of the policy scientist as a "pure scientist" or an "expert" creates a role conflict that can lead to the prevention of scientific advancement as the scientist's role gives way to the demands for governmental "experts."[26] Pure science becomes neglected as demands for policy expertise take precedence. Nevertheless, policy analysis is both practical and theoretical.

Third, policy studies are by definition and nature interdisciplinary with political scientists playing key roles. The type of policy under analysis often determines which disciplines are most involved. For example, economists are very likely to be involved in welfare policy evaluation, whereas political scientists are most heavily involved in defense policy analysis. One recent analysis found that political scientists, followed by economists, continue to dominate the field, although there has been a small increase in multidisciplinary authorship from 1975 to 1984.[27]

Fourth, policy analysis is concerned with both rigorous quantitative methods as well as simple, yet systematic, methods. For example, a study in the early 1980s found that only 43 percent of the articles surveyed on policy analysis were empirical and quantitative, whereas 57 percent were descriptive and rhetorical in nature.[28] This percentage of quantitative articles had dropped to 29 percent by the mid-1980s.[29] This change is related to the emerging consensus in policy analysis that multiple approaches are relevant and that the scientific approach, meaning the use of quantitative techniques, is not the only valid approach to policy analysis. We discuss various approaches to policy analysis in the next chapter.

In addition, Nagel notes that policy analysis is often criticized as being underutilized by emphasizing the many examples of policy analysis that have not been used in any way by policymakers. He suggests that highly rigorous methods of analysis may have contributed to a degree of nonutilization of policy analysis by decision makers. Researchers can perform externally valid research by using survey and sensitivity analysis as well as quantitative techniques.[30] The argument that policy analyses are underutilized need not be a primary concern for the policy analyst. The primary job of the analyst is to do valid research. Therefore, the focus should be on the variables that lead to nonuse. Such a focus leads to greater consideration of internal and external validity. We will discuss the utilization of policy analysis in Chapter 14 as well as the factors that affect use of policy analysis by decision makers.

Finally, policy analysis is neither inherently liberal or conservative. Instead, as Stuart Nagel notes, studies that begin with conservative assumptions about human nature and/or conservative goals will likely produce conservative results. Likewise, liberal conclusions stem from liberal assumptions and liberal goals. Thus, given different goals and assumptions, some policy analyses will arrive at conservative conclusions, and others will arrive at liberal conclusions. In the next chapter, we discuss several approaches to policy analysis, including liberal and conservative approaches and the assumptions of each.

THE POLICY CYCLE: EVOLUTION OF OUR UNDERSTANDING

As noted in Chapter 1, public policymaking is often viewed as a "conveyor belt" in which issues are first recognized as a problem. Then policies are adopted, implemented by agency officials, evaluated, and finally terminated or changed on the basis of their success or the lack of it. Certainly the process is much more complex than this rather simple image, but when we speak of the policy cycle we are talking about a political process through which most public policies pass. Although the reality of the policy process is very complex, it helps us to understand it by thinking of it as a series of discrete stages from agenda setting to policy termination and change. Over the past twenty-five years, we have made substantial progress in acquiring a better understanding of the policy cycle. This research also passes through several stages.

Stages in the Research Process

Our understanding of the policy cycle has evolved on the basis of a continuing and systematic research tradition. More specifically, research on various phases of the policy cycle seems to pass through several stages as scholars develop and extend the extant literature. Clearly, there is a pattern in the evolution of policy research. A review of the literature shows that our understanding of the policy cycle increases as each phase progresses through four stages. By identifying these four stages and illustrating how policy process research evolves, students may begin to appreciate how research is often cumulative and always evolutionary. These stages involve (1) an initial concern with concept development and an identification of factors that are thought to affect the behavior under study, (2) an attempt to develop a systematic framework for investigation, (3) a test of this framework, and (4) a synthesis and revision of the original concept and framework so that empirical research can progress.

Stage 1: Concept Development   The first stage in the development of our understanding of the policy cycle is the introduction of the concept itself. Martha Derthick and Jeffrey Pressman and Aaron Wildavsky are recognized as the individuals who first advanced the concept of policy implementation in the early 1970s.[31] They provided a wealth of details about all the inducements and constraints that can affect the actual carrying out of a federal mandate by local decision makers. For example, Pressman and Wildavsky provided a case study of the difficulties that the city of Oakland, California, encountered when trying to implement a federal manpower training program during the late 1960s. Specifically, they found that technical details involved with translating federal intent into local policy, confusing goals, inadequate funding, institutional fragmentation, and many other conditions like these frustrated policy implementation in the city of Oakland.[32]

Stage 2: Model Building   Usually after a number of case studies of a particular phenomenon have been published, another scholar will undertake a review and synthesis of those case studies with a view toward identifying the critical variables thought to affect the behavior they are attempting to explain. This will usually result in an analytical framework that categorizes these explanatory variables and tries to make some sense out of them in an organized way. This effort usually results in a new model of a particular phase of the policy cycle. For example, Donald Van Meter and Carl Van Horn did this in 1975 in the area of policy implementation. They identified six explanatory variables that seemed to affect policy implementation, based largely on earlier work by Derthick, Pressman and Wildavsky, and others. These variables included standards and objectives; implementation resources; interorganizational communication and enforcement activities; characteristics of the implementing agencies; economic, social, and political conditions in the locale where the policy was to be delivered; and the disposition of the implementors.[33] Several other scholars interested in policy implementation also attempted to model the process to facilitate empirical research by themselves and others.[34]

Stage 3: Model Testing   For the next phase, still other scholars (or sometimes the authors of the model themselves) will undertake an empirical test of the model. To do this, they will need to identify specific hypotheses stemming from the model, develop measures of each aspect of the model and its hypotheses, and then test the model in a particular substantive area and (it is hoped) across time. For example, a number of empirical tests have been conducted of the policy implementation model that was developed by Paul Sabatier and Daniel Mazmanian. Specifically, it was tested in a number of policy areas, including hazardous waste, coastal zone management, groundwater management, education, civil rights and welfare policy implementation, among others.[35] Essentially, this part of the research process is concerned with an attempt to refute the model's hypotheses by way of rigorous statistical tests.

Stage 4: Synthesis and Revision   Finally, after much testing of the models by several investigators, some scholars will attempt to revise the existing model on the basis of their own findings, develop an entirely new version of the model, or chart a new course, which then moves the research agenda back to stage three. For example, Malcolm Goggin and his colleagues reviewed existing analytical frameworks for policy implementation and, on the basis of their review of the literature, decided that a synthesis of both "top-down" and "bottom-up" models was needed to produce a much more comprehensive (and presumably more accurate) model of policy implementation.[36] Such efforts are important because they can facilitate an increased understanding of the concept and its empirical determinants by sensitizing us to new sources of data and hypotheses and by uncovering a more complete explanation than what was previously available.

SUMMARY

In summary, our understanding of each stage of the policy cycle has advanced over the last twenty-five years largely by moving through each of the four research stages discussed above. By examining various aspects of the policy cycle against this framework, we may see which phases are more fully developed than others and identify the next step in theory building for agenda setting, policy formulation, policy implementation, policy evaluation, policy termination, or policy change.

The preceding discussion has also provided us with an appreciation of how American public policy evolves over time. We noted some near-term changes in American values and longer-term changes in public policies. Finally, our understanding of the policy studies field has evolved as research has accumulated over the past twenty-five years. Although the policy studies subfield is still a young one, we have learned a great deal about the policy cycle and how public policy itself changes over time. In the next two chapters, we discuss various approaches to policy analysis as well as what we mean by "models" in policy analysis. These two chapters lay the groundwork for the following chapters on each phase of the policy cycle.

NOTES

1. See, for example, Virginia Gray, "Models of Comparative State Politics," *American Journal of Political Science* 20 (1976), pp. 235–256; Harvey Tucker, "Its About Time: The Use of Time in Cross-Sectional State Policy Analysis," *American Journal of Political Science* 26 (1982), pp. 176–196. Joseph Cooper and David Brady, "Toward a Diachronic Analysis of Congress," *American Political Science Review* 75 (1981), pp. 988–1006; Wayne McIntosh, "Private Use of a Public Forum: A Long Range View of the Dispute Processing Role of Courts," *American Political Science Review* 77 (1983), pp. 991–1010; and Edwin Amenta and Theda Skocpol, "Taking Exception: Explaining the Distinctiveness of American Public Policies in the Last Century," in *The Comparative History of Public Policy*, ed. Francis G. Castles, (New York: Oxford University Press, 1989).

2. See, for example, Paul A. Sabatier, "Knowledge, Policy-Oriented Learning, and Policy Change: An Advocacy Coalition Framework," *Knowledge: Creation, Diffusion, Utilization* 8 (June 1987), pp. 649–692; See also, Paul A. Sabatier and Hank C. Jenkins-Smith, *Policy Change and Learning: An Advocacy Coalition Approach* (Boulder, CO: WestviewPress, 1993); T. Alexander Smith, *Time and Public Policy* (Knoxville: University of Tennessee Press, 1988); and Malcolm Goggin, Ann O'M. Bowman, James P. Lester, and Laurence J. O'Toole, *Implementation Theory and Practice: Toward a Third Generation* (New York: HarperCollins, 1990).

3. Amenta and Skocpol, "Taking Exception," pp. 292–333. This constant shifting of values in American public policy reflects the ongoing conflict of "visions" on the nature of man. See Thomas Sowell, *A Conflict of Visions* (New York: William Morrow, 1987).

4. James P. Lester, "New Federalism and Environmental Policy," *Publius* (Winter 1986), pp. 149–165.

5. James L. Regens and Robert Rycroft, "Intergovernmental Issues in Managing Sunbelt Growth," in *The Future of the Sunbelt*, ed. Steven Ballard and Thomas James (New York: Praeger, 1983), p. 166.

6. "Both Political Parties Losing Trust, Poll Finds," *Denver Post*, 19 September 1990, p. A1.

7. William Ophuls, *Ecology and the Politics of Scarcity* (New York: W. H. Freeman, 1977).

8. Charles Stoddard, *Looking Forward* (New York: Macmillan, 1982), p. 18; see also Theodore Lowi, *The End of Liberalism* (New York: Norton, 1969); and Trudi G. Miller, "Normative Political Science," *Policy Studies Review* 9 (1990), pp. 232–246.

9. Stoddard, *Looking Forward*, p. 24.

10. Ibid., p. 25.

11. Robert Reinhold, "Politics of the Environment: California Will Test the Waters," *New York Times*, 27 April 1990, p. A1.

12. Leslie Phillips, "Term Limits a Possibility: Angry Voters Give More Thought to Reform," *The Coloradoan*, 13 October 1990, p., A8.

13. Sowell, *A Conflict of Visions*, chs. 1, 2, and 5.

14. Amenta and Skocpol, "Taking Exception," pp. 292–333.

15. James W. Lamare, *Texas Politics: Economics, Power, and Policy* (St. Paul: West Publishing Company, 1981).
16. Amenta and Skocpol, "Taking Exception," pp. 292–333.
17. Charles Murray, *Losing Ground: American Social Policy, 1950–1980* (New York: Basic Books, 1984).
18. Sowell, *A Conflict of Visions*.
19. Stuart Nagel, "Evaluating Public Policy Evaluation," *Policy Studies Journal* 16 (Winter 1987), pp. 219–233.
20. Susan B. Hansen, "Public Policy Analysis: Some Recent Developments and Current Problems," *Policy Studies Journal* (1983), pp. 218–220.
21. See Stuart Nagel, "Report of Membership," *Policy Studies Journal* 17 (Summer 1989), p. 983.
22. See James M. Rodgers, "Social Science Disciplines and Policy Research: The Case of Political Science," *Policy Studies Review* (1989), pp. 13–28; Janet A. Schneider et al., "Policy Research and Analysis: An Empirical Profile," *Policy Sciences* 15 (1982); and David M. Hedge and Jin Mok, "The Nature of Policy Studies: A Content Analysis of Policy Journal Articles," *Policy Studies Journal* 16 (Autumn 1987), pp. 49–61.
23. Nagel, "Evaluating Public Policy Evaluation," pp. 219–233.
24. Ibid., p. 220.
25. William A. Glazer, "The Type and Uses of Political Theory," *Social Research* 22, (1955) pp. 275–296.
26. Edward B. Portis and Dwight F. Davis, "Policy Analysis and Scientific Ossification," *PS: Political Science and Politics* 15 (Fall 1982), pp. 593–599.
27. Hedge and Mok, "The Nature of Policy Studies," pp. 49–61.
28. Schneider et al., "Policy Research and Analysis."
29. Hedge and Mok, "The Nature of Policy Studies."
30. Nagel, "Evaluating Public Policy Evaluation," pp. 219–233.
31. See Martha Derthick, "Defeat at Ft. Lincoln," *The Public Interest* (1970) pp 3–39; and Jeffrey Pressman and Aaron Wildavsky, *Implementation* (Berkeley: University of California Press, 1972).
32. Pressman and Wildavsky, *Implementation*, pp. 1–6 and 146–162.
33. Donald Van Meter and Carl Van Horn, "The Policy Implementation Process: A Conceptual Framework," *Administration and Society* 6 (1975), pp. 445–488.
34. George Edwards, *Implementing Public Policy* (Washington, D.C.: CQ Press, 1980); and Daniel Mazmanian and Paul Sabatier, *Implementation and Public Policy* (Glenview, IL: Scott, Foresman, 1983).
35. Paul A. Sabatier, "Top-Down and Bottom-Up Approaches to Implementation Research: A Critical Analysis and Suggested Synthesis," *Journal of Public Policy* 6 (1986), pp. 21–48.
36. See Goggin et al., *Implementation Theory*, pp. 13–28.

APPROACHES TO POLICY ANALYSIS

When we speak of approaches to policy analysis, we mean the various ways political and other social scientists go about "doing" policy analysis. Every policy analyst implicitly or explicitly adopts a research strategy that best suits him or her. Yet, no one has perfect vision as to the "proper" approach to policy analysis. Rather, policy analysts take many diverse approaches to the analysis of public policy. These alternative approaches are often based on one's primary objectives for conducting policy analysis. At the broadest level, Cook and Vaupel discuss three basic "research styles" in policy analysis: (1) policy analysis, (2) policy research, and (3) applied social science research.[1]

Policy analysis, according to their definition, refers to a staff memorandum on a narrowly defined problem. Such an analysis might take anywhere from days or weeks to prepare. The methods used in this instance are basic data collection techniques, including the compilation of readings and synthesis of many ideas into a coherent course of action. For example, such an analysis might be done to advise the Health and Human Services Department as to whether it should recommend a particular type of welfare policy.

Policy research, on the other hand, refers to a monograph on a broad problem, such as the feasibility of natural gas deregulation. This type of analysis might take a year or more to prepare, and the methods used might include decision analysis, cost-benefit analysis, systems analysis, or other sophisticated techniques. This type of policy analysis might be carried out by several analysts at the Brookings Institution or the Urban Institute for decision makers at the Department of Energy or perhaps those at the White House.

Finally, **applied social science research** refers to a scholarly assessment of the effects of a policy intervention on some narrowly defined set of outcomes, such as analyzing the effects of using seat belts on traffic fatalities in the state of Oklahoma. The research might be carried out by university researchers on behalf of a state agency that is interested in requiring such a law or assessing the impacts of a seat-belt law. The techniques used might be quantitative, such as multiple regression, or even less sophisticated techniques, such as case studies.

SPECIFIC APPROACHES TO POLICY ANALYSIS

There are many more specific approaches to policy analysis. For example, one may be interested in the analysis of either a part of the policy process (e.g., agenda setting, policy implementation) or a substantive area (e.g., environmental policy). One may rely on rigorous statistical approaches or more intuitive approaches. Finally, one may utilize prescriptive (what should be) or empirical (what is) approaches. In the following sections, each of these alternative approaches is discussed to give a better sense of the various options one has in approaching policy analysis. Of course, you are free to adopt any one, or a combination, of these approaches in your own work in public policy analysis.

The Process Approach

Perhaps the most commonly adopted approach is to identify stages in the policy process and then to analyze the determinants of each particular stage. This refers to the familiar conveyorlike concept of the policy cycle that was discussed in Chapter 1. As we mentioned there, it is called the **policymaking process approach.** In this approach, societal problems are first recognized as an issue for action, and then policies are adopted, implemented by agency officials, evaluated, and finally terminated or changed on the basis of their success or the lack of it. Certainly the process is much more complex than this rather simple image, but when we speak of the policy cycle we are talking about a political process through which most public policies pass. Although the reality of the policy process is very complex, it helps us to understand it by thinking of it as if it went through a series of discrete stages such as those discussed in the first chapter. Over the past twenty-five years, we have made substantial progress in acquiring a better understanding of the policy cycle. Various authors have examined particular aspects of the policy cycle and have advanced our understanding of each phase. Some of the aspects of the policy cycle have been more heavily studied than others (e.g., policy formulation), whereas others are just beginning to be further developed by research that seeks to advance the concepts involved or test a series of hypotheses that explain a particular aspect of the policy cycle (e.g., policy change). For example, John Kingdon's work on agenda setting has provided a rich explanation of the central determinants of this phase. Future research will be directed to testing his model and other models of each phase of the policy cycle. Work is just beginning on examining the politics of policy change.[2]

The Substantive Approach

Many policy scientists become substantive specialists in a particular area. For example, they might analyze the determinants of environmental policy formulation, implementation, or change.[3] Others become educational policy specialists, health-care policy specialists, energy policy specialists, crime policy specialists, or welfare policy specialists.[4] These individuals may stay within the context of a single substantive area for much of their professional careers or, alternatively, they may delve into policy in a particular area for a short time and later move on to yet another policy area. According to a recent study of articles published in leading journals of political science, the most often studied areas from a substantive perspective are economic policy (14.5%), science/technology policy (14.1%), and foreign policy (13.7%).[5] An earlier study, however, concluded that health and natural resource/energy/environmental policy studies were the most studied areas of interest during the period 1975–1984.[6]

Some policy scientists argue that expertise within a substantive area is highly desirable and gives one much more credibility than a "generic" policy analyst who is a welfare policy specialist one month and a crime policy specialist the next. To acquire expertise in a substantive area often requires that one become familiar with both the technical and the political aspects of a policy area. For example, when Charles O. Jones wrote his classic book on air quality policy in the 1970s, he had to become very familiar with the technical issues as well as the political issues associated with clean air.[7] By doing so, he was able to produce a very fine book that combined policy analysis skills with substantive expertise.

On the other hand, some policy scientists argue that substantive knowledge is not necessary to be a good policy analyst; instead, they argue that one need only to be skilled in the process and methods of public policy; substance is relatively unimportant.[8] To the contrary, it is our belief that substance is important as it can give one insight into what questions to ask in conducting a policy analysis. This substantive knowledge is necessary, we think, to understand and to interpret one's empirical findings. At any rate, there will always be those who argue either for or against substantive knowledge in policy analysis. This is an area of individual choice for budding policy scientists.

The Logical-Positivist Approach

The **logical-positivist approach,** often called the **behavioral approach** or the **scientific approach,** advocates the use of deductively derived theories, models, hypothesis testing, hard data, the comparative method, and rigorous statistical analysis. "Scientific" in this context means several things. First, it means clarifying key concepts used in the analysis of policy. For example, we must define concepts such as policy implementation more carefully than has been done in the past. Previously, implementation was defined as a yes/no dichotomy rather than as a process of drafting guidelines, appropriating funds, monitoring performance, and revising statutes. Second, it means working from an explicit theory of policy behavior and testing this theory with hypotheses. Third, it means using hard data, developing good measures of various phenomenon, and (ideally) examining various explanations across time.[9] This approach really began with the "behavioral revolution" in social science shortly after World War II. It has endured over fifty years and has become the dominant epistemological approach in political science.

It is not without its critics, however, who argue that the scientific approach misunderstands the policy process by treating it as a "rational project."[10] That is, the policy process is much more complex than this conveyorlike perspective, and thus it does not lend itself to highly sophisticated techniques of analysis. The criticism has taken the form of a postpositivist deconstruction of traditional behavioral methods and instead has argued for more intuitive or participatory approaches to the analysis of public policy. We discuss these latter approaches below.

The Econometric Approach

The **econometric approach,** sometimes called the **public choice** approach or the **political economy** approach, is primarily based on economic theories of politics in which human nature is assumed to be "rational," or motivated by purely personal gain. This approach assumes that people pursue their own fixed weighted preferences regardless of collective outcomes.[11] Essentially, it integrates the general insights of public policy research with the methods of public finance. For example, it assumes that the preferences of individuals are narrow and diverse, which requires that these individuals aggregate or "log-roll" their preferences into majorities that can command governmental action. Recently, John Chubb used such an approach to study policy implementation.[12]

This approach has recently gained much respect in the policy sciences, although it has been criticized for being a somewhat narrow approach to policy analysis.[13] Specifically, some argue that this approach is not completely wrong, but that it is very incomplete in its assumptions about human nature and political power. Specifically, humans are also altruistic (not just rational or selfish) and are thus occasionally motivated to serve the public or collective interest.[14]

The Phenomenological (Postpositivist) Approach

As noted above, recent years have seen a growing disenchantment with the utility of scientific methods (including logical-positivism and econometric approaches) in the study of public policy.[15] Those who oppose the scientific (behavioral) study of public policy prefer an approach whereby *intuition* is more important than positivist/scientific approaches. This approach is called the **phe-nomenological, naturalistic,** or sometimes the **postpositivist approach.**[16] Essentially, this approach argues that we need to adopt "a respect for the disciplined employment of sound intuition itself born of experience not reducible to models, hypotheses, quantification, hard data," and the like.[17] Methodologically, these analysts treat each piece of social phenomenon as a unique event, with ethnographic and other qualitative indices becoming paramount.[18] This alternative view is described by its concern with understanding rather than prediction, with working hypotheses rather than rigorous hypothesis testing, and with mutual interaction between the inquirer and the object of study rather than detached observation on the part of the analysts. To gather "evidence," this approach favors the continued use of case studies, rather than more sophisticated techniques of analysis.[19] In short, it substitutes a concern for scientific rigor with intuition and total immersion in relevant information. Table 3–1 compares the positivist approach with the postpositivist (naturalistic) approach.

The naturalistic approach may be criticized for its lack of rigor and for its movement away from the scientific approach advocated by the behavioralists and economists. It is almost as if these postpositivist scholars want us to return to the prebehavioral approaches of the 1940s and 1950s, in which descriptive, nonscientific, and intuitive studies characterized much of what passed for policy analysis.

The Participatory Approach

The **participatory approach**, recently associated with Peter DeLeon and others, is closely related to the postpositivist challenge, and involves a greater inclusion of

TABLE 3–1   Contrasting Positivist and Naturalist Axioms

Axioms About	Positivist Paradigm	Naturalist Paradigm
The nature of reality	Reality is single, tangible, and fragmentable.	Realities are multiple, constructed, and holistic.
The relationship of knower to the known	Knower and known are independent, a dualism.	Knower and known are interactive, inseparable.
The possibility of generalization	Time- and context-free generalizations (nomothetic statements) are possible.	Only time- and context-bound working hypotheses (idiographic statements) are possible.
The possibility of causal linkages	There are real causes, temporally precedent to or simultaneous with their effects.	All entities are in a state of mutual simultaneous shaping, so that it is impossible to distinguish causes from effects.
The role of values	Inquiry is value-free.	Inquiry is value-bound.

Source: Yvonna S. Lincoln and Egon G. Guba, *Naturalistic Inquiry* (Newbury Park, CA: Sage Publications, 1985) p. 37, copyright © by Sage Publications, Inc. Reprinted by permission of Sage Publications Inc.

the interests and values of the various stakeholders in the policy decision-making processes.[20] It is presumably closer to what Harold Lasswell called the "policy sciences of democracy," in which an extended population of affected citizens would be involved in the formulation and implementation of public policy through a series of discursive dialogues.[21] It would involve extensive open hearings with a broad range of concerned citizens, in which these hearings would be structured in such a way as to prompt individuals, interest groups, and agency officials to contribute to policy design and redesign. The declared purpose of participatory policy analysis is to gather information so that policymakers can make better (i.e., more completely informed) recommendations and decisions. As an approach to analysis, it encourages us to consider a greater number of players and values in the policymaking process and to thus have a better catalog of the various perspectives being brought to bear on the policy under consideration.[22]

Critics of participatory approaches, on the other hand, often argue that increased citizen involvement will lead to an increase in group dissensus over program goals and procedures, that it will lead to needless delays in policy formulation and implementation, that the costs of policymaking and implementation will increase dramatically, and that dissaffected interests will seek to obstruct programs through litigation or recourse to Congress.[23] Moreover, where such participatory experiments have been tried previously, confusion and conflict increases.[24]

Participatory approaches may be more useful as a guide to agenda setting, policy formulation, and policy implementation rather than any other stages in the process. In some respects, it is more of a prescription for policy design or redesign rather than an empirical approach to understanding policy formation or implementation. The next section describes what we mean by a prescriptive approach.

The Normative or Prescriptive Approach

Still others adopt a **normative** or **prescriptive** approach and define their task as a policy analyst as one of defining a desirable "end state" and perhaps arguing that this prescription is both desirable and attainable. They often advocate a policy position and use rhetoric in a very skillful way to convince us of the merits of their position.[25] Some examples or this type of policy analysis would be work by Henry Kissinger, Jeane Kirkpatrick, or other practicing political scientists. Essentially, they use skillful argumentation and (sometimes) selective use of data to advance a political position and to convince us that their position is a desirable policy choice. Sometimes, this type of policy analysis leads to the charge that policy analysts often disguise their ideology as science.[26]

The Ideological Approach

Although not all policy analysts explicitly adopt a liberal or conservative point of view, they almost always have such a view embedded somewhere in their policy analysis. Thomas Sowell calls these ideological approaches "visions" and identifies two competing perspectives.[27]

The "constrained vision" is a picture of egocentric human beings with moral limitations. The fundamental social and moral challenge, therefore, was to make the best of possibilities that existed within that constraint, rather than to dissipate energies in a vain attempt to change human nature. By this logic, then, we should rely on incentives, rather than dispositions, to obtain the desired behavior.[28] The prospect of rewards or the fear of punishments provided the incentives to obtain desirable behavior. Fundamentally, then, this results in a conservative view of human nature and will lead us to more conservative policy positions if we assume that the primary constraints come from within the individual rather than being imposed from the environment outside the individual.

The "unconstrained vision," on the other hand, provides us with a view of human nature in which understanding and human dispositions are capable of intentionally creating social benefits.[29] Under this perspective, humans are capable of directly feeling other people's needs as more important than their own, and therefore consistently acting impartially, even when their interests or those of their family are involved.[30] This view of human nature, then, is often associated with the liberal view that human nature is no constraint; rather constraints are imposed by the environment outside the individual. Both of these visions are illustrated in the substantive chapters of this book.

The Historical Approach

Many public policy scholars are increasingly turning their attention to the evolution of public policies across time.[31] As we examine American public policies from the perspective of a hundred years or more, we begin to see certain patterns in the contours of public policy that were previously unrecognized due to rather short time frames of analysis (i.e., either cross-sectional analyses or analyses limited to a decade or less). Only by examining public policies from the standpoint of a longer period of time can we gain a much better perspective about patterns that exist in the making of public policy in the United States.

Extant research along these lines suggests two rather opposing perspectives on the nature of American policymaking. The first is that American policymaking tends to follow a **cyclical** or **zigzag** pattern in which more conservative tendencies follow more liberal tendencies and then this pattern is repeated across time.[32] This perspective suggests a reactive approach to policymaking that is repetitive and, in some respects, nonrational over time. Others suggest an **evolutionary** explanation in which American public policy reflects policy learning as we evolve toward more thoughtful (and by implication more rational) policymaking.[33] Table 3–2 briefly describes each of these approaches.

Still Other Approaches

Other scholars have identified approaches that are quite similar to the above. For example, Dubnick and Bardes identify five distinct approaches, some of which

TABLE 3–2   Approaches to Policy Analysis

Type of Approach	Primary Objective
1. Process approach	1. To examine a part of the policy process
2. Substantive approach	2. To examine a substantive area
3. Logical-positivist approach	3. To examine the causes and consequences of policy using scientific methods
4. Econometric approach	4. To test economic theories
5. Phenomenological (postpositivist) approach	5. To analyze events through an intuitive process
6. Participatory approach	6. To examine the role of multiple actors in policymaking
7. Normative or prescriptive approach	7. To prescribe policy to decision makers or others
8. Ideological approach	8. To analyze from a liberal or conservative point of view
9. Historical approach	9. To examine policy over time

overlap with our discussion above.[34] Their approaches are identifed in Table 3–3. They provide a very comprehensive set of ways in which analysts approach their jobs.

Scientific policy analysts engage in the search for the "causes and consequences" of public policies rather than the prescription of policies. They use scientific rigor to analyze policies and make an effort to develop and test general propositions and to accumulate reliable research findings of general relevance.[35] This approach is much the same as the logical-positivist approach identified earlier and is represented by such analysts as Thomas R. Dye, Richard Hofferbert, Paul Sabatier, and many others.

The **professional** policy analyst is one who studies public policy to improve it. Austin Ranney, for example, describes this approach as the study of public policy that seeks to apply scientific knowledge to the solution of practical problems.[36] These analysts believe that policy studies will eventually develop a "policy science" that is capable of informing decision-makers by (1) effectively defining and diagnosing policy problems, (2) proposing policy alternatives, (3) developing models that can aid in the achievement of desired ends and methods for testing those models, (4)establishing intermediate goals, and (5) estimating the feasibility of various policy programs.[37] This approach is represented by policy analysts trained at policy institutes (e.g., the Rand Corporation) who tend to practice in think tanks as opposed to universities.

The **political** policy analyst, on the other hand, sees the function of policy analysis as a mechanism to advocate the "right" policy position. The primary task, under this perspective, is to give credence to certain policy positions or to challenge others. Teaching policy analysis within this perspective would stress fundamental research skills and instruction in the rhetorician's methods of

TABLE 3–3   Dubnick and Bardes's Approaches to Policy Analysis

Type of Policy Analyst	Public Policy Problem	Motivation	Approach	Relevant Training
1. Scientist	Theoretic	Search for theory, regularities, "truth"	Scientific method, objectivity, pure analytics	Basic research methods, canons of social science research
2. Professional	Design	Improvement of policy and policymaking	Utilization of knowledge, strategic	Strategic; benefit-cost analysis; queuing, simulation, decision analysis
3. Political	Value maximization	Advocacy of policy position	Rhetoric	Gathering "useful" evidence; "effective" presentation
4. Administrative	Application	Effective and efficient policy implementation	Strategic, managerial	Strategic; same as professional with stress on those talents useful in implementation
5. Personal	Contention	Concern for policy impacts on life	Mixed	Use of many models and techniques from other approaches; less sophisticated

Source: Melvin J. Dubnick and Barbara A. Bardes, *Thinking About Public Policy: A Problem-Solving Approach* (New York: Wiley, 1983), p. 264. Reprinted with permission.

rationalization and argumentation.[38] It is much like the normative or pre-scriptive approach described above.

The other two categories of policy analysis Dubnick and Bardes describe are the **administrative** and the **personal** policy analyst. The administrative analyst is primarily interested in helping to achieve effective and efficient policy implementation and tends to adopt the same methods and goals of the professional policy analyst, whereas the personal policy analyst is reflected in the citizen and lay person's use of policy skills to "reach tentative solutions to some of the basic policy related problems."[39] In effect, this last category is a residual category that involves lay persons who adopt policy analysis but who are not members of any other category, such as the scientific, professional, political, or administrative categories.[40]

In summary, approaches to policy analysis are numerous. In actual practice, scholars often cleverly combine several approaches in various ways. For example, an analyst might write a book that advocates the formulation of a type of employment policy that is clearly redistributive (liberal) in its intent, using (albeit selectively) empirical data that substantiates his or her position. In such a policy analysis, the approach combines the process, substantive, positivist, normative, and ideological or political approaches. By knowing these various approaches to public policy, we acquire the ability to recognize a type of policy analysis for what it is when we see it. We may then evaluate it on its own terms, rather than by applying criteria that are inappropriate to a specific policy analysis or by failing to evaluate it at all. From this discussion, the student should know that there are many options in conducting policy analysis.

Although we do not support the view that there is one "correct" approach to policy analysis, we do believe that the student should nevertheless select an approach that he or she deems most appropriate to the objectives of the analysis. The approach to policy analysis that is selected should be one with which the analyst feels most comfortable, and this approach should be made explicit in the analysis. Each of these approaches is appropriate in certain contexts.

Recently a number of attempts have been made to identify trends over time in approaches to policy analysis. These evaluations show that policy analysis is becoming more scientific (logical-positivist) in approach, although there are continuing elements of prescriptive and qualitative research.[41] Although positivist (especially quantitative) policy analysis, according to studies by Schneider et al. and by Hedge and Mok, is increasingly characteristic of policy studies, it still represents the minority approach compared to more descriptive (qualitative) and rhetorical (prescriptive) approaches. Policy analysis is also becoming more multidisciplinary, along with more analysis of state and local policy, especially natural resource issues and taxing/budgetary issues.[42]

ON BECOMING A BETTER POLICY SCIENTIST

No matter which of these approaches one finally selects, there are several things that one can do to become a better policy analyst. Political scientist Yehezkel Dror identifies several things that one can do over the course of one's professional career to become "more of a policy scientist."[43] First, one should **gain historical and comparative perspectives.** He argues that "present and emerging realities cannot be understood and handled within thin slices of time-space."[44] An ignorance of history thus condemns one to misperceptions of reality and severely limits one's understanding due to the insight provided by analysis over time. Therefore, one must read extensively and broadly. One should always, therefore, know the complete history of the policy area one is researching. Such an understanding can aid in identifying trends over time and in predicting the future of policy in that substantive area. This recognition guides our chapters in the last section of this book.

Second, one should **know policymaking realities.** Very distorted views of policymaking can be obtained from "popular" theories or theories not well-related to practice. Here Dror is openly criticizing the reliance on the economic approach (public choice) to policy analysis. He is simply saying that it is not a good idea to attach oneself to a single approach to policy analysis for there is the danger that such an approach could become dogmatic and therefore restrict your capacity as a policy scientist to discover "objective truth."

Third, **study your own society in depth.** "At the very least," says Dror, "predicaments must be understood within the broader context of societal problem-handling processes: main social institutions and their dynamics must be seen within historic configurations; and main facts of present situations must be known fully with alternative interpretations and within comprehensive alternative futures. . . ."[45] Sometimes, it is necessary to leave one's current operational context to more fully understand it. He encourages us to travel to gain perspective on our own country and its institutions and values.

Fourth, **take up grand policy issues** and work on diverse issues.[46] All too often, Dror feels, policy scientists fail to take on grand policy issues by opting for "micro-issues" that easily fit into extant methods. He advocates taking on grand policy issues, such as those written about by Herman Kahn, Amitai Etzioni, and Robert Reich. In addition, to build policy skills, one must gain experience on a wide variety of issues and public policy problems. Specialization within a single substantive area may be desirable for a time but, over the long term, it is better to broaden one's expertise.

Fifth, **move into metapolicymaking**.[47] By this he means that one should work on efforts to improve policymaking as opposed to just attempting to explain policymaking. In this sense, then, the policy analyst must think like a practitioner at times and try to see the world from this perspective. Such a different worldview helps the analyst to work to improve policymaking.

Sixth, **build an appropriate philosophy of knowledge and action**. He encourages us to reject positivism as the *exclusive* methodology recognized as "scientific." Rather, "clinical skills, subjective knowledge based on immersion in applied work and theoretic study, tacit understanding, and similar partly explicated bases of insight are a legitimate source of policy sciences knowledge and a partly acceptable basis for policymaking."[48] For example, the study of classical political thought and philosophy can enhance one's ability to understand and assess the normative choices implied in many policy decisions.

Seventh, **broaden one's methodology and experience** by moving to different work locations, by spending some time in another culture, and by studying a major language. Over the course of one's lifetime, it is possible to understand and utilize many different techniques, such as those from defense analysis or futures research. Moreover, every striving policy scientist, he argues, should spend at least two to three years in each of three types of work locations: a public policy school doing research and teaching, a policy analysis unit within government, and a think tank working on major policy issues. One should also try to live in a culture as different as possible from one's own country. No substitute exists, he argues, "for working a few years in another culture to broaden one's cognitive maps, to see one's own society in a different and more correct way, and to gain a sense of crucial dimensions of human predicaments and policy issues. . . ."[49]

Finally, he encourages us to **multiply our disciplinary bases** and to **be careful about professional ethics.** Understanding another discipline besides political science, such as economics or sociology, is very useful. Ideally, striving policy scientists should study an additional discipline that is contrary in basic assumptions to the discipline that he or she knows best. Last, but not

TABLE 3–4   On Becoming a Better Policy Scientist

1. Gain historical and comparative perspective.
2. Know policymaking realities.
3. Study your own society in depth.
4. Take up grand and diverse policy issues.
5. Move into metapolicymaking.
6. Build up an appropriate philosophy of knowledge and action.
7. Broaden one's methodology and experience.
8. Multiply your disciplinary bases.
9. Be careful about professional ethics.

Source: Adapted from Y. Dror, "On Becoming More of a Policy Scientist," *Policy Studies Review* 4 (August 1984), pp. 13–21. Reprinted by permission of the publisher.

least, personal professional ethics must be a matter of concern for every policy scientist. One must decide for him- or herself whether to work for every interesting (or paying) client that comes along or work only for clients whose values the analyst respects. In addition, one must balance loyalty to one's clients with overriding values and the public interest. Finally, when working with elites, one must balance essential functions of providing emotional support with the task of presenting often unwelcome (or counterintuitive) analyses and findings.[50] Table 3–4 summarizes Dror's main points.

All these considerations provide useful advice for anyone considering the policy sciences as a profession. In fact, the number of openings for policy analysts within research institutes, universities, and within local, state, or national governmental agencies is growing. The decade of the 1990s will require many more policy analysts as the number of policy problems proliferate. If you decide to become a policy analyst, you will have chosen a very exciting career and one that will doubtless become even more important over the coming decades.

NOTES

1. See Philip J. Cook and James W. Vaupel, "What Policy Analysts Do: Three Research Styles," *Journal of Policy Analysis and Management* 4 (Spring 1985), p. 427.
2. See Paul A. Sabatier and Hank Jenkins-Smith, "Policy Change and Policy-Oriented Learning," *Policy Sciences*, 21 (1988), pp. 123–277. and Paul A. Sabatier and Hank C. Jenkins-Smith, eds., *Policy Change and Learning: An Advocacy Coalition Approach* (Boulder, CO: WestviewPress, 1993).
3. See James P. Lester, ed., *Environmental Politics and Policy: Theories and Evidence*, 2d ed. (Durham, NC: Duke University Press, 1995).
4. See, for example, John E. Chubb and Terry M. Moe, *Politics, Markets, and America's Schools* (Washington, D.C.: The Brookings Institution, 1990); Frances Fox Piven and Richard A. Cloward, *Regulating the Poor* (New York: Pantheon, 1971); James Q. Wilson and Richard J. Herrnstein, *Crime and Human Nature* (New York: Simon and Schuster, 1985); David H. Davis, *Energy Policy* (New York: St. Martins Press, 1993); or Malcolm Goggin, *Policy Design and the Politics of Implementation* (Knoxville: University of Tennessee Press, 1988).

5. James M. Rodgers, "Social Science Disciplines and Policy Research," *Policy Studies Review* 9 (Autumn 1989), pp. 13–28.

6. Hedge and Mok, "The Nature of Policy Studies: A Content Analysis of Policy Journal Articles," *Policy Studies Review* 16 (Autumn 1987), pp. 49–61.

7. Charles O. Jones, *Clean Air* (Pittsburgh: University of Pittsburgh Press, 1975).

8. Richard Hofferbert, for example, has often advanced this view in discussions of the role of substance in policy analysis.

9. See Malcolm L. Goggin, Ann O'M. Bowman, James P. Lester, and Laurence J. O'Toole, *Implementation Theory and Practice: Toward a Third Generation* (New York: HarperCollins, 1990) for an example of this approach in implementation research.

10. Deborah A. Stone, *Policy Paradox and Political Reason* (New York: HarperCollins, 1988).

11. Trudi C. Miller, "Normative Political Science," *Policy Studies Review* 9 (Winter 1990), pp. 232–246.

12. John E. Chubb, "The Political Economy of Federalism," *American Political Science Review* 79 (1985), pp. 994–1015.

13. Miller, "Normative Political Science," p. 237–238.

14. Ibid., p. 237.

15. Gregory A. Daneke, "On Paradigmatic Progress in Public Policy and Administration," *Policy Studies Journal* 17 (Winter 1988–1989), pp. 277–296; Frank Fischer, "Beyond the Rationality Project: Policy Analysis and the Postpositivist Challenge," *Policy Studies Journal* 17 (Summer 1989), pp. 941–951.

16. In its most exteme forms, it is referred to as the "antipositivist" approach, or the "critical" approach.

17. Charles J. Fox, "Implementation Research: Why and How to Transcend Positivist Methodologies," in *Implementation and the Policy Process*, ed. Dennis J. Palumbo and Donald J. Calista (Westport, CT: Greenwood Press, 1990), pp. 199–212.

18. Daneke, "On Paradigmatic Progress," p. 282.

19. E. G. Guba, "The Context of Emergent Paradigm Research," in *Organizational Theory and Inquiry: The Paradigm Revolution*, ed. Y. S. Lincoln (Beverly Hills, CA: Sage, 1993).

20. Peter DeLeon, *Advice and Consent: The Development of the Policy Sciences* (New York: Russell Sage, 1988); and Peter DeLeon, "Participatory Policy Analysis: Prescriptions and Precautions," *The Asian Journal of Public Administration* 12 (June 1990), 29–54; see also Benjamin R. Barber, *Strong Democracy* (Berkeley: University of California Press, 1984); and Jayne Mansbridge, *Beyond Adversary Democracy* (Chicago: University of Chicago Press, 1983).

21. See Harold D. Lasswell, *A Pre-View of Policy Sciences* (New York: Elsevier, 1971).

22. See, for example, John S. Dryzek, "Policy Sciences of Democracy," *Polity* 22 (Fall 1989), 97–118; and John S. Dryzek, *Discursive Democracy: Politics, Policy, and Political Science* (New York: Cambridge University Press, 1990).

23. Walter A. Rosenbaum, "The Paradoxes of Participation," *Administration and Society* 8 (1976), pp. 355–383.

24. Dorothy Nelkin, *Technical Decisions and Democracy* (Beverly Hills, CA: Sage, 1977).

25. See, for example, John Dryzek, *Rational Ecology* (New York: Basil Blackwell, 1987).

26. See Laurence H. Tribe, "Policy Science: Analysis or Ideology," *Philosophy and Public Affairs* (Fall 1972), pp. 66–110.

27. Thomas Sowell, *A Conflict of Visions* (New York: William Morrow, 1987).

28. Ibid., pp. 19–23.
29. Ibid., pp. 23–25.
30. Ibid.
31. See scholars noted in endnote 2, chapter 2.
32. Arthur Schlesinger, "America's Political Cycle Turns Again," *Wall Street Journal*, 10 December 1987, and "Reaganism is Dead—Long Live Liberalism," *Manchester Guardian Weekly*, 8 May 1988.
33. See work by T. Alexander-Smith and others in endnote 2, chapter 2.
34. See Melvin J. Dubnick and Barbara A. Bardes, *Thinking About Public Policy* (New York: Wiley, 1983).
35. Thomas Dye, *Understanding Public Policy* (Englewood Cliffs, NJ: Prentice-Hall, 1987).
36. See Austin Ranney, ed., *Political Science and Public Policy* (Chicago: Markham, 1968).
37. Duncan MacRae, "Policy Analysis: An Applied Social Science Discipline," *Administration and Society* 6 (1975), pp. 376–380. Also cited in Dubnick and Bardes, *Thinking About Public Policy*.
38. Dubnick and Bardes, *Thinking About Public Policy*, p. 259.
39. Ibid., p. 261.
40. Ibid., pp. 261–262. In addition, three other approaches are identified in Donald T. Paris and William Reynolds, *The Logic of Policy Inquiry*, (New York: Longman, 1983), including the behavioral, the economic, and the interpretive approaches.
41. See Janet A. Schneider et al., "Policy Research and Analysis: An Empirical Profile," *Policy Sciences* 15 (1982), pp. 99–114; Susan B. Hansen, "Public Policy Analysis: Some Recent Developments and Current Problems," *Policy Studies Journal* 11 (1983): 14–42; David Hedge and Jin W. Mok, "The Nature of Policy Studies: A Content Analysis of Policy Journal Articles," *Policy Studies Journal* 16 (1987), pp. 49–61; and James M. Rodgers, "Social Science Disciplines and Policy Research: The Case of Political Science," *Policy Studies Review* 9 (1989): 13–28.
42. Hedge and Mok, "The Nature of Policy Studies," pp. 49– 61; Schneider et al., "Policy Research and Analysis," pp. 99–114.
43. Yehezkel Dror, "On Becoming More of a Policy Scientist," *Policy Studies Review* 4 (1984), pp. 13–22.
44. Ibid., p. 13.
45. Ibid., p. 14.
46. Ibid.
47. Ibid.
48. Ibid., p. 15.
49. Ibid., p. 19.
50. Ibid., p. 18.

MODELS AND PUBLIC POLICY STUDIES

". . . the major advantage of using formal models is the precision and clarity of thought which these models require, and the depth of argument which they allow."

MORRIS FIORINA

Before major development projects are undertaken, builders often construct a scaled-down model of the entire development project so that anyone interested can see beforehand what the project will look like when it is completed. Similarly, to analyze public policy, we often employ certain conceptual tools that help us to visualize reality. Among the conceptual tools that are most common and most useful to the policy analyst are **models** and **typologies**. These mental constructs allow us to better understand the formation or implementation of policies. That is, we need some conception of reality to guide our analysis. According to Thomas Dye, a model is "a simplified representation of some aspect of the real world."[1] Moshe Rubenstein suggests that we frequently use models to "facilitate understanding and enhance prediction."[2] Essentially, a model provides us with a "lay of the land" or a graphical representation of some aspect of the policy process. We are all model builders in the sense that we need to see some sort of pattern in the world around us, and thus we tend to interpret events in terms of a perceived pattern. In this way we *create* reality rather than simply observe it. In this chapter, we discuss various types of models and their usefulness in analyzing public policy.

MODELS

The Uses and Forms of Models

Models help us to "see" an abstraction of reality by indicating relationships among a number of determinants that are thought to cause some phenomenon. Sometimes, models use novel methods of representation, "while at other times models may constrain one's insight on reality."[3] By simplifying policy problems, models help us to better understand reality; on the other hand, they may inherently contribute to a distortion of reality. At any rate, these models may be expressed as concepts, diagrams, graphs, or mathematical equations and may be used to describe, explain, or predict elements of a particular phenomenon. The types of models include descriptive models, normative models, verbal models, symbolic models, procedural models, surrogate models, and perspective models.[4] However, the most common distinctions are between descriptive and normative models and between "hard" and "soft" models.

Descriptive Models The purpose of descriptive models is "to explain and/or predict the causes and consequences of policy choices."[5] For example, a model of the determinants of welfare spending in the fifty American states found that economic variables were more important than political variables in explaining variation among the states' spending patterns.[6] Much of the so-called determinants-of-public-policy approach uses descriptive models to explain and predict the causes and consequences of public policy.[7] One of the most well-known examples of descriptive models is the Coleman Report in which various explanations of student performance are assessed against each other.[8] This report found that family background factors, such as the amount of reading material in the home, parent's education, and so on were the most important determinants of student achievement as opposed to such factors as faculty quality or the amount of resources devoted to the school. In short, descriptive models are very common in the public policy literature.

Normative Models Alternatively, the purpose of normative models "is not only to explain and/or predict but also to provide rules and recommendations for optimizing the attainment of some value."[9] For example, let's say that we are interested in ascertaining the best way to prevent world hunger. We examine several policy options, such as food aid, monetary assistance, birth-control devices, and education, in terms of their contribution to alleviating hunger. We may find that food aid was counterproductive to alleviating hunger; in fact, it may have contributed to increased population growth, which in turn increased the amount of hunger. By contrast, birth-control technology and education may have been more effective in reducing hunger. Therefore, such a model explains and predicts as well as suggests a way to optimize a value—in this case alleviating hunger in the developing world.

Hard and Soft Models Another useful distinction to be made about models is between those that are "hard," in "which actual phenomena are being symbolized" and those that are "soft" or "representations of purely theoretical or hypothetical conceptual matters of imagined characteristics of some event of our concern."[10]

For example, consider a road map that represents the actual geography of the land-scape and is accurate (presumably) with respect to reality. On the other hand, consider a textbook diagram of a political system in which there are inputs, conversion mechanisms, and outputs. The latter is an attempt to take a very abstract concept such as a political system and convert it into a series of linkages between these hypothetical elements in the system.

The important thing to remember about models, whether descriptive or normative, hard or soft, is that they are imperfect representations of reality. As such, they may help to guide our thinking and to better understand some phenomenon, but they are still only abstract tools with which to interpret reality.

Criteria for Evaluating Models

How do you know whether models are helping or not? Usefulness, rather than the type of model being used, is the best criterion for evaluating a model's utility. That is, a "good model, like a good map, is rich; it guides us, under suitable interpretation, to many true statements . . . and facilitates understanding."[11] If we are going to use models in thinking about public policy, then we need to have a number of criteria for evaluating the usefulness of models. Thomas Dye has suggested a number of such criteria for evaluating models.[12]

1. Does the model *order and simplify* political life so that we can think about it more clearly and understand relationships in the real world? If the model is so simple that it leads to misunderstandings in our thinking about reality, or if it is so complex that it confuses us, then the model may not be of much help in explaining public policy.

2. Does the model *identify* the most important aspects of public policy? That is, the model should focus on the most salient aspects of a political phenomenon, such as the causes or consequences of public policy, and not be concerned with irrelevant variables or conditions. Essentially, the model should direct our attention to what is really significant about public policy.

3. Is the model *congruent with reality*? By this we mean does the model bear a strong relationship to reality or is it so idealized or abstract that it is unrelated to the real world? A good model should incorporate real-world empirical referents and facilitate a greater understanding of a particular policy situation or process.

4. Does the model *communicate* something meaningful in a way that we all understand? Does the model have the characteristic of intersubjective agreement, in which a concept used in the model is one that we all can understand? If the model communicates a concept for which there is no common understanding, then it is judged to have little intersubjective agreement and it will not help us better understand a phenomenon.

5. Does the model *direct inquiry and research* into public policy? A good model should suggest a number of testable relationships (hypotheses) that can be

observed, measured, and verified. We must be able to apply the model in a way that allows for empirical testing; the model is of little use if there are no testable propositions derived from it or if these relationships cannot be measured and tested with real-world data.

6. Does the model *suggest an explanation* of public policy? A model that merely describes public policy is not as useful as one that explains public policy. Does the model set forth a series of verifiable relationships that add up to a fairly complete explanation of some public policy phenonenon? Two of the best examples of such models are the elitist and pluralist models of community power and public policy.[13]

Some Examples of Models

To better understand the usefulness of models and what constitutes a good model, let's consider two of the best-known models in the public policy literature, the **elitist model** and the **pluralist model**.

The Elitist Model   Elite theory is based on the idea that public policy is the result of the preferences and values of a governing elite.[14] Thomas Dye and Harmon Zeigler summarize the ruling elite model as follows:

1. Society is divided into the few who have power and the many who do not. Only a small number of persons allocate values for society; the masses do not decide public policy.

2. The few who govern are not typical of the masses who are governed. Elites are drawn disproportionately from the upper socioeconomic strata of society.

3. The movement of nonelites to elite positions must be slow and continuous to maintain stability and avoid revolution. Only nonelites who have accepted the basic elite consensus can be admitted to governing circles.

4. Elites share a basic consensus on behalf of the basic values of the social system and the preservation of the system. In America, the bases of elite consensus are the sanctity of private property, limited government, and individual liberty.

5. Public policy does not reflect demands of the masses but rather the values of the elites. Changes in public policy will be incremental rather than revolutionary.

6. Active elites are subject to relatively little direct influence from apathetic masses. Elites influence masses more than masses influence elites.

7. Thus, public policy is directed from the top to the bottom rather than the reverse. Power flows upward and decisions flow downward.[15] A representation of the elite model is provided in Figure 4–1.

Some evidence indicates that the elite model is a good characterization of community decision making. Research by Robert and Helen Lynd in the 1920s and the 1930s, as well as Floyd Hunter in the 1960s (and again in the 1980s),

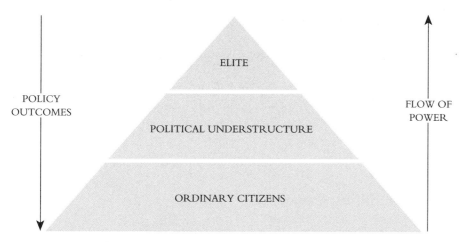

FIGURE 4–1   The Elitist Model

found that this model of community power was an accurate representation of reality.[16] Critics of the ruling elite model, however, challenged the empirical findings and put forth their own version of reality in an alternative pluralistic model.[17]

The Pluralist Model   An alternative model of decision making in America is the pluralist model. The proponents of this model of community power and public policy include Robert Dahl and David Truman.[18] It may be briefly summarized as follows:

1. Power is an attribute of individuals in their relationship with other individuals in the process of decision making.
2. Power relationships do not necessarily persist; rather they are formed for a particular decision and after this decision is made they disappear to be replaced by a different set of power relationships when the next decision is made.
3. No permanent distinction exists between "elites" and "masses." Individuals who participate in decision making at one time are not necessarily the same individuals who participate at another time. Individuals move in and out of the ranks of decision makers simply by becoming active or inactive in politics.
4. Leadership is fluid and highly mobile. Wealth is an asset in politics, but it is only one of many kinds of assets.
5. There are multiple centers and bases of power within a community. No single group dominates decision making in all issue areas.
6. Considerable competition exists among leaders. Public policy thus reflects bargains or compromises reached between competing leadership groups.

A representation of the pluralist model is found in Figure 4–2. It is similar to an unsolved Rubic's cube, in which political power is highly fragmented and widely dispersed over different actors, different types of policy, and different points in time.

These are two of the best-known models of public policymaking. They provide us with a mental image of the political processes that characterize public policy. Although both have been criticized for their shortcomings, they remain useful as a means of thinking about how power is distributed in the making of American public policy.[19]

Steps in Building Conceptual Models

How are models developed in the public policy literature? In the following chapters, we present several alternative models of agenda setting, policy formulation, policy implementation, and policy change. It would be useful at this point, however, to begin to understand how these models are derived. We discussed in Chapter 2 the evolutionary process that the public policy literature undergoes over time. A key step in that evolution is model building in which the builder works with the extant literature, as well as his or her insights, to construct a model of some public policy phenomenon. In constructing a model, one must utilize several distinct steps. According to Dubnick and Bardes, these steps include the following:[20]

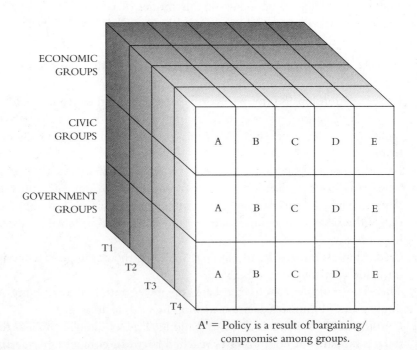

A' = Policy is a result of bargaining/
compromise among groups.

FIGURE 4–2   The Pluralist Model

Step 1. Examine the problematic phenomenon or situation carefully and proceed to factor (i.e., divide) it into simpler, more manageable problems.[21]   You cannot tackle all public policy problems at once; rather you must define your dependent variable (what you are seeking to explain) very carefully and precisely. For example, you might be interested in explaining what factors influence policy implementation or policy termination. You might want to develop a model that explains the changes in public policy over time, or you might be interested in explaining environmental policy formation. You probably could not, on the other hand, develop a model that at once explains the entire policy process. Some models are more comprehensive than are others, but one must be careful to avoid trying to tackle too much with a single model. Parsimony, or the ability to explain the most with the least, is a useful guide in the construction of policy models.

Step 2. Establish the purpose of the model.   What is the model supposed to do for you? Is it a descriptive or a normative model? That is, does it seek to predict and explain? Does it seek to prescribe policy solutions? No single model is expected to do everything. Rather, you should decide what kind of a model you are seeking to construct and define the model's objectives very carefully. How will the model be used by others?

Step 3. Observe facts relevant to the problematic phenonenon or situation.   The best way to begin at this stage is to read all that has been written about a particular policy phenomenon. Usually, the extant literature is based on case studies about the determinants of some phenomenon. By accumulating these materials, you may be able to begin to piece together multiple explanations about this behavior. As you become familiar with the causes and effects of this phenomenon, you will begin to see a pattern that will lead you to later construct a model.

Step 4. List the elements that may relate to the model's purpose. Select those that are believed to be the most relevant to the problem at hand. Arrange these relevant elements into chunks or clusters that reflect strong structural, functional, or interactive connections.   For example, let us say that we are interested in explaining the utilization of policy analysis by decision makers. The existing literature suggests that there are three broad categories of factors that determine the degree of knowledge utilization: factors related to the environment within which the policy analysis takes place, factors related to the policy analysis itself, and factors related to the potential users of this information. These three categories of factors may be identified and together they suggest a testable explanation of this particular phenonenon.

Step 5. Consider these aggregates and the facts they represent relative to the purpose of your proposed model. Try to find patterns or relationships among these factors that will aid you in fulfilling that purpose.   This is the most creative part of model building. In this stage, you are looking for the pattern of interrelationships

that characterize your model. In the earlier stage, you were simply trying to identify all the kinds of factors that explained your phenonenon, whereas at this stage
you are looking for interactions in the categories of factors you identified earlier. For example, a well-known model of political development hypothesizes
that urbanization leads to industrialization and education, which in turn leads to
political development. In this stage cause and effects are very important in the
sense that some of the factors you identified earlier will precede others and cause
certain effects. Every relationship you identify here is a theoretical statement in
your model, so you should be careful and have strong evidence to support the
posited relationships.

   ***Step 6. Elaborate on the constructed model where necessary and simplify where
   possible.***   As you work with your model, you will begin to see the need for
minor corrections and alterations. These alterations may be based on actual tests
of the model, from additional fieldwork that identifies "left-out" variables, or it
may be a function of subtleties in your original design that you overlooked in
developing the model. At any rate, it is likely (and even desirable) that you will
make changes in your model on the basis of experience with it. These refine-
ments may also come from work by others who use your model in their studies
of public policy.

   In sum, model construction is very important to the advancement of public
policy studies; indeed, it is a key stage in the evolution of the subfield.

TYPOLOGIES

In addition to models, sometimes we use **typologies** to analyze public policy. A
typology is a way of organizing phenomena into discrete categories for systematic analysis. For example, in 1964, Theodore Lowi proposed a typology that he
thought would facilitate our understanding of public policymaking.[22] He argued
that what was needed was a general framework that could convert discrete facts
from case studies into a body of research that could be evaluated, weighed, and
cumulated. His main thesis was that a political relationship in policymaking is
determined by the type of policy at stake; that is, every type of policy has a distinctive type of political relationship. In developing this typology, he argued that
public policy may be categorized into three types: regulatory, distributive, and
redistributive. Regulatory policies attempt to limit the number of specific service
providers (e.g., airline regulations) or to protect the public by setting forth conditions under which private activities may occur (e.g., environmental regulation).
Essentially, regulatory policy involves a direct choice as to who will be indulged
and who will be deprived. Because of this, various groups will engage in conflict, bargaining, and negotiation over who should win and who should lose.
   Distributive policies are those policies that are aimed at promoting, usually
through subsidies, private activities that are judged to be socially desirable. This

type of public policy does not have winners or losers; there is no direct con-frontation at all and everybody benefits equally (e.g., educational policy).

Finally, redistributive policies are an effort to distribute wealth or other valued goods in society. Essentially, these policies redistribute benefits from one group to another (e.g., welfare policy). Therefore, redistributive policy tends to be char-acterized by ideological concerns and often involves class conflict.

Lowi argues that these three areas of policy or government activity constitute real "arenas of power." Each arena tends to develop its own characteristic politi-cal structure, political process, elites, and group relations (i.e., its own politics). For example, regulatory policy is characterized by coalitions of interest groups that are often in conflict with each other and are very unstable as they seek to bar-gain and compromise. Thus, pluralism characterizes this arena of power. In the distributive policy arena, decisions are characterized by logrolling rather than conflict; power relations are stable and there is very little conflict. The elitist model thus characterizes this arena of power. Finally, in redistributive policy, there is much conflict but it is more likely to take place among elite organizations. Lowi's major contribution was to suggest that we cannot generalize across all types of policy with a single model (e.g., elitist or pluralist). Rather, we should focus our investigation within a particular type of policy and develop general-izations by policy type as opposed to broad generalizations that are expected to hold across the entire range of public policy.

The Lowi typology has been criticized on a number of grounds. Some argue that it is difficult to separate regulatory from distributive and redistrib-utive policy.[23] Moreover, policy is more complex than Lowi's simple typology as policies are first one type of policy, then become another. Recently some of the defenders of the Lowi typology assert, on the other hand, that his typology retains its usefulness if we think of it as a continuum rather than dis-crete categories. Some policies are more purely regulatory than are others (e.g., crime policy) and some policies are more purely redistributive than are others (e.g., progressive income tax).[24] Nevertheless, today the Lowi typology remains one of the most useful conceptual tools in the study of public policy and has been applied very creatively over the past three decades.[25]

In addition, other scholars have developed typologies that categorize public policies. For example, Mancur Olson distinguishes between public goods and private goods.[26] Public goods are those goods that are available to everyone and no one may be excluded from their use, whereas private goods are divisible in the sense that others may be kept from benefiting from their use or be charged for benefitting from these goods. Lewis Froman also developed a means for dis-tinguishing policies from one another. He differentiates between policies that are areal and those that are segmental.[27] Areal policies are those that affect a total population of a geographical area by a single policy, whereas segmental policies are those that affect different people at different times in separate areas of a pop-ulation. Similarly Eulau and Eyestone distinguish between adaptive and control policies.[28] Adaptive policies are policies that are designed to meet the needs of a group, whereas control policies are those that attempt to direct the environment. In summary, these policy typologies are meant to be helpful to us as we begin to analyze public policy. Whether they help or not has a lot to do with several evaluative considerations.

Criteria for Evaluating Typologies

How do we know whether a typology is a useful one? How do we evaluate typologies? Although it is difficult to evaluate typologies in any comprehensive way, Lewis Froman has proposed a number of criteria for evaluating typologies.[29] Among these criteria are the following:

1. *Inclusiveness.* Does the scheme cover all possible forms of the phenomenon in its categories? That is, have all dimensions of this phenomenon been included within the typology? Is the typology comprehensive?
2. *Mutual exclusivity.* Are the separate categories within the typology distinct so as to avoid overlap? Are the categories distinct from one another in such a way as to facilitate placement into one category or another?
3. *Validity.* Do the concepts used in the typology measure what they say they measure? For example, what do we mean by a federal, state, or local policy? Are not public policies often a mixture of all three levels of government? Is there a close fit between the typology and the empirical world that it purports to measure?
4. *Reliability.* Can the typology be used by others in a consistent manner? Does the typology have the characteristic of "intersubjectiveness," or the trait that implies everyone will use the typology in the same, or nearly the same, way?
5. *Level of measurement.* Does the typology employ an appropriate level of measurement? For example, nominal-level measurement is used to classify cases; ordinal-level measurement is used to order cases; and interval-level data are used for more specific differentiation between items on a scale of measurement.
6. *Operationalization.* Can a phenomenon be measured by a set of attributes? Does the typology lend itself to being measured? Can the concepts used in the typology be measured?
7. *Differentiation.* Are the categories being used in the typology significant and theoretically fruitful?

WHERE DO WE GO FROM HERE?

In the first section of this book, we have introduced students to the context of public policy studies. To gain some perspective on the study of public policy, we examined how the subject has evolved over time, paying particular attention to the evolutionary process by which the literature and subject matter develop. Many approaches may be used to study public policy and the choice over the single "best" approach must be left to the student. One of the most useful approaches is the policy process approach, in which we study agenda setting, policy formulation, policy implementation, policy evaluation, policy termination, and policy change. This is the approach that guides the next section of this text. We will examine the development of the public policy literature in each of these areas of the policy process, paying particular attention to how this literature has evolved over time.

At the moment, a lively debate characterizes the policy studies field over the most appropriate approach (the positivists versus the postpositivists) to the analysis of public policy. Implicit in this book is a preference for the positivist approach, though we also recognize that qualitative approaches have merits as well. The policy process is terribly complex, but we will attempt to make some sense of it by working with prevailing models of each aspect of the process. Thus, we introduced the topic of models for helping us to understand the policy process. In the following section, we examine how these models help us to understand agenda setting, policy formulation, policy implementation, and policy change. In some areas of the policy process, the available literature is less developed (e.g., policy evaluation and policy termination) in terms of model building. Nevertheless, the stage has been set for a thorough review of the evolution of our thinking in several phases of the policy process. By remembering that policy studies are constantly evolving, we begin to appreciate how our knowledge base (both substantive and procedural) expands over time. Based on substantive analyses, we also develop a better understanding of how the process works. In doing so, we also acquire some means of affecting policy outcomes over time.

NOTES

1. Thomas R. Dye, *Understanding Public Policy,* 8th ed. (Englewood Cliffs, NJ: Prentice-Hall, 1995), p. 18.
2. Moshe F. Rubenstein, *Patterns of Problem Solving* (Englewood Cliffs, NJ: Prentice-Hall, 1975), p. 19.
3. Stephen Toulmin, *The Philosophy of Science: An Introduction* (New York: Harper and Row, 1960), pp. 34–35.
4. William N. Dunn, *Public Policy Analysis: An Introduction* (Englewood Cliffs, NJ: Prentice-Hall, 1981), pp. 110–118.
5. Ibid., p. 111.
6. Richard E. Dawson and James A. Robinson, "Inter-Party Competition, Economic Variables, and Welfare Policies in the American States," *Journal of Politics* 25, no. 2 (May 1963), pp. 265–289.
7. See Kent E. Portney, *Approaching Public Policy Analysis* (Englewood Cliffs, NJ: Prentice-Hall, 1986).
8. James S. Coleman, *Equality of Educational Opportunity* (Washington, D.C.: U.S. Government Printing Office, 1966).

9. Dunn, *Public Policy Analysis*, p. 111.

10. Marc Belth, *The Process of Thinking* (New York: David McKay, 1977), pp. 15–19.

11. David Hawkins, *The Language of Nature: An Essay in the Philosophy of Science* (Garden City, NY: Doubleday, 1967), pp. 38–39.

12. Dye, *Understanding Public Policy*, pp. 40–41; see also Daniel C. McCool, *Public Policy Theories, Models, and Concepts* (Englewood Cliffs, NJ: Prentice-Hall, 1995), pp. 12–18.

13. Thomas R. Dye and Harmon Zeigler, *The Irony of Democracy* (Monterrey, CA: Brooks/Cole, 1981).

14. Thomas R. Dye, *Understanding Public Policy*, 6th ed. (Englewood Cliffs, NJ: Prentice-Hall, 1987), p. 29.

15. Dye and Zeigler, *The Irony of Democracy*.

16. Robert S. Lynd and Helen M. Lynd, *Middletown* (New York: Harcourt Brace, 1929) and *Middletown in Transition* (New York: Harcourt Brace, 1937). See also Floyd Hunter, *Community Power Structure* (Chapel Hill: University of North Carolina Press, 1969); and Floyd Hunter, *Community Power Succession: Atlanta's Policy-makers Revisited* (Chapel Hill: University of North Carolina Press, 1980).

17. Robert Dahl, *Who Governs* (New Haven, CT: Yale University Press, 1961).

18. David B. Truman, *The Governmental Process* (New York: Knopf, 1951); and Dahl, *Who Governs*.

19. See Robert A. Dahl, "A Critique of the Ruling Elite Model," *American Political Science Review* 52, no. 2 (June 1958), pp. 463–469; Peter Bachrach and Morton S. Baratz, "The Two Faces of Power," *American Political Science Review* 66, no. 4 (December 1962), pp. 947–952; Theodore Lowi, *The End of Liberalism* (New York: Norton, 1969); see also Clarence Stone, "Systemic Power in Community Decision-Making," *American Political Science Review* 74, no. 4 (December 1980), pp. 978–990.

20. Melvin J. Dubnick and Barbara A. Bardes, *Thinking About Public Policy: A Problem-Solving Approach* (New York: Wiley, 1983), pp. 44–48.

21. The following six steps draw heavily from William T. Morris, "On the Art of Modeling," in *The Process of Model-Building in the Behavioral Sciences*, ed. Ralph M. Stogdill (New York: Norton, 1970), pp. 83–84.

22. Theodore Lowi, "American Business, Public Policy, Case Studies, and Political Theory," *World Politics* 16 (July 1964), pp. 677–715.

23. See G. D. Greenberg et al., "Developing Public Policy Theory: Perspectives from Empirical Research," *American Political Science Review* 71, no. 4 (December 1977), pp. 1532–1543.

24. Robert Spitzer, "Promoting Policy Theory: Revising the Arenas of Power," *Policy Studies Journal* 15, no. 4 (June 1987), pp. 675–689.

25. See Randall Ripley and Grace Franklin, *Congress, the Bureaucracy, and Public Policy* (Homewood, IL: Dorsey Press, 1980).

26. Mancur Olson, *The Logic of Collective Action* (Cambridge, MA: Harvard University Press, 1965).

27. Lewis Froman, "An Analysis of Public Policy in Cities," *Journal of Politics* 29, no. 1 (February 1967), pp. 94–108.

28. Heinz Eulau and Robert Eystone, "Policy Maps of City Councils and Policy Outcomes," *American Political Science Review* 62, no. 1 (March 1968), pp 124–143.

29. Lewis Froman, "The Categorization of Policy Contents," in *Political Science and Public Policy*, ed. Austin Ranney (Chicago: Markham, 1968), pp. 46–48.

PART TWO

ANALYSIS IN THE POLICY PROCESS

AGENDA SETTING

"We know more about how issues are disposed of than about how they came to be issues on the governmental agenda in the first place, how the alternatives from which decision makers choose were generated, and why some potential issues and some likely alternatives never came to be the focus of serious attention."

JOHN W. KINGDON

Where do public policy proposals come from? Why do decision makers pay more attention to some issues than to others? In this chapter, we begin an analysis of the policymaking process as a series of developmental stages. Before we begin this analysis, we need to define a couple of terms. **Policy formation** means the total process of creating or forming a public policy, whereas **policy formulation** refers to the more discrete stage of adopting a proposed course of action for dealing with a public problem.[1]

Until very recently, most public policy research focused on the policy adoption aspect of the policy cycle. This phase of the policy cycle was the first to be explored by researchers. Many models were developed to explain policy adoption. Now, more emphasis has been placed on how issues get onto the agenda in the first place. We simply want to know why some issues are more likely to get onto the agenda than others. This is a key aspect of the policy cycle and an extremely important one. In answering this question, it seems that issues get onto the agenda if several conditions are met. First, if the issue has reached *crisis proportions* and can no longer be ignored, it will be placed on the agenda. Second, if the issue has achieved *particularity*, in which the issue exemplifies and dramatizes a larger issue, such as ozone depletion and global warming, it will receive attention. Third, if the issue has an *emotive* aspect, or attracts media attention because of a "human interest angle," it will receive agenda attention. Fourth, if the issue has *wide impact*, it will be placed on the agenda. Fifth, if the issue raises questions about *power and legitimacy* in society, it will get onto the agenda. Finally, if the issue is *fashionable*, it will receive attention.[2] All these factors seem to be necessary conditions for items being placed on the agenda. Still, we need to explore these conditions (and others) in greater depth. In this initial chapter on the policy process, we will examine how policies get onto the public, or governmental, agenda. Agenda setting is crucial, because if an issue cannot be placed on the agenda, it cannot be considered for action. Problems must be recognized before a policy choice can be made.

Cobb and Elder define agenda setting as "a set of political controversies that will be viewed as falling within the range of legitimate concerns meriting the attention of the polity; a set of items scheduled for active and serious attention by a decision-making body."[3] Others, such as John Kingdon, define agenda setting as "the list of subjects or problems to which government officials . . . are paying some serious attention at any given time."[4] Still others, such as Baumgartner and Jones, distinguish between "policy images" (how policies are understood and discussed) and "policy venues" (the institutions or groups that have the jurisdictional authority over the issue).[5] The process of agenda setting, according to Barbara Nelson, is where "public officials learn about new problems, decide to give them their personal attention, and mobilize their organizations to respond to them."[6] Essentially, agenda setting involves getting an issue to be recognized. Each stage of the policy process is theoretically distinct, but they nevertheless merge together in practice. For example, the nature of the problem affects whether or not it gets onto the agenda, as well as whether or not a course of action gets finally enacted into law. Generally speaking, once a proposal is before Congress in the form of a public law, it may be said to be on the agenda. Let us examine agenda setting in a bit more depth.

THE NATURE OF POLICY PROBLEMS

A **policy problem** may be defined as a "condition or situation that produces needs or dissatisfaction on the part of people for which relief or redress is sought."[7] In effect, the tractability of public policy problems varies greatly. Some public policy problems are very easy to define and solve, such as energy conservation; others, such as reducing crime, are more difficult to assess and diagnose. Consider, for example, the following list of public policy problems Kirkpatrick Sale has identified:

> An imperiled ecology, a deepening suspicion of authority and distrust of established institutions, the decline of community, a contempt for law, deteriorating cities, megalopolitan sprawls, ghettoes, overcrowding, traffic congestion, untreated wastes, smog and soot, budgetary insolvency, inadequate schools, mounting illiteracy, declining university standards, dehumanizing welfare systems, police brutality, overcrowded hospitals, clogged court calendars, inhuman prisons, racial injustice, sex discrimination, poverty, crime, alcoholism, divorce, violence, defense overspending, nuclear prolifera-

tion, the arms race, unemployment, inflation, the energy crisis, mounting personal debt, maldistribution of wealth, worldwide inflation, international instability, and the end of the American imperial arrangement, to name a few.[8]

The personal debt problem, for example, may be remedied much more easily than the crime problem or the poverty problem. In many areas of public policy, we simply do not know how to "solve" the problem with an appropriate policy solution. This is primarily because we often do not understand the cause-and-effect relationship between the problem and its policy solution. Cause and effect are open to interpretation and widely different perceptions. Policy analysts must consider the characteristics and dimensions of the problems if they are to be helpful in designing effective solutions. Yet, many problems are taken as "givens" and little attention is directed toward understanding the problem in the first place. The current debate on welfare policy is illustrative of this. Michael Harrington's *The Other America* and his more recent book, *Poverty in America*, argues that poverty is "caused" by external or structural factors, such as changes in employment opportunities. Charles Murray, in *Losing Ground*, on the other hand, argues that poverty is "caused" by our current welfare programs, which offer more incentives to remain on welfare than to get off of it. Others, such as Edward Banfield, argue that individual shortcomings predispose some to a life of poverty rather than a hostile external environment or structural determinants of poverty.[9]

As our understanding of a problem develops over time, we often define the problem very differently. For example, until very recently, we pursued a reactive policy response to the environmental problem. Some environmental problem would be identified, such as toxic waste, and we would formulate a response to it. The passage of the Comprehensive Environmental Response, Compensation, and Liability Act of 1980 (CERCLA), or Superfund, is an example of this kind of strategy. More recently, we are attempting to design environmental policies that are *preventive*, rather than reactive, in nature. We are attempting to anticipate the problem and prevent the buildup of pollutants rather than clean them up after the fact. The passage of the Pollution Prevention Act of 1990 is an example of this preventive strategy.

Policy problems are continually being redefined on the basis of new information or a new understanding of the problem. The recent and emerging concern for wetlands is a good example of this phenomenon. In addition, there are several types of agendas to deal with these policy problems.

TYPES OF AGENDAS

Cobb and Elder distinguish several types of agendas, including **systemic agendas** and **institutional agendas**. Systemic agendas consist of all those issues that might be subject to action or that are already being acted on by government. These issues can include pseudo-issues, or issues discussed just to placate clientele groups but without any serious attempt to make policy choices. Systemic agendas are the universe of issues that might be considered for governmental action, whereas institutional agendas are those sets of issues explicitly up for active and serious consideration by decision-making bodies, such as the legislative calendar or the court docket.[10] The institutional agenda is also referred to as the **public** or **government** agenda as opposed to the **popular** or **decision** agenda (other names for the systemic agenda), which consists of all the issues under consideration by the mass public or professional class.[11] The point is that there are two types of agendas, depending on whether issues have been formally placed on the agenda or are being discussed in the background, waiting to be placed on the agenda.

TYPES OF ISSUES

Many types of issues are placed on the systemic or institutional agendas. For example, **subject issues** are relatively broad, such as air pollution, water pollution or health-care issues. Issues surrounding specific legislation, such as the Clean Air Act of 1990 (CAA) or the Comprehensive Environmental Response, Compensation, and Liability Act of 1980 (CERCLA) are called **policy issues**. **Project issues** relate to a specific project or locality, such as the Denver International Airport issue.[12]

New issues are those that are newly emergent, such as radon issues and indoor air pollution. **Cyclical issues** occur regularly, such as the annual budget. Finally, **recurrent issues** reemerge because of the failure of previous policy choices, such as welfare issues.[13]

Now that we have discussed various types of agendas and various types of issues, it is useful to discuss the evolution of the literature on the agenda-setting process. Through this brief review, we may appreciate how our conceptual understanding has developed over time on this stage of the policy cycle.

EVOLUTION OF THE LITERATURE ON THE AGENDA-SETTING PROCESS

In the early 1970s, the first important work on agenda setting defined the agenda-setting process as a link between mass participation and elite decision making.[14] This research sought to explain the movement of an issue from the systemic agenda to the formal or institutional agenda. The fundamental proposition was that the greater the size of the audience to which an issue may be appealed, the greater the likelihood that the issue will attain status on the systemic agenda and later move to the formal or institutional agenda. Essentially, the process is based on the fundamental assumption that if the issue has several characteristics, such as specificity, social significance, temporal relevance, complexity, and categorical precedence, then it will be more easily expanded to a larger audience and hence have a much better chance of reaching the formal or institutional agenda.[15] Specificity refers to how abstractly or concretely an issue is defined. The more broadly an issue is defined, the greater the likelihood that the issue will remain on the institutional agenda. For example, the issue of toxic waste has been linked broadly to include human health as well as environmental issues. Social significance refers to whether an issue is peculiar to the immediate disputants or has more general significance. The cleanup of abandoned toxic waste sites has social significance in that the costs greatly exceed the resources of the locality where the sites exist, so federal and state participation are required. Temporal relevance reflects the extent to which an issue has short-range, circumstantial importance or whether it represents more enduring, fundamental concerns. If an issue contains implications for the management of problems that go beyond the conduct of current program activities, then the issue has a greater likelihood of remaining on the institutional agenda. For problems to be considered temporally relevant, they must have a potential effect on future generations. Complexity refers to how an issue is delineated along a continuum from the highly complex to the simple and easily understood. The less the complexity, the greater the likelihood an issue will remain on the institutional agenda. Finally, categorical precedence refers to the extent to which an issue is a routine matter with clear precedents or whether it is extraordinary, with no clear precedents. The more an issue is defined as lacking a clear precedent, the greater the likelihood that the issue will remain on the institutional agenda. The issue of acid rain, for example, had no clear precedent in the Clean Air Act of 1970 and the amendments of 1977.

Before an issue reaches the institutional agenda, it must reach the systemic agenda. According to Cobb and Elder, three prerequisites were thought to be necessary for an issue to first obtain status on the systemic agenda: (1) widespread attention to or at least awareness of the issue; (2) a shared concern of a sizable portion of the public that some type of action is needed to remedy this problem; and (3) a shared perception that the matter is an appropriate concern of some governmental unit and falls within the bounds of its authority.

A second major contribution to the understanding of the agenda-setting process was offered by Davies.[16] He argued that the agenda-setting process consisted of three phases: (1) initiation, (2) diffusion, and (3) processing. In the initiation stage, a public problem creates a demand for action. In the diffusion stage, these demands are transposed into issues for government. In the processing stage, issues are converted into agenda items. A central part of Davies' argument was that the type of issue is an important determinant that affects whether an issue becomes (or fails to become) an agenda item. Davies also argued that many issues were initiated within government itself rather than the common assumption that issues arose within the general public and worked their way onto the governmental agenda.[17]

The next major contribution to this area of research came from Cobb, Ross, and Ross in which they identified three different models of agenda setting.[18] Their first model was the outside initiative model, which was very similar to the original model proposed by Cobb and Elder. Their second model was the mobilization model, where issues were initiated inside government and eventually achieved agenda status. This second model was similar to the one suggested earlier by Davies. Their third model was called the inside initiative model, which described a process whereby issues arose within government but were not expanded to the general public. The issue's supporters desired to keep the issue within the governmental arena exclusively.[19]

Yet another major contribution to this literature was made by Barbara Nelson. According to Nelson, the process of agenda setting may be divided into four discrete stages: (1) issue recognition, (2) issue adoption, (3) issue prioritization, and (4) issue maintenance.[20] In the issue recognition phase, a problem is first noticed and then perceived to have potential for governmental action. In this phase, the issue must be important enough for governmental actors to seriously consider. In the issue adoption phase, the decision is made to respond (or not to respond) to the public policy problem. The primary concerns are whether there is a perception that the government has a legitimate responsibility to act on this issue and whether an appropriate response is available. If the problem is adopted as a potential issue, then the agenda must be reordered to accommodate the new issue, which is the focus of the prioritization phase. Essentially the new issue must be viewed within the context of other older issues already on the agenda. In the issue maintenance phase, the issue advances to the stage of decision making. Proposals are put forth to be considered by the decision makers. As long as these proposals are being considered, the issue has been maintained on the institutional agenda. If the issue fails to retain interest by the decision makers, then the issue no longer is maintained on the agenda.

Nelson's first stage corresponded to what had been viewed as agenda setting in previous works. Her remaining three stages added new materials to our understanding of the agenda-setting process. She argued that two conditions had to be present for an issue to achieve issue adoption: (1) a shared perception of the legitimacy of government responsibility for action on this issue, and (2) a belief that an appropriate response could be found if the issue were to be adopted for consideration by government actors.[21] She expanded our understanding of the process by making some careful distinctions about the process itself and building on the works of those before her.

Perhaps the most extensive work on the topic of agenda setting is by John Kingdon. His view of the process is by far the most comprehensive to date. Figure 5–1 illustrates his view of the agenda-setting process. His conceptual model is based on the notion of three "streams" of information: (1) the problem stream, (2) the policy stream, and (3) the political stream.[22] The problem stream is concerned with the definition of the problem to be addressed. It includes such things as crisis events that focus attention on the problem as well as budgetary constraints and how the problem is conceptualized in the first place. For example, the Love Canal crisis in 1978 focused attention on the toxic waste issue. In that case, the discovery that twenty-one thousand tons of hazardous chemicals deposited decades earlier were leaching into the groundwater and into the prop-

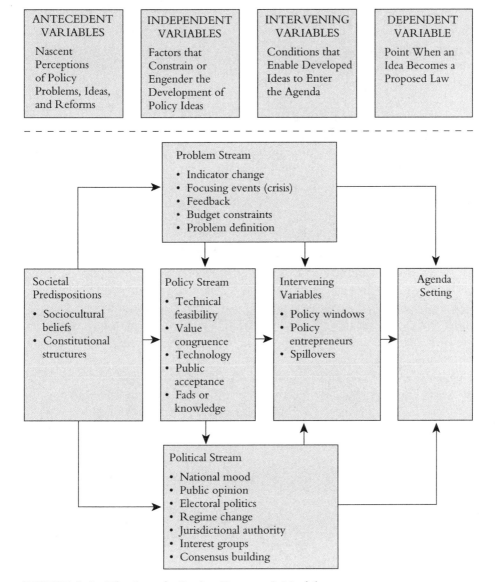

FIGURE 5–1   The Agenda-Setting Process: A Model

Source: Adapted from John W. Kingdon, *Agendas, Alternatives, and Public Policies* (Boston: Little, Brown, 1984). Reprinted by permission of the publisher.

erty and homes around the canal was the crisis. It was officially recognized as such when President Carter declared Love Canal a national emergency and when a preliminary study of health problems that might have been caused by the chemicals was leaked to the *New York Times*.

The policy stream has to do with the technical feasibility of dealing with the problem, the availability of technology to deal with it, and the public degree of acceptance of a solution, among other things. Essentially, the policy stream includes various proposals that are developed to deal with the issue, usually in the form of legislation. Although the study of the Love Canal situation yielded inadequate evidence to conclude that the chemicals had led to health problems among residents, a perception of government insensitivity led to President Carter's decision to relocate 710 persons.

The political stream has to do with the politics affecting the solution to the issue. This includes such considerations as the national mood, public opinion, electoral politics, and interest-group activity. When these three streams come together, "policy windows" of opportunity are open. In addition, policy entrepreneurs "are responsible not only for prompting important people to pay attention, but also for coupling solutions to problems and for coupling both problems and solutions to politics."[23] In the Love Canal case, the ultimate solution was new environmental legislation to clean up abandoned hazardous waste sites.[24]

Prior to these three streams are "societal predispositions" (values, political culture, etc.), which set the context for issues getting on the agenda. Finally, such things as "spillovers" affect agenda status as well. Spillovers refer to the fact that sometimes an issue from one area affects another issue's ability to get onto the agenda.

Simply put, there are times when issues are "ripe" for solutions, and there are individuals who can move an issue to agenda status by virtue of their political clout in the decisional arena, such as a key congressperson or president. Sometimes, spillovers from other policy areas affect agenda status as well. For example, the issue of dumping wastes at sea affected the status of burning wastes at sea. The former issue affected the latter issue by sensitizing the public to the potential for harm. (Chapter 9 explores this example in greater depth.)

WHO SETS AGENDAS?

Concurrent with these frameworks for understanding agenda setting, a number of explanations about just who sets agendas have been advanced. These explanations include the following: (1) the elitist argument, (2) the pluralist argument, and (3) the subgovernment argument.

The Elitist Perspective

The power elite argument assumes the existence of a power elite that dominates public decision making. It argues that these elites (including business elites, military elites, and political elites) set the agendas. At any one time, one of these elite groups is dominant. For example, in the period following the Civil War, business-sector elites were dominant in agenda setting; in the New Deal era, politicians were dominant; and in the 1950s, the military elites were dominant.[25] A variant of this perspective—the neo-Marxist view—assumes that the dominant actors placing items on the agenda are the capitalists. These capitalists are believed to be in collusion with big labor against the interests of "the people" and are thus able to control policymaking by government. We have discussed the elitist model in the previous chapter, and Figure 4–1 illustrates this perspective.

The Pluralist Perspective

A second argument is that interest groups dominate the agenda-setting process. It sees the agenda-setting process as reacting to the activity expressed by dominant interest groups. These interest groups identify problems and then apply pressure to have them placed on the public agenda or to oppose their being placed on the agenda. The pluralist perspective was described in Chapter 4 and is illustrated in Figure 4–2.

The Subgovernment Perspective

Finally, a third perspective on who sets the public agenda is that it is shaped by three sets of actors: (1) key congresspersons on select committees dealing with the issue; (2) agency bureaucrats responsible for the policy in question, and (3) clientele groups with a stake in the issue. The term *subgovernment* was originally coined by Douglas Cater.[26] Other terms for this phenomenon include *subsystem, iron triangles,* or *cozy little triangles.* Cater used this term to describe networks of key actors that determined America's policy on sugar import quotas. He discovered that a close interlocking network of specialized congressional committees, middle-level executive branch bureaus, and powerful commercial interest groups together hammered out U.S. policy in this area. According to this argument, a subgovernment will likely evolve under the following conditions: (1) a relatively narrow policy field; (2) specialized congressional committees responsible for that field and deferred to by the rest of Congress; (3) unequally equipped interest groups in the field plus general apathy on the subject among the public; (4) relatively autonomous bureaucratic agencies able to cultivate ties of their own outside the executive branch of government.[27]

   The interest groups most capable of cultivating such intimate relationships with Senate and House committees and their bureau counterparts are those possessing at least the following attributes: (1) a clearly defined stake in the field of interest; (2) legitimacy in the eyes of congressional committee members; (3) money enough to afford offices in Washington and staffs able to conduct research of use to the committee's work; (4) additional funds with which to support individual committee members' election (and reelection) campaigns; and (5) organizational bases at the local level and elsewhere from which the committee members come (e.g., clubs, business firms).[28] Essentially, the subgovernment arrangement works by a series of "exchange relationships," whereby favorable votes for the clientele groups are traded for campaign contributions for congresspersons, information from agency officials to congresspersons is traded for favorable appropriations to the agency from Congress, and personnel exchanges occur between the clientele groups and the agency (i.e., many agency representatives later go to work for the very clientele groups they previously regulated). Figure 5–2 illustrates this perspective. A good example of a subgovernment is the relationships among the Bureau of Land Management (BLM), western cattlemen's associations, and congressional committees made up of western representatives who are beholden to the cattle industry. It

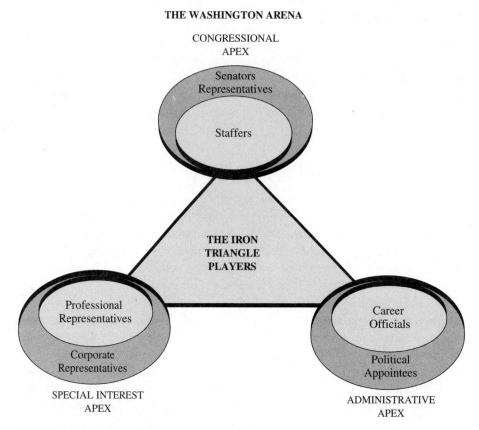

FIGURE 5–2   The Subgovernment Model

is argued that these three groups have protected cattle grazing on public lands and kept the grazing fees quite low.[29]

SUMMARY

Who sets agendas can best be explained by examining individual issue areas at specific points in time. For example, energy policy in the 1960s may best be explained by an elitist model; educational policy in the 1970s by a pluralistic model; and environmental policy in the 1980s by a subgovernmental model. In addition, as issues evolve over time and expand to include more public awareness and greater public attention, the scope and level of participation in agenda setting may evolve from elite-dominated to subgovernment to interest-group models. The key point is that issues evolve and the participants involved with an issue change over time.

The framework developed by John Kingdon contains all three perspectives within its unique framework. Elite involvement in agenda setting is represented in the concepts of policy stream and policy entrepreneurs. The pluralist perspective is reflected in Kingdon's political stream, and the subgovernmental perspective is contained with both the political stream and policy entrepreneurs.

CASE STUDIES

The following two case studies of agenda setting illustrate many of the points made in the preceding discussion. Using John Kingdon's model of agenda setting, we first explore the issue of toxic waste cleanup at the Love Canal and the enactment of Superfund (or the Comprehensive Environmental Response, Compensation, and Liability Act of 1980). Next, we explore the case of acid rain legislation that culminated in the passage of the Clean Air Act Amendments in 1990. These two case studies of agenda setting are useful in illustrating how an issue rises to the top of the policy agenda and becomes the basis for a new law.

Superfund

The Problem Stream   The problem stream, according to Kingdon's model, is concerned with how problems come to be recognized and how conditions come to be defined as problems. "Problems are brought to the attention of people in and around government by systematic indicators, by focusing events like crises and disasters, or by feedback from the operation of current programs."[30] Essentially, the release of hazardous waste from abandoned and inactive sites was brought to the attention of governmental decision makers by the disaster at Love Canal in 1978 and by the feedback from existing legislation. Love Canal was a community of 239 families whose homes were built within the area of a twenty-one thousand ton chemical waste site.[31] As early as 1942, Hooker Chemical Company, the original owner of Love Canal, began disposing of more than eighty compounds of chemicals in the abandoned Love Canal. In 1952, the Niagara Falls Board of Education bought land from Hooker for the sum of $1.00 and in 1954, the 99th Street School was built on the old site.[32] By 1959, there were reports of children being burned while playing near the Canal. In the 1960s, residents reported black sludge appearing on their basement walls, apparently coming from the waste site. The New York State Department of Environmental Conservation and the city of Niagara Falls conducted a number of inspections between 1976 and 1977, and they concluded that "a serious health hazard may exist in the area as a consequence of leaking chemicals."[33] These studies were severely criticized by Lois Gibbs, the president of the Love Canal Homeowners Association, for being done too quickly and for not recognizing what she and others thought was a much more serious problem than what was being reported by the state and local authorities. This crisis escalated during 1979 and 1980 as hearings were held by state, local, and federal authorities. All this focused attention on the need for a law that would provide monies for cleanups like the Love Canal problem. Beyond this crisis at the Love Canal, the Environmental Protection Agency (EPA) was estimating that 1,200 to 2,000 hazardous waste sites in the United States might present serious problems for individuals and the environment and that the costs for these cleanups would amount to $26.2 to $44.1 billion. Other states were beginning to report problems like the Love Canal problem in their neighborhoods.

In addition to this reporting of serious hazardous waste problems all across the nation was the problem that the existing legislation for hazardous waste regulation—the Federal Water Pollution Control Act of 1972 and the Resource Conservation and Recovery Act of 1976—was inadequate for handling the problem of cleaning up such abandoned waste sites as the Love Canal. For example, sections 311 and 504 of the Federal Water Pollution Control Act of 1972 addressed the cleanup of hazardous waste but its provisions only amounted to $5 to $10 million. A limitation of the Resource Conservation and Recovery Act was that it did not empower the Justice Department to subpoena witnesses and compel the production of documents for conducting investigations of violations of the two statutes; nor did it require the existence of a disposal site to be revealed or allow for monitoring of possible leakage from the inactive sites.[34] In sum, the Love Canal crisis, together with media attention to similar problems in other jurisdictions, and the inadequacies of existing legislation provided a problem stream that pushed this issue to the top of the governmental agenda in 1979 and 1980.

The Policy Stream   The policy stream, according to Kingdon, is concerned with the generation of policy proposals in the form of bill introductions, speeches, testimony, papers, and conversation. In that process, "proposals are floated, come into contact with one another, are revised and combined with one another, and floated again."[35] The proposals that survive must meet several criteria, such as their technical feasibility, their fit with dominant values and the current national mood, their budgetary workability, and the political support or opposition that they might experience as they are put forth by decision makers.[36]

On March 21, 1979, Representative James Florio of New Jersey introduced a bill for toxic waste cleanup (HR 5790) that failed to gain necessary support by the subcommittee he chaired. In 1980, he introduced HR 7020, a bill that provided $600 million for cleanup of abandoned toxic waste sites. In addition, President Jimmy Carter also developed a version of a Superfund bill, which included the cleanup of oil along with hazardous chemicals, and proposed a Superfund of $1.6 billion over four years. A Senate version (S 1480) was introduced in July 1979, and it provided for a $4.1 billion Superfund program over six years. As these three bills moved along in the "policy primeval soup," they were amended in order to gain more votes in the Senate and in the House of Representatives. One version of a bill compensated victims for medical costs not paid by insurance, liberalized existing rules for evidence so that it would be easier for victims to prove actual injury resulting from the chemical exposure, and made it easier to sue for damages. The chemical industry opposed this stringent version and eventually the version that passed (HR 7020) was weakened in terms of liability and victim compensation. In sum, the various actors in the policy stream were able to influence the final outcome of the bill that passed the House and Senate in late 1980.

The Political Stream   The political stream is composed of such factors as swings of national mood, administration or legislative turnover, and interest-group pressure. Potential agenda items "that are congruent with the current national mood, that enjoy interest group support or lack organized opposition, and that fit the orientations of the prevailing legislative coalitions or current administration are more likely to rise to agenda prominence than items that do not meet such conditions."[37]

The 1970s are often referred to as the "environmental decade." Beginning with the National Environmental Policy Act of 1969 (NEPA), environmental issues enjoyed wide support by the American people. Public opinion in support of the environment was at an all-time high in the late 1960s.[38] Although public support for environmental protection declined somewhat in the period 1973–1979, it began to climb again by the early 1980s.[39] In addition, several national environmental organizations, such as the Sierra Club, the National Wildlife Federation, the Audubon Society, and the Environmental Defense Fund, all enjoyed significant increases in membership in the late 1970s and early 1980s.[40] Although the Chemical Manufacturers Association (CMA) led the opposition to the Superfund bill, by September 1980, CMA President Robert Roland indicated that CMA supported the House bill over the Senate bill with a smaller fund and less in the way of liability provisions. Later, CMA sent letters to Congressman Florio stating that it did not support the final bill. This embarrassed many Senators and eventually led them to support what many considered to be a dead bill.[41]

At the same time, public support, due to many media reports on the problems at Love Canal in the summer of 1980, continued to focus attention on the problem of toxic waste cleanups. From mid-May to mid-June, problems at the Love Canal were reported daily on the major networks. On August 21, 1980, an ABC News feature titled *The Killing Ground* focused more attention on the problem. Eventually, this led to the direct involvement of President Carter in the toxic waste issue. His administration strongly supported environmental issues, and he personally called many undecided members of the House and Senate. In summary, all this media attention, the widespread public support for environmental issues in general and toxic waste issues in particular, together with the personal involvement of the Carter administration and Congressman James Florio led ultimately to the enactment of HR 7020, in place of S 1480, which became PL 96-510: The Comprehensive Environmental Response, Compensation, and Liability Act of 1980.

Policy Windows and Policy Entrepreneurs   Kingdon also stresses how separate streams of problems, policies, and politics come together at certain critical times. Policy solutions become joined to problems, and both of them are joined

to favorable political forces when **policy windows**—or opportunities for pushing pet proposals or conceptions of problems—are open.[42] Windows are opened
either by the appearance of compelling problems or by happenings in the political stream. In the case of Superfund, problems at the Love Canal and elsewhere
presented a compelling case for this legislation to be enacted promptly. Crisis
events compel responsive action on the part of key decision makers.

At the same time, Kingdon argues that **policy entrepreneurs,** or people
who are willing to invest their resources in pushing pet proposals or problems,
are responsible not only for prompting important people to pay attention to the
problem, but also for coupling solutions to problems and for coupling both problems and solutions to politics.[43] Although governmental agendas are set in the
problems or political streams, the chances of items rising on a *decision* agenda are
enhanced if all three streams are coupled together by policy entrepreneurs.[44]

In this case, Representative James Florio (D–New Jersey) was an active policy
entrepreneur. New Jersey was one of the worst states as far as toxic waste
cleanups were concerned, yet Representative Florio solicited support for a
Superfund bill from the chemical industry. In addition, he chaired the relevant
congressional committee hearings on this issue and carefully guided the eventual
bill (HR 7020) around industry adversaries and kept the bill viable by amending
it as necessary. He clearly exhibited the characteristics of a policy entrepreneur
as Kingdon defines this role.

This brief case study illustrates Kingdon's model of agenda setting. The next
brief case study of acid rain also illustrates how an issue rises to agenda status and
remains there for some time.

Acid Rain

The problem of acid rain may be one of the most polarizing yet least understood
environmental issues of the 1980s and 1990s. It has implications for both environmental quality and national energy policy, especially regarding the increased
use of coal as a substitute for imported oil. According to one view, acid rain is one
of the most serious and deadly environmental problems that humans have ever
faced. Others charge that acid rain is a nonissue that is blown out of proportion
by antigrowth environmental extremists seeking a rationalization for a continuing
attack on emissions. In the end, the former view won the debate, for a new Clean
Air Act was passed in 1990 that effectively dealt with the problem of acid rain.
The following case vignette uses Kingdon's model of agenda setting to explore
how this issue achieved agenda status and remained on the agenda for over ten
years before the Clean Air Act of 1990 was passed.

The Problem Stream   Although a Swedish scientist, Svante Oden, warned in
the 1960s that the increasing acidity of Swedish lakes was the result of atmospheric fallout of sulfur dioxides, acid rain first appeared as an American problem
when President Carter referred to it in his second annual environmental message

in 1979. Before his address, the subject of acid rain had been confined to a small group of American scientists who were worried about the potential problems of this phenomenon for our environment.[45] In his address, President Carter asked for additional research and development funds as well as possible control measures. By 1980, the director of the EPA, Douglas Costle, argued that the time had come to make the transition from further research to action. Initially, the General Accounting Office (GAO) characterized the problem as one that was confined to a small number of lakes and streams in the northeastern United States and southeastern Canada. After the election of President Reagan in 1980, the approach to acid rain was to call for more research. As time wore on, however, the seriousness of the acid rain problem became more apparent.

The Policy Stream   Starting in 1979, various acid rain control bills were introduced in the House and the Senate annually. Before passage of the Clean Air Act Amendments of 1990, at least seventy-four separate bills were introduced in Congress. Table 5–1 indicates how many acid rain bills were before Congress from 1979 to 1989. At least twenty-five pieces of legislation concerning acid rain were introduced in the 98th Congress (1983–1984) alone.

Support for or against these bills generally reflected the economic interests of the states represented by members of Congress. For example, senators from New England generally supported these bills, whereas those from polluting

TABLE 5–1   Number of Acid Rain Bills Introduced in Congress, 1979 to mid–1989

	Senate	House	Total
96th Congress			
1979	1	1	2
1980	0	1	1
97th Congress			
1981	2	4	6
1982	3	0	3
98th Congress			
1983	7	8	15
1984	1	9	10
99th Congress			
1985	5	6	11
1986	3	4	7
100th Congress			
1987	4	4	8
1988	2	4	6
101st Congress			
1989	2	3	5
TOTALS	30	44	74

Source: Leslie R. Alm, "Acid Rain and the United States Congress: A Case Study of Issue Maintenance and the Agenda-Setting Process" (Ph.D. diss., Colorado State University, 1990), p. 57. Reprinted by permission of the publisher.

states generally opposed the bills.[46] Senator Robert Byrd of West Virginia—one of the most polluting states—claimed that "acid rain has been found in ice cores in the Artic Circle . . . and my state would lose jobs under any scenario."[47]

Broadly speaking, the various pieces of legislation introduced were categorized as either control legislation that mandated reductions in air emissions or research legislation that proposed further study of the acid rain problem. For example, Senate Bill 769, introduced by Senator Robert Stafford (R-Vermont) in 1983, would have reduced emissions by twelve million tons annually within a thirty-one-state region over a twelve-year period. From 1979 to 1988, sixty-nine different acid rain bills were introduced in Congress. However, none passed.[48] In June 1989, President Bush sent Congress a new Clean Air Act in which provisions for acid rain were quite strong. His bill called for a ten million-ton-per-year reduction in sulfur dioxides. On November 15, 1990, President Bush signed the Clean Air Act Amendments of 1990, in which acid rain finally received statutory coverage. The new Clean Air Act of 1990 required coal-burning electric power plants to cut sulfur dioxide emissions by ten million tons, or roughly in half, by 2000, when emissions will be capped at 8.9 million tons a year.

The Political Stream   After the Democratic and Republican National Conventions in the summer of 1988, resistance to acid rain control diminished, especially among the utility companies and the unions. Fearing that both George Bush and Michael Dukakis would favor strong acid rain control laws, opponents of acid rain legislation sought a weaker bill, rather than a strong one. Although the various acid rain bills did not pass in 1988, the opposition softened its stance and focused on who would pay for control of acid rain.[49] The year 1988 represented a turning point in the struggle for acid rain controls. The election of President Bush, who had campaigned as an "environmental president," seemed to send a message to the polluting industries that the time had come for legislation to reduce acid rain.

Policy Windows and Policy Entrepreneurs   The Democrats in Congress dominated the sponsorship of acid rain bills by three to one. Most of the bills introduced in Congress favored control and/or reduction of emissions. Leading actors in the acid rain initiative in Congress included Senator George Mitchell (D-Maine) and Representative Henry Waxman (D-California). These individuals helped to keep the acid rain issue on the public agenda for years. Others, including Senator Robert Stafford of Vermont and Represenative Gerry Skiorski of Minnesota were instrumental as well.[50] Senator George Mitchell was the key spokesman for acid rain control in the Senate. He sponsored more acid rain bills than any other senator in Congress. As the senate majority leader, he was in a good position to play a strong role in this issue. Besides Senator Mitchell, Representative Waxman in the House also helped to move this issue to the point of policy adoption.[51]

In addition, President Bush played a major role. As mentioned earlier, he had promised during his 1988 campaign to be the "environmental president." Immediately after taking office, he pledged to a joint session of Congress that he would soon introduce legislation to reduce acid rain. The day after that speech, President Bush traveled to Canada where he repeated his promise to Prime Minister Mulroney and the Canadian people. On June 12, 1989, he proposed acid rain legislation to the Congress. The change in administration from the Reagan to the Bush administration provided the "window of opportunity" that was crucial for legislation on this issue. Moreover, with President Bush's support, Senator Mitchell and Representative Waxman were able to keep the issue before Congress and, ultimately, a new Clean Air Act was signed into law in November 1990.

These two case studies illustrate how John Kingdon's model of agenda setting can be used to analyze the agenda-setting process. In his model, we see how the problem stream, the policy stream, and the political stream combine to encourage an issue rising to the agenda-setting stage. In addition, windows of opportunity and policy entrepreneurs enhance the ability of an issue to reach the agenda and remain on the public agenda for some time. However, to use Kingdon's model of agenda setting, we need some *decision* in the form of a policy proposal. Sometimes, however, there are instances whereby decisions are never achieved, as policy issues are deliberately kept off the governmental agenda. That is the phenomenon called nondecision-making.

THE PROBLEM OF NONDECISIONS

Sometimes agenda items are deliberately kept off the institutional agendas by those who seek to control the agenda-setting process for political or economic reasons. Peter Bachrach and Morton S. Baratz identified a phenomenon called **nondecision-making**, which is defined as "a means by which demands for change in the existing allocation of benefits and privileges in the community can be suffocated before they are even voiced; or kept covert; or killed before they gain access to the relevant decision-making arena; or failing all these things, maimed or destroyed in the decision-implementing stage of the policy process."[52]

An example of a nondecision is the charge that the rubber industry and the oil companies have conspired to keep the possibility of rapid rail transportation off the institutional agenda; instead, these two industries want to promote highway transportation. It is sometimes argued that these industries forced the shutdown of much of the inner-city rail transportation to promote the use of automobiles. From time to time, there is some discussion of inter-city rapid transit using rail transportation, much like the European systems, but it is allegedly kept off the governmental agenda by those who would lose economically from the switch from highway to rail transit, including the bus industry, the gasoline industry, the tire industry, and the airlines.

CONCLUSIONS

The two case studies of Superfund and acid rain illustrate how John Kingdon's model may be used to explain agenda setting. Nevertheless, much work remains to be done in the area of agenda setting. What is needed at this point are more applications of existing frameworks on agenda-setting, such as the framework developed by John Kingdon. Kingdon's model needs to be applied in many areas of public policy formation so the various components of his model may be tested against real-world data. Some of his variables may be less important than others. It would be extremely useful to know, for example, if the problem stream is more important in explaining agenda setting than either the policy stream or the political stream. It may be that a policy entrepreneur is crucial in getting an item on the public agenda, but we will not know this until researchers test this argument against empirical data across many types of policy.

After an item gets onto the public agenda, the next step is for that policy to be enacted into law. That is the subject of the next chapter.

NOTES

1. James E. Anderson, *Public Policymaking: An Introduction* (Boston: Houghton Mifflin, 1990), p. 78.
2. Brian W. Hogwood and Lewis A. Gunn, *Policy Analysis for the Real World* (Oxford: Oxford University Press, 1984), p.68.
3. Roger W. Cobb and Charles D. Elder, *Participation in American Politics: The Dynamics of Agenda-Building* (Baltimore: Johns Hopkins University Press, 1972).
4. John W. Kingdon, *Agendas, Alternatives, and Public Policies* (Boston: Little, Brown, 1984).
5. See Frank R. Baumgartner and Bryan D. Jones, *Agendas and Instability in American Politics* (Chicago: University of Chicago Press, 1993), pp. 25–31.
6. Barbara J. Nelson, *Making an Issue of Child Abuse* (Chicago: University of Chicago Press, 1984), p. 20.
7. Anderson, *Public Policymaking*, pp. 78–79.
8. Kirkpatrick Sale, *Human Scale* (New York: G. P. Putnam Sons, 1982), pp. 21–22.
9. Michael Harrington, *The Other America* (New York: Viking Penguin, 1971); Charles Murray, *Losing Ground* (New York: Basic Books, 1986); and Edward Banfield, *The Unheavenly City Revisited* (Prospect Heights, IL: Waveland Press, 1990).
10. Cobb and Elder, *Participation in American Politics*, p. 14.
11. See Kingdon, *Agendas*, and Nelson, *Child Abuse*.
12. J. Clarence Davies, "How Does the Agenda Get Set?" in *The Governance of Common Property Resources*, ed. Edwin Haefele (Baltimore: Johns Hopkins University Press, 1974), p. 61.
13. Nelson, *Child Abuse*, p. 22.
14. Roger W. Cobb and Charles D. Elder, "The Politics of Agenda-Building," *Journal of Politics* 33, no. 4 (November 1971), pp. 892–915.
15. Cobb and Elder, *Participation in American Politics*, p. 110.

16. Davies.
17. Ibid., p. 61.
18. Roger Cobb, Jennie-Keith Ross, and March Ross, "Agenda Building as a Comparative Political Process," *American Political Science Review* 70 (1976), pp. 126–138.
19. Ibid, p. 127.
20. Nelson, *Child Abuse*, pp. 22–23.
21. Ibid.
22. See Kingdon, *Agendas*, pp. 20–21.
23. Ibid., p. 21.
24. Martin Linsky, *Impact: How the Press Affects Federal Policymaking* (New York: W. W. Norton, 1986), pp. 71–78.
25. See C. Wright Mills, *The Power Elite* (New York: Oxford University Press, 1956).
26. See Douglas Cater, *Power in Washington* (New York: Random House, 1965).
27. Ibid.
28. Ibid., and Cynthia H. Enloe, *The Politics of Pollution in a Comparative Perspective* (New York: McKay, 1975).
29. See Phillip O. Foss, *The Politics of Grass* (Seattle: University of Washington Press, 1960).
30. Kingdon, *Agendas*, pp. 20–21.
31. John A. Worthley and Richard A. Torkelson, "Managing the Toxic Waste Problem: Lessons from the Love Canal," *Administration and Society* 13 (August 1981), pp. 147–148.
32. For a complete story on the Love Canal situation, see Adeline G. Levine, *Love Canal: Science, Politics, and People* (Lexington, MA: Lexington Books, 1982).
33. Worthley and Torkelson, "Toxic Waste Problem," p. 152.
34. U.S. House of Representatives, Committee on Interstate and Foreign Commerce, Subcommittee on Oversight and Investigations, *Hazardous Waste Disposal* (Washington, D.C.: U.S. Government Printing Office, 1979), p. 721.
35. Kingdon, *Agendas*, p. 21.
36. Ibid.
37. Ibid.
38. See Riley Dunlap, "Public Opinion and the Environment," in *Environmental Politics and Policy: Theories and Evidence*, ed. James P. Lester (Durham, NC: Duke University Press, 1989).
39. Ibid., pp. 86–134.
40. See Helen Ingram and Dean E. Mann, "Interest Groups and Environmental Policy," in Lester, *Environmental Politics*, pp. 139–141.
41. Kathy Koch, "Superfund Cleanup Proposal Apparently Dead This Year," *Congressional Quarterly Weekly Report* (November 15, 1980), p. 3378.
42. Kingdon, *Agendas*, p. 21.
43. Ibid.
44. Ibid.
45. See, for example, Ellis B. Cowling, "Acid Precipitation in Historical Perspective," *Environmental Science and Technology* 16, no. 2 (February 1982), pp. 110–123.
46. James L. Regens, "Congressional Co-sponsorship of Acid Rain Controls," *Social Science Quarterly* 70, no. 2 (June 1989), pp. 505–512.

47. *Congressional Record*, 98th Congress, 2d Sess., 3 February 1984, p. 1783.

48. Leslie R. Alm, "Acid Rain and the United States Congress: A Case Study of Issue Maintainance and the Agenda-Setting Process" (Ph.D. diss., Colorado State University, 1990), p. 57.

49. Ibid.

50. Ibid.

51. Ibid.

52. Peter Bachrach and Morton S. Baratz, *Power and Poverty* (New York: Oxford University Press, 1970), p. 44; see also Matthew A. Crenson, *The Unpolitics of Air Pollution* (Baltimore: Johns Hopkins University Press, 1971).

POLICY FORMULATION

"At the core of every moral code there is a picture of human nature, a map of the universe and a version of history."
WALTER LIPPMAN

In this chapter, we examine how policies are formulated. By the term **policy formulation**, we mean the stage of the policy process where pertinent and acceptable courses of action for dealing with some particular public problem are identified and enacted into law.[1] Each of the stages in the policymaking process is theoretically distinct, but they nevertheless merge in practice. For example, the nature of the problem affects whether or not it gets onto the agenda, as well as whether or not a course of action gets finally enacted into law. Let us examine the policy formulation stage in a bit more depth.

THE NATURE OF POLICY SOLUTIONS

The expected result of policy formulation is some type of solution to a public problem. According to Deborah Stone, there are five types of policy solutions: (1) **inducements**, which can be either positive (tax credits) or negative (penalties for pollution); (2) **rules**, or other forms of mandated behavior such as regulations governing pollution; (3) **facts**, or using information to persuade target groups to behave in a certain way, such as community right-to-know information; (4) **rights**, which give certain people rights or duties, such as civil rights legislation; and (5) **powers**, whereby a decision-making body is charged with specific powers to improve decision making. An example of these powers would be legislative budgetary power whereby a legislature has the ability to affect the state budget. These policy solutions can be congressional legislation, executive orders, judicial decisions, or other forms of policy outputs.[2]

ACTORS IN POLICY FORMULATION

Who is involved in policy formulation? In this discussion of the actors involved in policy formulation, we pay particular attention to the national level of government.

Governmental Agencies

Contrary to conventional logic, most policy proposals are first developed in governmental agencies by career bureaucrats rather than in Congress. These officials have been involved in developing policy for decades, often have more expertise in specific areas of public policy than elected officials, and are in a particularly good position to engage in the formulation of policy.[3] Sometimes new agency proposals are designed to remedy previous legislation that has loopholes. For example, the Resource Conservation and Recovery Act of 1976 (RCRA) originally regulated businesses that produced 1,000 kilograms or more of hazardous waste per month. This threshold of toxic waste produced by these businesses omitted all those industries that produced less than this amount, such as dry cleaners, paint shops, printing shops, and others. Thus, the Environmental Protection Agency developed the Hazardous and Solid Waste Amendments of 1984 (HSWA), which was designed to amend RCRA to bring these smaller businesses within the regulatory regime. Under the provisions of HSWA, all businesses that produce at least 100 kilograms of toxic waste per month are within the purview of the new regulatory regime established by HSWA in 1984.

Government agencies often provide information to Congress and the executive branch that later becomes the basis for legislation. The General Accounting Office (GAO), for example, undertakes research on the effectiveness of previous policies in reaching their goals as defined by Congress. When problems in implementation are detected by the GAO, these shortcomings often become the basis for new legislation. For example, the GAO examined the toxic waste cleanup process under the Comprehensive Environmental Response, Compensation, and Liability Act of 1980 (CERCLA) and made suggestions for improving the process when CERCLA was amended in 1986 under the Superfund Amendments and Reauthorization Act (SARA). In sum, we often think that governmental agencies get involved only in policy implementation when, in fact, they usually are involved in the policy formulation process.

The Presidency

The president and/or executive offices are often involved in the policy formulation process. Such involvement includes presidential commissions, task forces, interagency committees, and other arrangements. Quite often, the president is personally involved in policy formulation. For example, President Jimmy Carter was known for his attention to details and for his interest in formulating policy. He preferred to be actively involved in the initiation of legislation and used his staff to help prepare much legislation for congressional review. On the other hand, President Lyndon Johnson used task forces to develop legislative proposals. He appointed over one hundred of these groups during his tenure in office as he believed that these groups would be more innovative in developing proposals for new policies than would the national bureaucracy.[4] Throughout history, there has been much variation in the amount of attention given to the policy formulation process by various presidents.

The Congress

Congress is the institution that is most commonly associated with policy formulation, either through the development of new legislation or through oversight and legislative review. For example, Congress was actively involved in the revision of the Clean Air Act in 1977 and again in 1990, as discussed in the previous chapter. Congressional committees and congressional staff, as well as several new organizations within Congress, also allow substantial involvement. These new organizations, including the Office of Technology Assessment (OTA), the Congressional Research Service (CRS), and the Congressional Budget Office (CBO), were created to give Congress a greater voice in the design of public policies. For example, during 1985 and 1986, the OTA and its Advisory Group on Waste Minimization helped to formulate legislation that would aid in promoting toxic waste reduction and waste minimization.

Interest Groups

Interest groups are extremely important in policy formulation in the United States. Although there are several alternative explanations of public policy formulation, one of the most frequently mentioned determinants is the role and influence of interest groups. Essentially, **pluralism** means that public policy is shaped by bargaining, negotiation, and compromise among various interest groups in American society. As V.O. Key once said, "group interests are the animating forces in the political process; an understanding of American politics requires a knowledge of the chief interests and their stake in public policy."[5]

The idea that interest groups are a major determinant in public policy may be traced back to the Founding Fathers. For example, James Madison, in *The Federalist*, warned against factions (interest groups) and suggested that a republican form of government with checks and balances would offer the best protection against the domination of public policy by interest groups. Later, Arthur Bentley, in *The Process of Government*, argued that "there are no political phenomena except group phenomena."[6] Most recently, Theodore Lowi has presented the argument that interest groups are very strong actors in the American policy process. He argues that "interest group liberalism" has produced a situation in which interest groups have undue power and are able to structure policy outcomes in a way that is characterized by corruption, backroom politics, a lack of long-range planning, and injustice.[7] For example, we discussed the role and influence of the Chemical Manufacturers Association in the development of Superfund legislation in Chapter 5.

In sum, all these actors and institutions are, at one time or another, involved in policy formulation. In the following discussion of models of policy formulation, we describe exactly how these organizations and actors exert their influence on public policy.

EXPLAINING POLICY FORMULATION

The literature on public policy formulation provides several alternative explanations of how policies are formulated in the United States. Because the core activity of policy formulation is choosing between alternatives for dealing with a policy problem, the alternative explanations are, in fact, models of decision making. The use of these explanations is critical to understanding policy formulation and policy analysis. Besides the elitist, pluralist, and subgovernment models (discussed earlier in Chapters 4 and 5), the rational-comprehensive, the incremental, and the systems models of policy formulation are some of the best-known examples.

The Rational-Comprehensive Model

A well-known model of decision making is the **rational-comprehensive model,** primarily based on the assumption that individuals make decisions on the basis of a rational calculation of costs and benefits. This model of policy choice usually includes the following components:

1. The decision maker is confronted with a given problem that can be separated from other problems or at least considered meaningfully in comparison with them.
2. The goals, values, or objectives that guide the decision maker are clarified and ranked according to their importance.
3. A complete set of alternative policies for dealing with the problem are prepared.
4. The consequences (costs and benefits, advantages and disadvantages) that would follow from the selection of each alternative are investigated.
5. Each alternative, and its attendant consequences, can be calculated and compared with the other alternatives.
6. The decision maker chooses that alternative that maximizes the attainment of his or her goals, values, or objectives.

Figure 6-1 illustrates the rational-comprehensive model. The net result of this process is the most rational decision or one that most efficiently achieves a desired end.

The rational-comprehensive model has been criticized on a number of grounds. First, it is extremely difficult to define the nature of a problem and to separate out the various aspects of a particular problem. For example, what is the nature of the crime problem? Are crimes "caused" by the environment, including such things as lack of employment opportunities, poor education, and the like? Or, is crime caused by individual defects, such as low IQs, lack of motivation to work, inherent tendencies toward violence, alcoholism, and so forth?

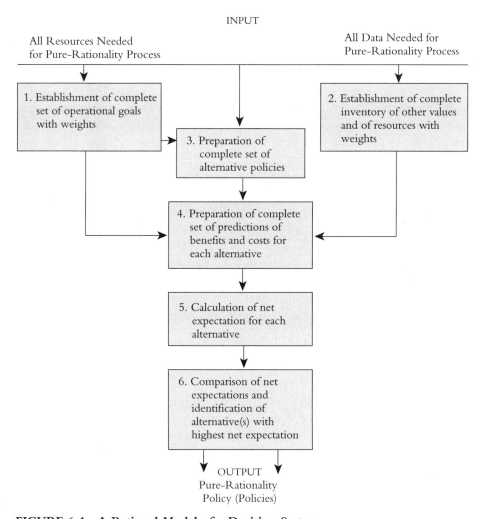

FIGURE 6-1   A Rational Model of a Decision System

Source: Thomas R. Dye, *Understanding Public Policy*, 8th ed., © 1995, p.29. Reprinted by permission of Prentice Hall, Upper Saddle River, New Jersey.

Until we know exactly what causes a problem, it is difficult to set forth alternatives that can be weighted and evaluated.

A second criticism of the rational-comprehensive model is the demands it places on the decision maker. It assumes that one has complete information on various alternatives for dealing with a problem and that one will be able to predict the consequences with complete accuracy; thus, one will be able to make cost-benefit comparisions of each alternative. In reality, this is seldom, if ever, the case. We can never have complete information on any alternative and be able to predict consequences with the kind of accuracy that this model assumes.

Third, even with the most advanced computerized analytical techniques, decision makers do not have the intellectual capacity, or judgment, to calculate cost-benefit ratios when a large number of diverse political, social, economic, and cultural values are at stake. In addition, decision makers are often motivated not by societal goals, but by self-serving goals; they are interested in an alternative that works for them rather than the one that achieves societal goals. Decision makers have personal needs, inhibitions, and inadequacies that prevent them from behaving in a highly rational manner.

Fourth, there is the problem of sunk costs. Previous decisions, commitments, and investments in existing policies and programs prevent decision makers from reconsidering alternatives that have been foreclosed by previous decisions. Moreover, uncertainty about policy consequences of new choices compel decision makers to stick closely to previous policies to reduce the possibility of errors in judgment.

Finally, the rational-comprehensive model assumes the existence of a unitary decision maker. This is rarely the case in that decisions are made by legislative bodies, plural-headed agencies, or multiple-member courts. Clearly, choices are almost never made by a single actor, even if all the other conditions were met. Although the rational-comprehensive model has been criticized for its many assumptions, most of which cannot be met, it nevertheless provides a prescription for the making of policy to which we may strive. That is, it provides a guide to follow in the attempt to design more rational public policy, if that is our objective.

The Incremental Model

Another model of policy formulation is represented by the **incremental model.** Incrementalism views public policy formulation as continuation of past government activities with only minor modifications. The constraints of time, intelligence, and cost prevent policymakers from identifying the full range of policy alternatives and their consequences. Incrementalism is conservative in that existing programs, policies, and expenditures are considered as a base and attention is concentrated on new programs and policies and on increases, decreases, or modifications of existing programs or policies. The key assumptions of this model are (1) that decision makers do not have sufficient predictive capabilities to know all the consequences of each alternative; (2) that decision makers accept the legitimacy of previous policies; (3) that sunk costs prevent serious consideration of all

policy alternatives and especially any radical change in policy; (4) that incrementalism reduces conflict and is politically expedient; and (5) that the characteristics of the decision makers themselves are more suited to the incremental model
in that humans are not value-maximizers, but more often they are "satisficers," or
they act to merely satsify particular demands. Thus, in the absence of agreed-
upon societal values, a pluralistic government can more easily continue existing
policies or programs than engage in overall policy planning toward specific policy goals. The key components of the incremental model are listed below:

1. The selection of goals or objectives and the empirical analyses of the action
   needed to attain them are closely intertwined with, rather than distinct
   from, one another.
2. The decision maker considers only some of the alternatives for dealing
   with a problem, which will differ only incrementally from existing policies.
3. For each alternative, only a limited number of important consequences are
   evaluated.
4. The problem confronting the decision maker is continually redefined.
   Incrementalism allows for countless ends-means and means-ends adjust-
   ments that have the effect of making the problem more manageable.
5. There is no single "best" solution for a problem. The test of a good decision is that various analysts find themselves directly agreeing on it, without
   agreeing that the decision is the most appropriate means to an agreed-
   upon objective.
6. Incremental decision making is essentially remedial and is geared more to
   the amelioration of present, concrete social imperfections than to the promotion of future social goals.[8]

This model has also been criticized on a number of grounds. First, some have
argued that this model does not explain dramatic policy change or reversals.
Nor does it explain recent governmental efforts at long-range planning, such as
the Global 2000 report in 1980, which was produced during the Carter administration and explored the relationships among population, resources, and the
environment between 1979 and 2000. Table 6-1 provides a comparision of the
incremental and rational-comprehensive models of decision making.

The Systems Model

The **systems model,** originally developed by David Easton, suggests that public policy formation is initially affected by demands for new policies or support
for the existing policies.[9] These demands and supports are then acted on by a
political system, or conversion mechanism, which converts these demands into
public policies or decisions, called outputs. Essentially, his model of policy formation proposes that inputs (demands and supports) are converted by the
processes of the political system (legislatures, the courts, etc.) into outputs (policies or decisions), and these in turn have consequences both for the system and

TABLE 6-1   Rational and Incremental Models: A Comparison

Rational Process	Incremental Process
1. The analysis of the situation.	1. The policymaker works directly on agreement on specific projects, policies, or programs, and *not* toward agreement on abstract goals.
2. End reduction and elaboration.	2. The policymaker is concerned with the comparison and evaluation of increments only.
3. The design of courses of action.	3. The policymaker considers only a restricted number of policy alternatives.
4. The comparative evaluation of consequences in light of ends.	4. Ends are adjusted to means, as well as the other way around. The problem is constantly redefined. Policy objectives are derived largely from an inspection of our means.
5. The selection of the preferable alternative.	5. Many alternatives are attempted in a series of "attacks" on the problem of concern.
6. The assessment of the action taken in light of both ends and means.	6. Assessment relies on experience and feedback because policymaking is remedial. In Lindblom's view: " . . . public problem solving [Proceeds] less by aspiration toward a well defined future state than by identified social ills that seem to call for remedy."[*] In short, ultimate ends are not of great concern.

[*]Charles Lindblom, quoted in Galloway, p. 179.

Source: Thomas D. Galloway, *The Role of Urban Planning in Public Policy-making: A Synthesis and Critique of Contemporary Procedural Planning Thought* (Ph. D. diss.(1971) Ann Arbor, Mich.: University Microfilms, 1974). The figure is drawn from material on pp. 71, and 175–180.

for the environment in which the system exists. Demands may be internal to the system (e.g., political parties or interest groups) or external to the system (e.g., ecology, the economy, culture, demography). Support, according to Easton, includes actions or orientations that help the system operate and help to sustain it. Support is derived from three directions: (1) the political community; (2) the regime or rules of the game; and (3) the government itself. A political system generates support by meeting demands of the polity and by political socialization. The outputs of the system (political decisions or public policies) create support when they satisfy day-to-day demands or when system members perceive the government as being generally favorable to their interests. On the other hand, persistent inability of a government to produce satisfactory outputs for the members of a system may lead to demands for changing the regime or for dis-

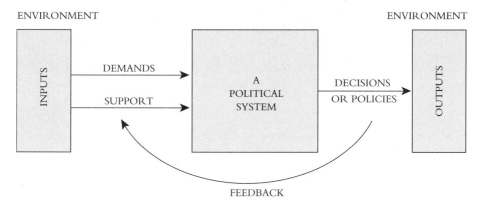

FIGURE 6-2   The Systems Framework
Source: David Easton, *A Framework for Political Analysis* (Chicago: The University of Chicago Press, 1979), Diagram 3, p. 112. © 1965, 1979 by David Easton. Reprinted with permission.

solution of the political community.[10] Figure 6-2 illustrates Easton's systems model.

Other scholars have attempted to modify the systems model for various purposes. Thomas Dye, for example, adapted the systems model for the study of American state politics. His model suggests that socioeconomic development variables in the states (e.g., urbanization, industrialization, income, and education) create demands or supports on the political system (e.g., constitutional framework, the electoral system, the party system, interest-group structures, elite or power structures, or political styles), which in turn produce state policy outcomes (e.g., welfare policies, highway policies, educational policies, tax policies).[11] Since the early 1970s, still others have attempted to elaborate on the systems model developed by Easton, and they have produced several useful additional versions of this model for the comparative analysis of public policy in the American states.[12]

The "mainstream" state politics model has been criticized on several grounds. Specifically, it is argued that the model does not allow for variation in "needs," or the severity of the problem, which in turn produces demands for a solution to some public problem. The model is also somewhat vague about whether political parties are "demands" or an institution. Finally, there is the boundary problem as to what should be included in the "environment" of the political system.[13]

In conclusion, there is no single "best" model of policy formulation. Rather, the models discussed above are more or less useful, depending on the objectives of the policy analyst and the criteria for a "good" model.[14] For example, if one seeks to explain the determinants of policy outputs among the fifty American states, then the systems model works rather well.[15] If one is interested in systematically approaching the task of decision making, then the rational-comprehensive model works rather well. The incremental model is useful in explaining budgetary decisions and/or minor changes in policy. The latter is not very useful, however, in explaining massive changes in public policy.

CASE STUDY

At-Sea Incineration of Toxic Waste

The case of designing and finalizing regulations for at-sea burning of toxic wastes provides a useful means for illustrating how the rational, pluralist, and elitist models are sometimes used.

Policy as Efficient Goal Achievement   The rational model suggests that policy-makers know all of society's preferences, that they know all the policy alternatives available, that they know all the consequences of each policy alternative, that they calculate the ratio of achieved to sacrificed societal values for each policy alternative, and that they ultimately select the most efficient policy alternative.

The Environmental Protection Agency (EPA) has been involved in at-sea incineration of toxic wastes for over fifteen years.[16] Beginning in 1974, a series of four research burns were conducted under EPA permits to gather scientific information about incineration of liquid hazardous wastes at sea and to evaluate ocean incineration as an alternative to land-based disposal options. These research burns were conducted under the authority of the Marine Protection, Research, and Sanctuaries Act of 1972, as amended, and the Convention on the Prevention of Marine Pollution by Dumping of Wastes and Other Matter (the London Dumping Convention, as it is commonly called).

Between October 1974 and January 1975, 16,800 metric tons of organo-chlorine wastes from the Shell Chemical Company's Deer Park manufacturing complex were incinerated in the Gulf of Mexico. In October 1976, Shell was issued a permit to incinerate up to 50,000 metric tons of mixed wastes at the Gulf Incineration Site. Approximately 29,100 metric tons of wastes were actually incinerated. In 1977, the U.S. Air Force incinerated its stock of herbicide orange at a site 322 kilometers west of Johnson Atoll in the Pacific Ocean. The last series of burns were performed in 1981 and 1982 when liquid PCB wastes were incinerated at the Gulf Incineration Site under a research permit issued to Chemical Waste Management and Ocean Combustion Services.[17]

Opposition to ocean incineration coalesced on October 21, 1983, when the EPA published a notice in the *Federal Register* announcing that Chemical Waste Management had been granted tentative approval to burn 79.7 million gallons of mixed liquid organic chemicals containing PCBs and DDT at a site 170 miles southeast of Brownsville, Texas. A public hearing was held on November 21, 1983, in Brownsville and another in Mobile, Alabama, during November 22 and 23, 1983. Reputed to be the largest example of citizen participation in EPA history, 6,488 people registered at those two public hearings and some threatened litigation if any permits were issued.[18]

As a result of these demonstrations, the EPA assistant administrator decided not to grant permits to Chemical Waste Management and Ocean Combustion Services to burn the wastes. Rather, the administrator deferred permit issuance until a more deliberative strategy could be developed for at-sea incineration of toxic wastes. Toward that end, he directed his staff to develop a research strategy that would respond to the need to develop more specific regulations for ocean incineration. EPA began to develop these regulations between 1985 and 1986. Using its experience with land-based incineration of toxic wastes, the EPA proposed rules that provided a regulatory framework for the ocean incineration program in February 1985. The proposed rules modified provisions in the Ocean Dumping Regulations regarding the issuance of permits and the designation of burn sites. Specifically, the rules required that 99.99 percent of the chemicals burned at sea should be destroyed in the process and, for PCBs and dioxin, burning efficiency should be 99.9999 percent. In addition, each ship would be required to carry a full-time EPA employee to monitor compliance with the conditions of the incineration permits. Thus, these proposed rules imposed stringent licensing and operating restrictions on operators of incinerator ships.

After receiving over 4,500 comments on these proposed rules, in November 1985 the EPA announced a tentative decision to permit the test burning of toxic wastes at sea off the New Jersey coast. However, in February 1986 the National Oceanic and Atmospheric Administration (NOAA) ordered a six-month delay in plans for burning hazardous wastes aboard Vulcanus II, a ship owned by Chemical Waste Management. As a reaction to this concern by NOAA, the EPA released a report on May 1, 1986, that raised more questions about the plan to burn toxic wastes off the mid-Atlantic coast. Finally, in late May 1986 the EPA announced its decision to deny the research permit and to grant no further permits for burning until it finalized its Ocean Incineration Regulations.

Thus, this behavior by the EPA illustrates the rational model of policy formation. The EPA carefully developed its plans for at-sea incineration according to the rational model of policy formation by attempting to develop complete information and carefully considering all policy alternatives in designing its final regulations. In that sense, it attempted to select the most efficient policy solution after receiving public comments and designing (and redesigning) its regime framework for ocean burning of toxic wastes.

Policy as Group Equilibrium   The pluralist model describes all meaningful political activity as competition between interest groups. Policymakers are seen as constantly reacting to group pressures and, as a consequence of these competing pressures, reaching policy compromises through bargaining and negotiation. Public policy outcomes reflect a "balancing" of competing group pressures.

The ocean incineration policy subsystem contained a large and diverse set of actors. Essentially, two coalitions developed in the debate over ocean incineration of toxic wastes. These two coalitions included the pro-incineration coalition and the anti-incineration coalition. The pro-incineration coalition was dominated by the waste incineration industry, including Chemical Waste Management (the owners of Vulcanus I and II incineration vessels), At-Sea Incineration (owners of Apollo I and II incineration vessels), Precision Conversion and Recovery, Inc., and Sea Burn, Inc. They were joined by the Institute of Chemical Waste Management and the state of Florida's Department of Environmental Regulation (DER), among others. They believed that incineration at sea was the best liquid chemical waste disposal technology available, that it was safe and valuable, and that it added little risk to the already heavy traffic of hazardous waste chemicals through American ports.[19]

The competing anti-incineration coalition was dominated by environmental groups including Greenpeace, the Cousteau Society, Friends of the Earth, and a number of others. It also included a number of attorneys general of various states, the Texas Shrimp Association, the Texas Rural Legal Aid Association, the Texas Environmental Coalition, some migrant farm workers, representatives of the land-based incineration industry, resort owners, and some members of the scientific community. This coalition believed that the ocean incineration technology was old and remained unproven; that incinerator stack emissions were toxic and capable of destroying Texas citrus orchards, cattle ranches, and shellfish grounds; and that an accidental or operational spill might devastate the coastal economy, including tourism.[20]

Each coalition attempted to influence the EPA on this issue through grassroots lobbying efforts, hearings, and demonstrations, especially between 1983 and 1985. The strategy of the pro-incineration coalition was to restore public confidence in the safety of at-sea incineration and to get the EPA to issue permits for incineration ships and for sites for burning hazardous wastes. The strategy of the anti-incineration coalition was to get the EPA to undertake additional research before approving procedures and/or to draft broad regulations for ocean incineration before granting permits for burning. At most, this coalition hoped to prevent the EPA from issuing permits for sites and ships for burning toxic wastes and to bring suit against the EPA challenging the agency's authority to issue final permits if the regulations were perceived as too lax.[21]

The evidence suggests that the EPA was affected by these two pressure groups' demands. The EPA decision to require more research before approving permits for burns reflected a "balancing" of the demands by each of these two groups. Thus, the pluralist model helps us to understand the formulation of EPA's policy for burning toxic wastes at sea.

Policy as Elite Preferences The elitist model suggests that elites (e.g., corporate elites, key politicians, or top military leaders) dominate public policy outcomes. According to elite theorists, the masses are largely passive, apathetic, and ill-informed; thus, mass sentiments are more often manipulated by elites who share a consensus on behalf of the basic values of the social system. Policy questions are seldom influenced by democratic institutions, such as elections or political parties; rather, policy outcomes come about as a result of redefinitions by elites of their own values.

Some argued that Chemical Waste Management developed a "cozy relationship" with the Environmental Protection Agency during the discussions over burning toxic wastes at sea. Moreover, Chemical Waste Management acknowledges recruiting six former EPA officials to its payroll, and several EPA officials involved in issuing test-burn permits were rebuked in a 1983 inspector general's report for keeping Chemical Waste Management calendars on their office walls, thus creating the appearance of favoritism.[22]

In general, the EPA favored at-sea incineration as a waste disposal option. The agency often said that the at-sea incineration process "will have minimal effects on the marine environment."[23] Moreover, the EPA initially announced a decision to permit the burning of toxic waste at sea at a site off the New Jersey coast; this project alone would have added roughly 8 percent to Chemical Waste Management's earnings, which in 1984 totaled $142.5 million.[24] In addition, some scientists contended that, in its haste to find a solution to the hazardous waste management problem, the EPA itself promoted incineration with "flimsy research." It was argued that EPA staffers deleted sections of an independent scientific advisory's report to make it appear more favorable to the agency's enthusiastic position on at-sea incineration. The EPA, according to many environmental groups, "continues to relentlessly push ocean incineration, with the assumption that siting a hazardous waste disposal facility at sea will avoid the controversy of locating a facility on land in someone's back yard."[25]

Thus, the elitist model of policy formulation finds some support in the preceding description of the EPA's policy for at-sea incineration. The EPA seemed to develop a cozy relationship with the chemical waste industry and favored its desire to burn wastes at sea, at least from 1983 to 1985.

THE EVOLUTION OF OUR UNDERSTANDING OF POLICY FORMULATION

We have learned a great deal over the past three decades about the process of policy formulation. In the 1970s, several scholars attempted to further develop the systems model and to test it within several alternative contexts.[26] These efforts attempted to put "politics" back in the analysis of public policy. By encouraging us to think about politics much like a biological system, Easton's systems model provided a new way of thinking about determinants of policy outcomes. Forces both outside the political system as well as within the "black box" affected public policy.

In the 1980s, a number of causal theories of substantially new portions of the policy process have emerged, including theories and models of agenda setting, policy implementation, policy termination, and policy change.[27] In the 1990s, we realize that policy formulation is never complete; we are constantly changing public policy through oversight and policy redesign. Thus, we are beginning to study policy change (the subject of Chapter 9). In this aspect of the policy cycle, we are interested in explaining why policies are changed from one type to another. Research from the 1950s until the present time has evolved so that we have a much more complete understanding of each aspect of the policy cycle. What is needed now, however, is a careful application and testing of existing models of the policy process so that they may be validated and accepted or falsified and rejected. We also need refinement and elaboration of many of these models and even the development of new ones, as necessary.[28]

SUMMARY

In conclusion, the policy formulation aspect of the policy cycle is the most "mature" in terms of existing literature. This is the point where scholars began their research on the policy process, although more recently we have turned our attention toward other aspects of the policy cycle, such as policy implementation.[29] In the next few chapters, we take up the subject of policy implementation, policy evaluation, and policy termination and change. These following chapters illustrate the evolution of our understanding in these more "youthful" areas of the policy cycle.

NOTES

1. James E. Anderson, *Public Policymaking: An Introduction* (Boston: Houghton Mifflin, 1990), p. 93.
2. See Deborah A. Stone, *Policy Paradox and Political Reason* (Glenview, IL: Scott, Foresman, 1988).
3. Anderson, *Public Policymaking,* p. 94.
4. Ibid., p. 96.
5. V. O. Key, *Politics, Parties, and Pressure Groups,* 5th ed. (New York T.Y. Crowell, 1964), p. 17.
6. Arthur Bentley, *The Process of Government* (Chicago: University of Chicago Press, 1908), p. 222.
7. Theodore Lowi, *The End of Liberalism* (New York: W. W. Norton, 1979).
8. Charles Lindbloom, "The Science of Muddling Through". *Public Administration Review* 19 (Spring, 1959), pp.79–88.
9. David Easton, "An Approach to the Analysis of Political Systems," *World Politics* 9, no. 3 (April 1957), pp. 383–400.
10. Ibid., p. 384.
11. Thomas R. Dye, "A Model for the Analysis of Policy Outcomes," in *Policy Analysis in Political Science,* ed. Ira Sharkansky (Chicago: Markham Publishing Company, 1970).
12. See, for example, Robert H. Salisbury, "The Analysis of Public Policy: A Search for Theories and Roles," in *Political Science and Public Policy,* ed. Austin Ranney (Chicago: Markham Publishing, 1968), and Richard I. Hofferbert, "Elite Influences in State Policy Formation: A Model for Comparative Inquiry," *Polity* 2, no. 3 (Spring 1970), pp. 316–344.
13. See Joyce Matthews Munns, "The Environment, Politics, and Policy Literature," *Western Political Quarterly* 28, no. 4 (December 1975), pp. 646–667; Charles O. Jones, *Political Science and State and Local Government* (Washington, D.C.: APSA, 1973); James P. Lester and Emmett N. Lombard, "The Comparative Analysis of State Environmental Policy," *Natural Resources Journal* 30, no. 2 (Spring 1990), pp. 301–319; and Stuart H. Rakoff and Guenther F. Schaeffer, "Politics, Policy, and Political Science," *Politics and Society* 1, no. 1 (November 1970), pp. 51–77.

14. See Daniel C. McCool, *Public Policy Theories, Models, and Concepts* (Englewood Cliffs: Prentice Hall, 1995) pp. 12–18.

15. See Daniel Mazmanian and Paul A. Sabatier, "A Multivariate Model of Public Policymaking," *American Journal of Political Science* 24, no. 3 (August 1980), pp. 439–468.

16. This section borrows heavily from an earlier article by James P. Lester and John C. Freemuth entitled, "The Formation of Ocean Incineration Policy: Some Predictions from Three Models," *Policy Studies Review* 6, no. 2 (November 1986), pp. 340–347.

17. "Ocean Incineration Regulation," Proposed Rule, *Federal Register* (February 28, 1985), pp. 8222–8280.

18. K. Schneider, "Ocean Incineration: The Public Fumes While EPA Fiddles," *Sierra* 69 (1984), p. 26.

19. R. Reinhold, "States Oppose Burning of Toxic Wastes in Gulf," *New York Times,* 16 June 1985, p. A14.

20. Ibid.

21. Schneider, "Ocean Incineration."

22. Ibid.

23. "E.P.A. to Permit Test of Burning of Toxic Waste Off Jersey Coast," *New York Times,* 27 November 1985, p. B2.

24. T. Petzinger and M. Moffett, "Plants That Incinerate Poisonous Waste Run Into a Host of Problems," *Wall Street Journal,* 26 August 1985, p. A1.

25. A. Narvaez, "Decision Due on Burning Toxic Waste Off Jersey," *New York Times,* 6 May 1986, p. B2.

26. See, for example, Richard I. Hofferbert, "Elite Influences in State Policy Formation: A Model for Comparative Inquiry," *Polity* 2, no. 3 (Spring 1970), pp. 316–344; and Mazmanian and Sabatier, "Multivariate Model."

27. See, for example, John Kingdon, *Agendas, Alternatives, and Public Policies* (New York: HarperCollins, 1995); Daniel Mazmanian and Paul A. Sabatier, *Implementation and Public Policy* (Glenview, IL: Scott, Foresman, 1983); and Paul A. Sabatier, "An Advocacy Coalition Framework of Policy Change and the Role of Policy Oriented Learning Therein," *Policy Sciences* 21, nos. 2-3 (1988), pp. 129–168.

28. Paul A. Sabatier, "Toward Better Theories of the Policy Process," *PS: Political Science and Politics* 24, no. 2 (June 1991), p. 153.

29. See Malcolm Goggin et al., *Implementation Theory and Practice: Toward a Third Generation* (New York: HarperCollins, 1990).

POLICY IMPLEMENTATION

"The principal aim of third generation research is to shed new light on implementation behavior by explaining why that behavior varies across time, policies, and units of government."

MALCOLM L. GOGGIN, ANN O'M. BOWMAN, JAMES P. LESTER, AND LAURENCE J. O'TOOLE, JR.

This chapter seeks to trace the evolution of implementation research and to discuss some of the concerns that affect progress in our understanding of policy implementation. Our discussion proceeds in three stages. First, we briefly discuss the concept of implementation, including what we mean by the term and the various activities it encompasses. Next, we discuss the evolution of public policy implementation research from 1970 to the present. Finally, we review some of the more relevant concerns with this research and provide some suggestions that will help to achieve further advances in our understanding of policy implementation over the next few years.

THE CONCEPT OF POLICY IMPLEMENTATION

By **implementation**, we mean the stage of the policy process immediately after the passage of a law. Implementation, viewed most broadly, means administration of the law in which various actors, organizations, procedures, and techniques work together to put adopted policies into effect in an effort to attain policy or program goals.[1] Previous definitions of implementation have ranged from this broad conceptualization to the more limited or dichotomous view that implementation is either achieved or not achieved. In addition to these two definitions, implementation can be thought of as a process, an output, and an outcome.[2] For example, implementation can be conceptualized as a **process**, or a series of decisions and actions directed toward putting a prior authoritative federal legislative decision into effect. More specifically, we know that five recurring activities or functions typically occur in the process of state implementation of a federal directive. First, state legislatures pass **state enabling laws** and initiate the hearings process associated with such legislation. Next, state agencies undertake **administrative rule making** and establish administrative routines for implementing the laws. Then, states appropriate **resources**, including the money and the human capital needed by the state to carry out the policy as intended. After this activity, legislators **monitor** and, through the application of sanctions and rewards, **enforce** local adherence to the laws and regulations. Finally, after some experience with its operations, lawmakers **redesign policies** in response to design flaws or to missed opportunities.[3] The essential characteristic of the implementation process, then, is the timely and satisfactory performance of certain necessary tasks related to carrying out the intent of the law. This is most often termed *compliance*. For example, in implementation of the Resource Conservation and Recovery Act of 1976 (RCRA), the process of implementation involves several tasks, such as enacting state enabling legislation that is consistent with the federal law, delegating the authority to run a program to a leading state agency, funding the program, and hiring sufficient staff to provide for adequate implementation.

Implementation can also be defined in terms of **outputs**, or the extent to which programmatic goals are supported, such as the level of expenditures committed to a program or the number of violations issued for failure to comply with the implementation directive. For example, in implementation of the Occupational Safety and Health Act (OSHA), notices of violations were issued to states that were not in compliance with the federal directive.

Finally, at the highest level of abstraction, implementation **outcomes** imply that there has been some measurable change in the larger problem that was addressed by the program, public law, or judicial decision. For example, have the toxic waste sites been cleaned up or is the air or water cleaner than before the policy was enacted?

In summary, implementation as a concept involves all these activities. Although it is a complex phenomenon, it may be understood as a process, an output, and an outcome. It also involves a number of actors, organizations, and techniques of control.

Who Implements Policy?

The Bureaucracy   Generally speaking, public policies in the United States are implemented by administrative agencies. Once Congress has enacted public laws and the president has signed them, the next step is for the various administrative agencies to begin the process of implementation. These agencies have a great deal of discretion in carrying out the public policies under their jurisdiction, because they often operate under broad and ambiguous statutory mandates from Congress. This situation exists because those who participate in the legislative process are often unable or unwilling to develop precise guidelines due to the complexity of the issue under consideration or because of lack of time, interest, or information.[4] For example, after the Resource Conservation and Recovery Act of 1976 was enacted into law, the EPA was charged with drafting the regulations for putting this law into effect. The EPA had to fill in the details of this legislation and reconcile the various conflicts embodied in the original legislation. The result was that this legislation was termed the most complex in the history of environmental protection policy.[5]

Although administrative agencies are the primary actors in public policy implementation, a number of other actors and institutions are also involved in the process. These include the legislature, the courts, pressure groups, and community organizations.

The Legislature   Traditionally, the assumption in much of the public administration literature was that politics and administration were separate activities. Politics was therefore concerned with the formulation of policy, which should be handled by the "political" branches of government, meaning the legislature and the executive branches. Administration of policy, on the other hand, was concerned with implementation of the decisions made by the more political branches and was to be handled by the various administrative agencies.[6] Today, this assumption has been called into question because administrative agencies are often involved in formulating, as well as implementing, public policy. For example, when administrative agencies draft regulations in support of existing legislation, they often are formulating policy. We saw this in the previous chapter on policy formulation in the case of at-sea incineration of toxic waste. Moreover, legislative bodies are often involved in implementing public policy when they draft very specific and detailed legislation. Increasingly today, legislative bodies are concerned with implementation and are thus drafting laws that are very specific when it comes to implementation. That is, legislators today are more concerned with details and are attempting to remove much of the bureaucratic discretion previously enjoyed by administrative agencies in the implementation of policy. This has become a functional necessity because many implementation failures are due to problems that were not addressed in the original drafting of the law.

The Courts   In many instances, public laws are enforced through the judicial branch. For example, in the *Roe* v. *Wade*, the Supreme Court declared a Texas statute prohibiting abortion unconstitutional because it violated the privacy protected by the First and Fourteenth amendments.[7] In 1989, the Supreme Court undermined *Roe* v. *Wade* in *Webster* v. *Reproductive Health Services*. In the latter case, the Court upheld a Missouri law that prohibited abortions in public facilities and the use of state funds for counseling women about abortion.[8] Since that time, the Supreme Court has agreed to hear several other cases on abortion. Thus, the Court will be involved in the implementation of laws governing abortion for some time to come.

The courts also get involved in implementation when various entities bring lawsuits in the federal district courts to enforce public laws. For example, during the 1980s and the early 1990s, the Environmental Defense Fund (EDF) has used the courts extensively to enforce environmental laws and regulations promulgated by the EPA.

Perhaps the courts' most important influence on implementation is through their interpretation of statutes and administrative rules and regulations and their review of administrative decisions in cases brought before them.[9] Affirmative action is a good example of the courts' involvement in implementation. In September 1965, Executive Order 11246 (during the Johnson administration) required "affirmative action" to foster equal opportunity for minorities and women. Specifically, this order required government contractors and others receiving government funds to take concrete measures to promote the hiring of blacks and other minorities. In the late 1960s, the Equal Employment Opportunity Commission (EEOC), acting as **amicus curiae** in civil suits, achieved a number of successes in getting its view of affirmative action accepted by the courts. In 1970, a federal court ruled that "specific hiring goals and time-tables" were "no more or less than a means for implementation of the affirmative action obligations of Executive Order 11246." This led to a view that affirmative action should be implemented with a goal of "proportional representation" of minorities in hiring decisions.[10]

Pressure Groups   Because administrative agencies have so much discretion in drafting regulations in support of legislation, they are besieged by various interest groups that seek to influence the guidelines and regulations in a way that will benefit them. Sometimes it is argued that various interest groups "capture" administrative agencies.[11] For example, some argue that the U.S. Coast Guard, which is the lead agency responsible for ocean pollution regulation, is involved in a "cozy" relationship with the U.S. shipping and oil interests. This close relationship between the U.S. Coast Guard and these business interests may have led to the United States's opposition to "double-bottoms" and the retrofitting of U.S. ships with segregated ballast during the 1970s and the 1980s, when the issues of tanker accidents and oil spills were on the agenda.[12]

Community Organizations   Finally, at the local level, community organizations often get involved in the implementation of public programs. An example of this kind of community involvement would include various advisory boards for toxic waste management under the Hazardous and Solid Waste Amendments of 1984, which required small businesses that produced at least 100 kilograms of toxic waste to comply with the federal law. Communities set up various advisory boards in an effort to take stock of the extent of small quantity generators (SQG) of hazardous waste so that they could design procedures for managing this low volume of waste within the community. Other examples include the various farmer committees under the price-support and soil conservation programs of the Department of Agriculture, advisory boards for the Bureau of Land Management, and representatives of the poor for Community Action agencies.[13]

Techniques of Policy Implementation

Implementors can use a number of devices to see that public laws are implemented according to the intent of Congress and/or the bureaucracy. Most recently, the debate has centered on two approaches: the **command and control** approach or the **economic incentives** (or **market**) approach. By command and control, we mean the use of mechanisms that are somewhat coercive, such as standard setting, inspections, and the imposition of sanctions on violators who fail to comply with the federal directive. By economic incentives, we mean the use of tax credits, subsidies, or other rewards or penalties that encourage private interests to comply. Opponents of the command and control approach argue that it dictates behavior, discourages private initiative and innovation in attaining policy goals, and wastes or misuses societal resources. The incentive system, on the other hand, "lets individuals make their own decisions, thus enhancing freedom and voluntarism, and . . . achieves desired goals at the lowest possible cost to society."[14]

The debate between the two approaches can be illustrated in the area of environmental policy. The incentive or market approach to pollution is to tax companies that discharge pollutants into the air or water according to how much they discharge and how toxic their pollutants are. The standards approach, on the other hand, is to set permissible levels of discharge for various pollutants (called performance standards) and then fine companies that do not comply with these standards.[15] The fundamental difference between these two approaches lies in the use of variable prices (or taxes) in the market approach and relatively fixed prices (or penalties) in the other.

Whatever approach is used ultimately depends on good faith between the various actors involved in implementation. No scheme for compliance will work if the implementors and those charged with compliance fail to agree on the goals of implementation. Implementation goals will necessarily involve bargaining and negotiation among the various parties involved, including the interests of the wider community affected by these goals and standards.

THE EVOLUTION OF POLICY IMPLEMENTATION RESEARCH

The study of policy implementation has grown substantially since Pressman and Wildavsky's case study of the difficulties that the city of Oakland, California, encountered when trying to implement a federal personnel training program during the late 1960s.[16] There is now an abundance of good theories and analytical frameworks and at least two major approaches, the "top-down" and the "bottom-up" approaches.[17] This research has resulted in demonstrable progress in at least two respects: first, there is now a better understanding of what implementation is and how it varies across time, policies, and units of government; and second, advances have been made in linking certain characteristics of the policy's design and setting on the one hand with implementation performance on the other. There is no shortage of variables thought to explain implementation. Yet despite the progress to date, the "critical" variables have not yet been identified, and the measurement of key variables, as well as the careful testing of hypotheses, has only just begun.[18] In this regard, implementation research in the mid-1990s is at approximately the same stage of development as was public policy research more generally a decade ago.[19]

For the most part, implementation research has been concerned with acquiring a better understanding of the political, economic, organizational, and attitudinal factors that influence how well (or how poorly) a policy or program has been implemented. Two generations of research have sought to understand the determinants of implementation. First-generation studies of implementation were, for the most part, detailed accounts of how a single authoritative decision was carried out (i.e., a case study). This body of research was primarily directed toward describing the numerous barriers to effective policy implementation.[20] Second-generation studies were concerned with explaining implementation success or failure. A more detailed fashion of analyzing these two generations of research may be suggested by four distinct stages between 1970 and 1995: (1) the generation of case studies; (2) the development of policy implementation frameworks; (3) the application of frameworks; and (4) synthesis and revision. In the following pages, we briefly discuss these four phases of implementation research, paying careful attention to key contributions during each stage of theoretical development.

Case Studies, 1970–1975

In the early 1970s, very little research was available on public policy implementation. This situation existed though many new public programs were being implemented; moreover, "little knowledge was available to assist in the implementation process, and only a few observers even appreciated the need to understand why implementation failed or succeeded."[21] As one scholar of implementation notes, "initial studies of implementation were, for the most part, detailed accounts of how a single authoritative decision was carried out, either at a single location or at multiple sites."[22] These pioneering studies, such as the one by Martha Derthick, came to the pessimistic conclusion that government-sponsored programs seldom achieved their objectives.[23] Little or no attempt was made to develop any dynamic model of the implementation process that could explain such failures or to provide any real guidance about how to relieve the problems. Moreover, the case study approach, used almost exclusively by the early researchers, made it exceedingly difficult for investigators to either introduce the element of control for multiple explanations or generalize from their findings. Early investigators were plagued by the problem of too many variables and too few cases. Therefore, they could not really extract much from their findings. By the mid-1970s, however, policy implementation scholars began to turn their attention toward the next stage of intellectual development—model building.

Policy Implementation Frameworks, 1975–1980

Although describing the numerous barriers to effective implementation was extremely useful, it did not result in the development of useful theory about policy implementation. However, the second broad category of implementation literature sought to develop analytical frameworks that identified factors that contributed to the realization (or nonrealization) of policy objectives. The work conducted in this area can be broadly classified into "top-down" and "bottom-up" approaches.[24] Essentially, the top-down approach starts with a policy decision by central government officials and then asks:

1. To what extent were the actions of implementing officials and target groups consistent with (the objectives and procedures outlined in) that policy decision?
2. To what extent were the objectives attained over time (i.e., to what extent were the impacts consistent with the objectives)?
3. What were the principal factors affecting policy outputs and impacts, both those relevant to the official policy as well as other politically significant ones?
4. How was the policy reformulated over time on the basis of experience?[25]

The first such top-down effort was undertaken by Donald Van Meter and Carl Van Horn.[26] Their model—as depicted in Figure 7-1—posited six variables that were believed to shape the linkage between policy and performance. Their variables included the following: (1) policy standards and objectives; (2) policy resources (e.g., funds or other incentives); (3) interorganizational communication and enforcement activities; (4) characteristics of implementing agencies (e.g., staff size, degree of hierarchical control, organizational vitality); (5) economic, social, and political conditions (e.g., economic resources within the implementing jurisdiction, public opinion, interest-group support); and (6) the disposition of the implementors.[27]

Other top-down models included those developed by Sabatier and Mazmanian and by Edwards.[28] The most comprehensive list of factors thought to affect the success of implementing a program can be found in the work of Sabatier and Mazmanian, as shown in Figure 7–2. They identified sixteen

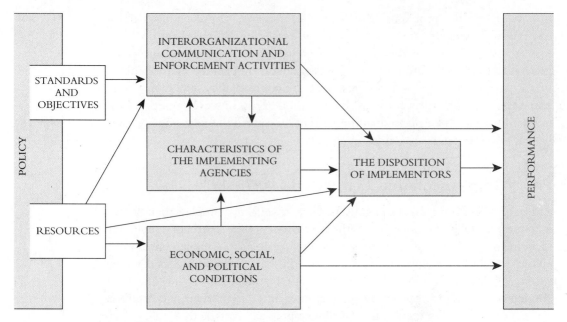

FIGURE 7–1   A Model of the Policy Implementation Process
Source: Donald Van Meter and Carl Van Horn, "The Policy Implementation Process: A Conceptual Framework," *Administration and Society* 6 (1975), p. 463, copyright © 1975 by Sage Publications, Inc. Reprinted by permission of Sage Publications, Inc.

independent variables within three major categories: (1) the tractability of the problem; (2) the ability of the statute to structure implementation; and (3) nonstatutory variables affecting implementation. All the variables mentioned in Figure 7–2 were thought to affect implementation.

Thus, the number of variables thought to affect implementation ranged from four to sixteen, and although some of these models were able to explain implementation behavior with very few determinants, all were criticized for failing to identify which variables were likely to be most important and under what circumstances.[29] In addition to this criticism, others criticized the top-downers for assuming "that the framers of the policy decision (i.e., the people who drafted the statute) are the key actors and that others are basically impediments. This, in turn, leads the top-downers to neglect strategic initiatives coming from the private sector, from street level bureaucrats or local implementing officials, and from other policy subsystems."[30]

In the light of these criticisms, a competing model of policy implementation, often termed "backward mapping," or the bottom-up approach, was developed by several scholars working independently from one another. These individuals included Richard Elmore, Michael Lipsky, and Benny Hjern and his associates.[31] In contrast to the top-down approach, the bottom-up approach starts by identifying the network of actors involved in service delivery in one or more local areas and asks them about their goals, strategies, activ-

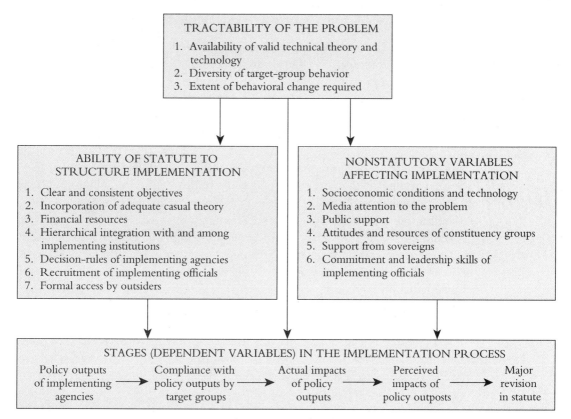

FIGURE 7–2   Skeletal Flow Diagram of the Variables Involved in the Implementation Process

Source: From *Implementation and Public Policy* by Daniel H. Mazmanian and Paul A. Sabatier (New York: HarperCollins, 1983), Figure 2–1, p.22. Copyright © 1983 by Scott Foresman & Company. Reprinted by permission of HarperCollins College Publishers, Inc.

ities, and contacts. "It then uses the contacts as a means for developing a network technique to identify the local, regional, and national actors involved in the planning, financing, and execution of the relevant governmental and nongovernmental programs."[32] Rather than control by central decision makers, policy is determined by the bargaining (explicit or implicit) between members of the organization and their clients. Therefore, "programs must be compatible with the wishes and desires, or at least the behavioral patterns, of those lower echelon officials."[33]

Similarly, this approach received a great deal of criticism for assuming that policy implementation occurs (or should occur) in a decentralized policymaking environment. Thus, the bottom–up approach was somewhat flawed by accepting a rather limited explanation of implementation behavior as both a desirable form of implementation and the only analytical approach for a complex organizational and political problem. For the next five years, various scholars were involved in testing these top–down or bottom–up models.

Applications of the Frameworks, 1980–1985

Most of the major implementation frameworks were tested by their authors or by others during the period 1980–1985. According to Carl Van Horn, four broad lessons can be drawn from these empirical studies. First, the frameworks were quite useful in constructing general explanations for policy implementation success and failure. Second, implementation researchers demonstrated that time periods are very important in implementation research (i.e., results varied depending on whether they were limited to only a few years of investigation or longer time frames). Third, some programs were successfully implemented (i.e., the case studies of the late 1960s and early 1970s emphasized failure, whereas later implementation studies suggested a more optimistic outcome). Finally, "scholars found that even simple, modest programs can fail."[34]

Although both first- and second-generation implementation research have added much to our knowledge of what implementation is and how and why it varies as it does, it has been much less helpful in differentiating among types of implementation outcomes, or in specifying the explanations associated with these outcomes, the frequency with which these patterns occur, and the relative importance and unique effects of each of the various independent variables that are part of any adequate analysis of implementation performance. Thus, these criticisms have led to recent efforts by various scholars to synthesize what we have learned and to suggest some promising revisions for future research.

Syntheses and Revisions, 1985–Present

Most recently a number of scholars have provided a synthesis and critique of the implementation literature.[35] These syntheses have produced a number of criticisms of both the top-down and bottom-up models of policy implementation and have led to at least three attempts to incorporate the best features of each of the two approaches.

The first such attempt (in the United States) was developed by Richard Elmore in which he combined his previous work on "backward mapping" with what he terms "forward mapping." In this initial synthesis, he argued that policymakers need to consider both the policy instruments and other resources at their disposal (forward mapping) with the incentive structure of ultimate target groups (backward mapping), because program success is contingent on combining both these two considerations. He does not, however, provide a graphic model of the policy implementation process that could be used by scholars to explain this particular phenomenon.[36]

A more ambitious approach was recently developed by Paul Sabatier.[37] His synthesis combines the "bottom-uppers'" unit of analysis (i.e., a whole variety of public and private actors involved with a policy problem) with the "top-downers'" concerns over the manner in which socioeconomic conditions and legal instruments constrain behavior. He then applies this synthesized perspective to the analysis of policy change over periods of a decade or more. His model is primarily concerned with the development of theory rather than with providing policy advice to practitioners. Figure 7–3 illustrates his model of policy change (i.e., policy formulation, policy implementation, and policy reformulation).

Finally, a third attempt to synthesize elements of both the top-down and bottom-up approaches was developed by Malcolm Goggin and his associates.[38] In their model of intergovernmental policy implementation, they argue that state implementation is in turn a function of inducements and constraints provided to (or imposed on) the states from elsewhere in the federal system—above or below—as well as of the states' own propensity to act and their capacity to effectuate their preferences. Moreover, state choices are not those of a single rational actor, but may be the result of bargaining among parties above them (the national level) as well as those below them (the local level) who are involved in state politics.

Thus, this approach assumes that state implementation of federal programs ultimately depends on both top-down and bottom-up types of variables. This synthesis yields the conceptual framework displayed in Figure 7–4.

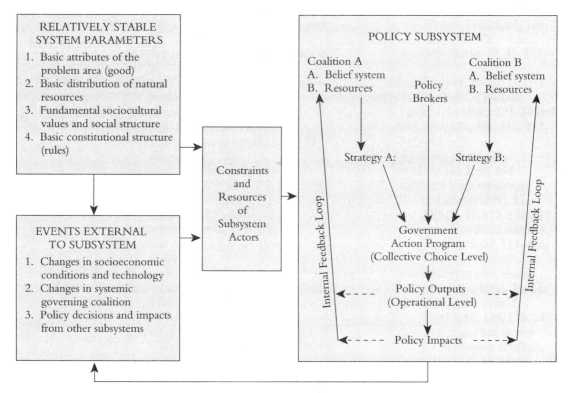

FIGURE 7–3   General Overview of Conceptual Framework of Policy Change

Source: Approximately one page from *Policy Change and Learning: An Advocacy Coalition Approach* by Paul A. Sabatier and Hank C. Jenkins-Smith (Boulder, CO: WestviewPress, 1993), p 18. Copyright © 1993 by WestviewPress. Reprinted by permission of WestviewPress.

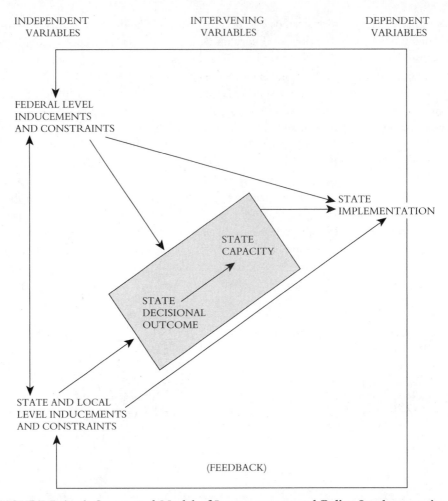

INDEPENDENT
VARIABLES

INTERVENING
VARIABLES

DEPENDENT
VARIABLES

FEDERAL LEVEL
INDUCEMENTS
AND CONSTRAINTS

STATE
IMPLEMENTATION

STATE
CAPACITY

STATE
DECISIONAL
OUTCOME

STATE AND LOCAL
LEVEL INDUCEMENTS
AND CONSTRAINTS

(FEEDBACK)

FIGURE 7–4   A Conceptual Model of Intergovernmental Policy Implementation
Source: From *Implementation Theory and Practice: Toward a Third Generation* by Malcolm L. Goggin et al.(New York: HarperCollins, 1990). Fig. 1–1, p. 32. Copyright © 1990 by Malcolm L. Goggin, Ann O'M. Bowman, James P. Lester, and Laurence J. O'Toole, Jr. Reprinted by permission of HarperCollins College Publishers.

Their approach is predicated on the notion that there is no single explanation for differences in implementation. The national decision that triggers an
implementation process constrains by its form and content, to varying degrees,
the choices and behaviors of those states and cities that have to execute the legislation.. State responses to federal inducements (or local responses to state
inducements) and constraints vary, depending on the nature and intensity of
the preferences of several key participants (inclusive of the local level) in the
state policy process at different points in time. Finally, state responses are also
constrained by the state's capacity to act.[39]

In the aftermath of these recent syntheses and revisions, we have come to a
crossroads in the study of policy implementation. One direction, suggested by

Paul Sabatier, takes us down the path of studying the "politics of policy change." This line of research "is primarily concerned with theory construction rather than with providing guidelines for practitioners or detailed portraits of particular situations."[40]

An alternative path is suggested by Elmore and by Goggin and his colleagues. Although both are concerned with policy implementation, Elmore is primarily concerned with aiding policy practitioners, whereas the framework suggested by Goggin and his colleagues is explicitly directed toward *both* theory development and useful advice for policy practitioners.[41] However, a number of conceptual and methodological issues must be addressed before any of these approaches provide either an advance in theory development or useful advice for decision makers.

WHERE ARE WE NOW? THE CURRENT STATUS OF IMPLEMENTATION RESEARCH

Today the study of public policy implementation presents many exciting opportunities for research that could enhance our understanding of the concept. In the mid-1990s, we are poised for exciting new breakthroughs in our understanding of the determinants of implementation. We have progressed to the point whereby we can apply these new frameworks to better understand the key determinants (or critical variables) in the process of implementing public policies. We now know that implementation is affected by top-down as well as bottom-up kinds of variables. For example, implementation of public programs is influenced by federal-level factors, such as the clarity of the message (the law itself or regulations) that the federal government sends to the states. In addition, the amount of resources (money) that the federal government provides to the states is crucial to the successful implementation of public programs. Some states are more dependent on federal intergovernmental aid than are other states. California, for example, is not very dependent on federal intergovernmental aid for implementation of its environmental programs, whereas Mississippi is very dependent on federal aid for implementing its environmental programs. In this instance, Mississippi's ability to implement federal mandates in the environmental area would be adversely affected by federal cutbacks in the level of intergovernmental aid in support of Mississippi's environmental programs. These kinds of top-down variables are important determinants of the success or failure of state implementation efforts.

At the same time, there are bottom-up conditions that also affect state success or failure in implementation. Such factors include state and local political and economic conditions, state capacities (including resources and personnel) for implementation, and the dispositions of state and local implementors. For example, the "liberalness" or the "conservativeness" of a state's political environment will obviously affect the ease with which a policy is implemented. Welfare policies might be more easily implemented in a more liberal state than a more conservative one. On the contrary, a "get-tough" crime policy might be more easily implemented in a conservative state. Furthermore, wealthier states are more likely to implement some policies that require huge expenditures of state funds than poorer states.

In addition to these factors, states vary in terms of their institutional and resource capacity to implement federal policies. For example, the availability of staff to implement federal mandates varies greatly among states. In the environmental program capacity, the state of New Jersey has considerably more personnel to implement environmental programs than does a state such as Nevada or Wyoming.[42] Similarly, the amount of state resources, meaning funds available, to implement federal programs also varies greatly from state to state. States having more fiscal resources are much more likely to implement public programs than states with fewer fiscal resources.

Finally, we also know that the dispositions of state and local implementors is a crucial determinant of implementation. That is, if state and local implementors favor the policy or program, then implementation will fare much better than one where state and local implementors are hostile to the policy or program.[43] For some implementation scholars, the disposition of the implementors is the most important factor influencing implementation of federal or state programs. For almost all implementation scholars, this factor is an important one and is incorporated in many of their frameworks.

In summary, we know a great deal about public policy implementation. Undoubtedly, we can learn much more in the future as scholars turn their attention toward the next generation of implementation research. However, before the next generation is successful in bringing us to a greater level of understanding, we will need to address some concerns.

WHERE ARE WE GOING? TOWARD A THIRD GENERATION OF RESEARCH

Virtually all scholars of policy implementation now agree that the next phase of research must be directed toward theory development. In addition, new questions have to be addressed that are designed to illuminate what we know so little about (i.e., the full range of outcomes that lie between the extremes of implementation success and failure, the various causal paths leading to each type of outcome, the frequency with which they occur, and their relative importance in historical analyses of implementation outcomes). This third generation of implementation studies, nonetheless, will have to first overcome a number of conceptual and methodological difficulties.

First, future research will have to specify the activities that are clearly **implementation** activities, so that we can say with certainty when implementation has occurred and when it has not. We must agree on what we mean by the term *implementation,* (i.e., when it begins and when it ends). Typically, past research has viewed implementation in terms of a success/failure dichotomy, frequently on the basis of a one-time determination during the take-off stage of the implementation period. Yet, as mentioned earlier, implementation can be thought of as a process, an output, and an outcome.

Second, as discussed above, there is no shortage of variables believed to explain implementation, but the crucial variables have not yet been identified. For example, it could be argued that the **policy** itself (i.e., its form and content) is the first critical independent variable and the **setting** (i.e., the people and organizations involved in implementing a policy) is the second critical independent variable.[44] In any case, we need to move beyond our current checklist of presumably important variables that are thought to explain implementation toward a systematic identification of the fewest number of independent variables that consistently explain implementation behavior across time.

Third, despite an impressive growth in the quantity and quality of implementation research in recent years, such studies are typically either bottom-up investigations of how local communities or school districts (including street-level bureaucrats), for example, negotiate with federal, regional, and state agency personnel and elected representatives and the environment to arrive at a mutually satisfying policy or top-down studies of how a federal mandate (e.g., a public law or Supreme Court decision, for example) constrains choices at the state or local government level. Often neglected in these two approaches are the American states, which are caught between pressures from above and below. Thus, there is a need to combine elements of both the top-down and bottom-up frameworks into a single model of intergovernmental policy implementation which, in turn, could help to provide us with a richer and more accurate understanding of the policy implementation process. Recently, scholars have recognized the need to compare and evaluate the relative merits of these two approaches in various settings, and they have proposed combining the variables and insights of both in empirical work.[45] However, none of these scholars have yet undertaken such a project. It is, in fact, a mark of the immaturity of policy implementation research that these two perspectives have developed in relative isolation, with so little effort to incorporate the variables and insights of each in a more fully developed empirical theory.

Finally, many of the insights and conceptual developments that have resulted from the study of comparative state politics and policy have yet to be applied to the study of policy implementation. Over the last twenty-four years, the literature of comparative state politics has developed considerable sophistication regarding the relative importance of socioeconomic and political process variables in explaining state policy outputs.[46] There are many reasons to expect state-level factors to be as important in the implementation process as in the process of policy formulation. Yet, very few of these ideas and findings (and their implications) have been introduced into the literature on policy implementation.[47] Thus, future research on policy implementation could benefit from using research designs from the comparative state policy literature, namely, by adopting designs that are genuinely **comparative** (i.e., across the fifty American states), **diachronic** (i.e., across periods of a decade or more), and **across policy types** (i.e., distributive, redistributive, and regulatory).

CASE STUDY

Toxic Waste Management

The implementation of two major laws governing toxic waste management illus-trates the difficulty and importance of the implementation phase of the policy process. The Resource Conservation and Recovery Act (RCRA) of 1976 is pri-marily responsible for the safe management of toxic waste today. Although it is a federal law administered by the EPA, it is implemented by the individual states. To receive authorization from the EPA to implement the law, a state must first do sev-eral things: provide adequate staffing, establish institutional responsibility, and allo-cate resources to carry out the intent of the law. Although the implementation process has proceeded at a snail's pace, all but six states have received final autho-rization during the period 1984–1995. Some of the states moved very quickly to achieve compliance, whereas others were slower but still very deliberate in their attempts to provide for adequate implementation. Yet, other states were "foot-draggers" or outwardly defiant in terms of implementation styles. Delaware was one of the first states to achieve compliance, whereas Wyoming never intends to attain authorization status. What explains this variation among the fifty states?

Part of the answer lies in the ability of a state to hire sufficient staff to imple-ment the Resource Conservation and Recovery Act. Some states, such as New Jersey, have sufficient staff to monitor compliance whereas other states, such as Nevada, have very few personnel. In addition, some states have sufficient finan-cial resources for implementing RCRA (e.g., Florida), whereas others do not (e.g., Mississippi).[48] In addition to these reasons, other research indicates that states dominated by the petrochemical industry (e.g., Texas, Oklahoma, Louisiana) are very slow to implement RCRA.[49] Finally, state implementors who are experiencing communication difficulties with their federal counterparts report that these communication problems have hindered the implementation of RCRA.[50] Thus, through this brief illustration of RCRA implementation, we see how the implementation models can help us to discover conditions that facili-tate or hinder implementation of public policy.

Another example of implementation problems concerns the extent to which we have cleaned up abandoned toxic waste sites under the federal Superfund program. As of 1995, only 8 percent of the more than 1,200 Superfund sites have been completely cleaned up. Why is there so much variation in the speed of compliance by the fifty states? Are there conditions within the states themselves that affect implementation success or failure? Is the federal government a major determinant of states' responsiveness? These are the kinds of policy questions that implementation research seeks to address.[51]

SUMMARY

If we recognize the limitations of implementation research as it has been prac-ticed in the past and attempt to design research strategies that address some of

the weaknesses noted above, we should improve our understanding of the implementation process. The results of these new investigations should also allow us to
improve implementation outcomes by using the results from these studies to
redesign policies so that they "work" better. That is, policymakers and managers
should be able to use the knowledge generated from this third generation of
studies of implementation to design or redesign policies so that implementation
is facilitated. Thus, the future of implementation research is an optimistic one and
one that should greatly improve our understanding of this terribly important
phase of the policy cycle.

NOTES

1. James E. Anderson, *Public Policymaking: An Introduction* (Boston: Houghton Mifflin, 1990), p. 172.
2. Malcolm Goggin, Ann Bowman, James Lester, and Laurence O'Toole, *Implementation Theory and Practice: Toward a Third Generation* (New York: HarperCollins, 1990), p. 34.
3. Goggin et al., *Implementation Theory*, pp. 46–47.
4. Anderson, *Public Policymaking*, p. 174.
5. James P. Lester, "Hazardous Waste and Policy Implementation: The Subnational Role," *Hazardous Waste and Hazardous Materials* 2, no. 3 (Fall 1985), pp. 381–397; see also James P. Lester and Ann O'M. Bowman, eds., *The Politics of Hazardous Waste Management* (Durham: Duke University Press, 1983), pp. 9–11.
6. Frank J. Goodnow, *Politics and Administration* (New York: Russell and Russell, 1900).
7. *Roe* v. *Wade*, 410 U.S. 113 (1973).
8. See *New York Times*, 4 July, 1989, pp. A1, A8–12.
9. Anderson, *Public Policymaking*, p. 177.
10. Charles Murray, *Losing Ground* (New York: Basic Books, 1984), pp. 93–95; see also Nathan Glazer, *Affirmative Discrimination: Ethnic Inequality and Public Policy* (New York: Basic Books, 1975).
11. Marver H. Bernstein, *Regulating Business by Independent Commission* (Princeton: Princeton University Press, 1955).
12. James P. Lester, "Domestic Structures and International Technological Collaboration: Ocean Pollution Regulation," *Ocean Development and International Law Journal* 8 (1980), pp. 299–335.
13. Anderson, *Public Policymaking*, p. 178.
14. This discussion draws on Deborah A. Stone, *Policy Paradox and Political Reason* (Glenview, IL: Scott, Foresman, 1988), pp. 224–230.
15. Ibid., p. 225.
16. Jeffrey Pressman and Aaron Wildavsky, *Implementation* (Berkeley: University of California Press, 1973). This discussion draws heavily on James P. Lester et al., "Public Policy Implementation: Evolution of the Field and Agenda for Future Research," *Policy Studies Review* 7, no. 1 (Autumn 1987), pp. 200–216.
17. Paul A. Sabatier, "Top-Down and Bottom-Up Approaches to Implementation Research: A Critical Analysis and Suggested Synthesis," *Journal of Public Policy* 6, no. 1 (1986), pp. 21–48.

18. Laurence O'Toole, "Policy Recommendations for Multi-Actor Implementation: An Assessment of the Field," *Journal of Public Policy* 6 (1986), pp. 181–210; Malcolm Goggin, "The Too Few Cases/Too Many Variables Problem in Implementation Research," *Western Political Quarterly* 38 (1986), pp. 328–347; and James P. Lester and Ann O'M. Bowman, "Implementing Environmental Policy in a Federal System: A Test of the Sabatier-Mazmanian Model," *Polity* 21, no. 4 (Summer 1989), pp. 731–753.

19. George D. Greenberg et al., "Developing Public Policy Theory: Perspectives from Empirical Research," *American Political Science Review* 71 (1977), pp. 1532–1543.

20. Steven H. Linder and B. Guy Peters, "A Design Perspective on Policy Implementation: The Fallacies of Misplaced Prescription," *Policy Studies Review* 6 (1987), pp. 459–475.

21. R. K. Yin, "Studying the Implementation of Public Programs," in *Studying Implementation: Methodological and Administrative Issues*, ed. Walter Williams (Chatham: Chatham House Publishers, 1982), p. 37.

22. Goggin, "Too Few Cases."

23. Martha Derthick, "Defeat at Ft. Lincoln," *The Public Interest* 20 (1970), pp. 3–39; Pressman and Wildavsky, *Implementation*; and Eugene Bardach, *What Happens After a Bill Becomes a Law* (Cambridge: MIT Press, 1977).

24. Sabatier, "Implementation Research"; and Linder and Peters, "Design Perspective."

25. Sabatier, "Implementation Research."

26. Donald Van Meter and Carl Van Horn, "The Policy Implementation Process: A Conceptual Framework," *Administration and Society* 6 (1975), pp. 445–488.

27. Ibid., pp 462–464.

28. George Edwards, *Implementing Public Policy* (Washington, D.C.: CQ Press, 1980); and Daniel H. Mazmanian and Paul A. Sabatier, *Implementation and Public Policy* (Glenview, IL: Scott, Foresman, 1983).

29. Helen Ingram, "Implementation: A Review and Suggested Framework," in *Public Administration: The State of the Field*, ed. Aaron Wildavsky and Naomi Lynn (Chatham: Chatham House, 1987).

30. Sabatier, "Implementation Research," p. 30.

31. Michael Lipsky, "Street Level Bureaucracy and the Analysis of Urban Reform," *Urban Affairs Quarterly* 6 (1971), pp. 391–409; Benny Hjern and David O. Porter "Implementation Structures: A New Unit of Adminstrative Analysis," *Organization Studies* 2/3 (1981), pp. 211–227; and Richard Elmore, "Backward Mapping: Implementation Research and Policy Decision," *Political Science Quarterly* 94 (1979), pp. 606–616.

32. Sabatier, "Implementation Research," p. 32.

33. Linder and Peters, "Design Perspective."

34. Carl Van Horn, "Applied Implementation Research" (paper presented at the annual meeting of the American Political Science Association, Chicago, Illinois, 1987).

35. Elmore, "Backward Mapping," Sabatier, "Implementation Research," and Goggin et al., *Implementation Theory*; see also Robert Stoker, *Reluctant Partners: Implementing Federal Policy* (Pittsburgh, PA: University of Pittsburgh Press, 1992).

36. Richard Elmore, "Forward and Backward Mapping: Reversible Logic in the Analysis of Public Policy," in *Policy Implementatin in Federal and Unitary Systems*, ed. K. Hanf and T. Toonen (Dordrecht: Martinus Nijhoff, 1985), pp. 33–70.

37. Sabatier, "Implementation Research."

38. Goggin, et al., *Implementation Theory*.
39. Ibid., pp. 31–33.
40. Sabatier, "Implementatin Research," p. 39.
41. Elmore, "Forward and Backward Mapping," and Goggin et al., *Implementation Theory*.
42. On this point see James P. Lester, "A New Federalism? Environmental Policy in the States," in *Environmental Policy in the 1990s*, 2d ed., ed. Norman Vig and Michael E. Kraft (Washington, D.C.: Congressional Quarterly Press, 1994), esp. Table 3–1.
43. On this point, see Hjern, "Implementation Structures."
44. Goggin, "Too Few Cases," p. 332.
45. See, for example, Goggin et al., *Implementation Theory*.
46. Jack M. Treadway, *Public Policymaking in the American States* (New York: Praeger, 1985); and James P. Lester and Emmett N. Lombard, "The Comparative Analysis of State Environmental Policy," *Natural Resources Journal* 30, no. 2 (Spring 1990), pp. 301–319.
47. Some notable exceptions include, for example, Patricia M. Crotty, "The New Federalism Game: Primacy Implementation of Environmental Policy, "*Publius* 17 (1987), pp. 53–67; Frank Thompson and Michael J. Scicchitano, "State Implementation Effort and Federal Regulatory Policy," *Journal of Politics*, 47 (1985), pp. 686–703; and Pinky Wassenberg, "Implementation of Intergovernmental Regulatory Programs: A Cost-Benefit Perspective," in *Intergovernmental Relations and Public Policy*, ed. J. Edwin Benton and David Morgan (Westport: Greenwood Press, 1986).
48. See James P. Lester, "Federalism and State Environmental Policy," in *Environmental Politics and Policy: Theories and Evidence*, 2d ed., ed. James P. Lester (Durham, NC: Duke University Press, 1995).
49. James P. Lester and Ann O'M. Bowman, "Implementing Environmental Policy in a Federal System: A Test of the Sabatier-Mazmanian Model," *Polity* 21 (Summer 1989), pp. 731–753.
50. See Ann O'M. Bowman and James P. Lester, "Policy Implementation in a Federal System: A Comparative State Analysis," in *State Policy Problems*, ed. Ralph Baker and Fred Meyer (Chicago: Nelson-Hall, 1993).
51. For studies that seek to answer these questions, see Daniel H. Mazmanian and David L. Morell, *Beyond Superfailure: America's Toxics Policy for the 1990s* (Boulder, CO: WestviewPress, 1992); Thomas W. Church and Robert T. Nakamura, *Cleaning Up the Mess: Implementation Strategies in Superfund* (Washington, D.C.: Brookings Institution, 1993); and John A. Hird, *Superfund: The Political Economy of Environmental Risk* (Baltimore: Johns Hopkins University Press, 1994).

POLICY EVALUATION

". . . feeling good is not what science is all about. Getting it right, and then basing social decisions on tested and carefully weighted objective knowledge, is what science is all about."
EDWARD O. WILSON

Public policies are intended to have some effect on a particular policy problem. Moreover, many people often assume that once we pass a law, create a bureaucracy to administer it, and fund the program, the problem will be remedied. Unfortunately, that is not often the case. If we had perfect understanding of what causes a public policy problem and perfect administration of laws intended to remedy the problem, there would be no need for judging how well a program has (or has not) worked. However, programs often fail to achieve their intended effects even after huge sums of money have been invested in funding the public program. Our experiences with many programs in the 1960s suggest the need for careful appraisal of the impact of these programs. The federal government often wants to know how much money was spent for a given program, how many persons were serviced by the program, how much these services cost, and how effective the programs were in relation to this cost. On other occasions, the government wants to know whether a program resulted in positive benefits or, to the contrary, made the problem worse.

The purposes of this chapter are to discuss the evolution of evaluation research, to identify some types of evaluation and who does it, to describe some research designs in evaluation research, to discuss some problems in evaluating the impact of public policies, and to discuss some of the obstacles that affect the utilization of evaluation research by decision makers.

THE CONCEPT OF POLICY EVALUATION

In its simplest form, **policy evaluation** is concerned with learning about the consequences of public policy. It means evaluating alternative public policies as contrasted with describing them or explaining why they exist. Essentially, there are two distinctive tasks in policy evaluation. One task is to determine what the consequences of a policy are by describing its impact, and the other task is to judge the success or failure of a policy according to a set of standards or value criteria.[1] Robert Haveman claims that the central tenet of policy evaluation research is its focus on the activities of the public sector and its influence on society. As such, it is the "effort to understand the effects of human behavior and, in particular, to evaluate the effects of particular programs (such as the Great Society Programs) on those aspects of behavior indicated as the objectives of this intervention."[2] Other definitions have been offered: "Policy evaluation is the assessment of the overall effectiveness of a national program in meeting its objectives, or an assessment of the relative effectiveness of two or more programs in meeting common objectives."[3] Still another definition is that "the evaluation of agency programs or legislative policy is the use of scientific methods to estimate the successful implementation and resultant outcomes of programs or policies for decision-making purposes."[4] What differentiates policy evaluation from other types of policy analysis (e.g., policy formulation) is the focus on policy results or consequences as opposed to policy characteristics or causes.[5]

The Evolution of Evaluation Research

Early strains of evaluation research were present in the late 1800s. For example, an actual evaluation study was reported by an educator named J. M. Rice in 1897. Rice used a standardized spelling test to relate the length of time spent on drill to spelling achievement.[6] By comparing schools that varied in their emphasis on drill, he generated data that were used to argue that an emphasis on drill did *not* lead to improved achievement among the students.[7]

Between 1920 and 1940, several attempts were made to use empirical research to determine the effects of social programs in various settings. One of the best-known examples of evaluation research in this period is Stuart Dodd's study of the effects of a health education program on hygiene practices in rural Syria in 1934.[8] He examined the effects of educational clinics on the adequacy of public health practices in experimental and isolated control villages. Other attempts included studies of changes in industrial plant organization and their impact on worker morale.[9] Until World War II, what little evaluation research existed was the domain of the disciplines of sociology, psychology, and public health; economists and education researchers made few contributions.[10]

After World War II and until 1965, a number of evaluation research studies were conducted by social psychologists concerned with social issues. For example, the experimental work of Ronald Lippitt on the effects of autocratic and democratic leadership styles on the performance of groups of children is well known.[11] Similarly, work by Kurt Lewin and his associates on the effects of programs designed to change attitudes toward minorities was prominent during this period.[12] This research was not very sophisticated—the use of experimental designs, baseline interviews, and controls for attrition and other forms of selectivity were basically nonexistent.[13]

However, more sophisticated policy evaluation can find its genesis in the aftermath of the War on Poverty programs of the 1960s. The War on Poverty–Great Society developments initiated in 1965 represented a level of social intervention that was unprecedented.[14] Although social science scholars did evaluation research prior to the 1960s, as noted above, there was nothing that could be identified as a unique approach or a particular set of questions that evaluation studies should ask.[15] By the late 1960s, however, scholars began to use experimental designs, economics, and statistics in their research. Requirements for program evaluation were written into almost all federal programs in the 1960s and the 1970s. Congress established new organizations for evaluation and steadily increased their personnel and funding during this period. Nevertheless, the support for evaluation research declined as the Nixon administration reduced some budgets for this purpose. The Carter administration attempted to revive some of these functions by instituting a system of zero-based budgeting, but this movement never gained substantial backing. The Reagan administration cuts deeply affected policy evaluation.[16] For example, the Department of Commerce had collected data on state spending for environmental protection from 1969 to 1980, but the Reagan budget cuts in 1981 curtailed this data collection effort. This made it difficult to evaluate the states' efforts to protect the environment. If we do not have longitudinal data on the levels of state spending, especially after the federal budget cutbacks in the early 1980s, it is difficult to know what effects the cutbacks had on state efforts in this area.

What Does Evaluation Research Study?

Earlier we stated that evaluation research focuses on the consequences of public policy. Having said that, we still need to know exactly what evaluators study when conducting their evaluations. First, they may examine **policy outputs**, such as funds, jobs, material produced, services delivered, and the like.[17] These outputs are the most obvious results of some public policy, but they are by no means all that evaluators study. Another category of results is the impact of the policy on specific target groups or the state of affairs the policy was intended to produce. For example, some policies are intended to increase student performance or encourage energy conservation. In this sense, then, we are concerned about the policy's **performance**. When analyzing these consequences, we are examining how the policy performed in relation to some stated objective.[18]

In addition, policy evaluators are concerned with the ability of the policy to improve some societal condition, such as reducing environmental pollution or reducing crime. These consequences are analyzed as **policy outcomes**, in which the policy is supposed to result in the improvement of a general condition in society.

Finally, evaluators are sometimes concerned with policy consequences in the form of **policy feedback**, or the repercussions of a government action or statement on the policymaking system or on some policymakers.[19] For example, the attempt by the federal government to reduce automobile emissions by requiring emission control devices on cars may in turn, through feedback, reduce air pollution in general.

Each of these types of policy consequences provides the policy analyst with a reasonably clear focus for study. Moreover, we can easily see the relationships between these policy consequences: government action programs produce *policy outputs*, which are then carried out in the form of *policy performance*, causing *policy outcomes*, which, in turn, trigger *policy feedback*.[20]

Types of Policy Evaluation

There are several types of policy evaluation. For example, Bingham and Felbinger identify four types of evaluations. First, there is what is known as **process evaluation**.[21] Process evaluation focuses on the means by which a program or policy is delivered to clients or the way in which a program is implemented.[22] This type of evaluation focuses on an assessment of program activities and client satisfaction with services. Basically, these evaluations attempt to uncover management problems or to assume that none are occurring. They ask such questions as, Are the contractual obligations being met? or, How could this service be done more efficiently?

The second type of evaluation is **impact evaluation**. This evaluation is concerned with the end results of a particular program. For example, such evaluations are focused on whether the program's or policy's objectives have been met in terms of outputs. That is, did the program or policy produce the intended result on the target population? For example, how many clients were served by the program? How many workers were trained? This type of evaluation is more straightforward. It is easier to assess outcomes than the process of evaluation. In addition, some impact evaluations are concerned with measuring effectiveness, which is concerned with such questions as, Was the program cost effective? or, What would have happened to the target population in the absence of the program?[23] Most evaluations are of this type.

A third type of evaluation is **policy evaluation**. This type of evaluation is concerned with the impact of the policy or program on the original problem to which the program or policy was addressed. For example, Has the problem (e.g., poverty, illiteracy, pollution) been reduced as a result of the policy or program?[24]

Finally, there are **metaevaluations**. These evaluations are syntheses of evaluation research findings. They look for commonalities among results, measures, and trends in the literature.[25] Metaevaluations are very similar to literature reviews in that they are concerned with cumulating the extant findings and looking for patterns in the findings across numerous evaluations. For example, Laurence J. O'Toole conducted a metaevaluation of implementation studies to see whether he could identify the crucial variables that affected the success or failure of public policy implementation.[26] In his review of over a hundred implementation studies, he concluded that the availability of fiscal resources was a key variable that affected implementation success or failure.

Who Does Evaluation?

Institutions that perform policy evaluations are widespread. They include **internal evaluators**, such as those governmental organizations concerned with congressional oversight, including the General Accounting Office (GAO), as well as those that provide research support to the Congress, such as the Congressional Research Service (CRS), the Office of Technology Assessment (OTA), and the Congressional Budget Office (CBO). Other governmental agencies conduct evaluations as well. For example, executive branch evaluations are conducted by assistant-secretary-level divisions for planning and evaluation, regulatory bodies, inspectors general, boards of inquiry, high-level advisory boards, commissions, panels, and others.[27]

A major advantage of internal evaluation is that insiders will have the detailed knowledge of just what is involved in delivering the policy or program.[28] However, there are several major disadvantages as well. First, the insiders may not have the specialized skills necessary to do a good evaluation. Second, a number of different organizations may be involved in policy delivery so that a complete evaluation cannot be obtained by examining the results of the activity in one organization. Finally, the evaluation may be affected by the insider's unwillingness to make major changes in the policy or program suggested by the evaluation. Existing personnel have a stake in maintenance of the status quo and may be threatened by implied changes suggested by the evaluation.[29]

In addition, **external evaluators**, such as private research organizations, the communications media, pressure groups, and public-interest organizations, conduct evaluation studies of policies that have effects on the public or government officials. For example, the Brookings Institution, the Urban Institute, the American Enterprise Institute, the Hoover Institution, and the Rand Corporation have conducted numerous evaluations. In addition, CBS News (e.g., *Sixty Minutes*) and Common Cause or the Citizens Clearinghouse on Hazardous Waste conduct evaluations. Finally, several schools offer programs providing undergraduate, and especially graduate, training in policy analysis, including policy evaluation. Professors from these schools often conduct policy evaluations:

1. The Graduate School of Public Policy, The University of California–Berkeley

2. The Institute of Public Policy Studies, The University of Michigan
3. The School of Urban and Public Affairs, Carnegie-Mellon University
4. The Woodrow Wilson School of Public and International Affairs, Princeton University
5. The John F. Kennedy School of Government, Harvard University
6. The Maxwell School of Citizenship and Public Affairs, Syracuse University
7. The Lyndon B. Johnson School of Public Affairs, The University of Texas
8. The Hubert H. Humphrey Institute of Public Affairs, The University of Minnesota

These schools offer training in the methods of policy evaluation, including microeconomics, experimental design, survey research, statistical analysis, causal modeling, decision models, benefit-cost analysis, and implementation.[30]

External evaluation has advantages and disadvantages as well. For example, outside evaluation has the advantage that the chances of change in the policy or program may be improved if the evaluator has involved the internal staff in discussions about objectives and effectiveness of the programs or policy. Second, outside evaluators may have the necessary skills that insiders lack. Thus, they may be much better equipped to conduct systematic policy or program evaluation. However, there are disadvantages as well. Outsiders may have an ideological axe to grind; that is, they may be ideologically predisposed one way or another and their analysis may reflect this bias. In addition, the users of evaluation research often complain that evaluations are neither timely nor relevant to their decision making. Other times, users complain that they do not understand the methods used by policy evaluators in professional organizations or universities.

In an article that critiques evaluation of social policies, James Q. Wilson formulates two general laws about policy evaluation:

Wilson's First Law: All policy interventions in social problems produce the intended effect—if the research is carried out by those implementing the policy or their friends.

Wilson's Second Law: No policy intervention in social problems produces the intended effect—if the research is carried out by independent third parties, especially those skeptical of the policy.

He argues that

Studies that conform to the First Law will accept an agency's own data about what it is doing and with what effect; adopt a time frame that maximizes the probability of observing the desired effect; and minimize the search for other variables that might account for the effect observed. Studies that conform to the Second Law will gather data independently of the agency; adopt a short time frame that either maximizes the chance for the desired effect to appear or, if it does appear, permits one to argue that the results are "temporary" and probably due to the operation of the "Hawthorne Effect"; and maximize the search for other variables that might explain the effects observed.[31]

In spite of this rather cynical observation about policy evaluations, there are a number of alternative research designs that are used in policy evaluations. These research designs are an attempt to systematically evaluate the effects of various public policies on some societal problem. Let us examine a few of these designs.

Research Designs in Evaluation Research

Systematic evaluation involves **comparisons**—comparison designed to estimate what changes in society can be attributed to the policy or program that has been implemented. We simply want to know whether changes in some identifiable behavior in the individual (e.g., better scholastic performance) or condition in society (e.g., crime rates) actually took place and whether the program or policy itself produced the change in behavior or the condition. A number of research designs may be used to answer these questions.

Preexperimental Designs   These designs include the "one-shot case study" and the "before-and-after studies." **One-shot case studies** are intensive analyses of what happened in the course of implementing the policy and after its implementation to try to determine whether there was any change in the behavior or condition. This approach is the most common in the political science literature. It examines one group, one event, or one phenomenon at one point in time and has no controls over rival explanations or side effects.

The One-Shot Case Study

X   0

For example, Martha Derthick's study of a housing project in the Washington, D.C., area is an illustration of a case study that sought to determine why the project failed.[32] She identified a host of factors that lead to the failure of this proposed remedy for low-cost housing. Her research was valuable for pointing out all the possible things that can go wrong in implementing a low-cost housing program, but there were no controls for rival explanations.

Before-and-after studies are a bit more sophisticated. They compare results in a jurisdiction at two points in time—one before the program was implemented and the other some time after implementation. Usually, only the target groups are examined; thus, it is difficult to know whether the observed changes were due to the program or policy itself or due to some other condition in society that occurred at the same time.[33] For example, we might be interested in knowing whether using seat belts lowered highway fatalities. So, we measure the highway fatality rate before the introduction of a mandatory seat-belt law and then measure the fatality rate after the introduction of the seat-belt law. A lowering of the fatality rate is attributed to the seat-belt law.

The One-Group Pretest-Posttest Design

0   X   0

True Experiments   The "classic" research design, or **true experiment**, involves the random selection of both control and experimental groups. These two groups are compared in terms of changes within each group before and after the introduction of the policy or program. That is, careful measurements are taken for each group prior to the introduction of the program, and then post-program differences between the experimental and control groups are carefully measured. Ideally, the experimental group would show marked improvements due to the program that the control group did not experience. With randomization, this design has strong controls for both internal and external validity.

The Pretest-Posttest Control Group Design

R   0   X   0   (Experimental Group)
R   0   0   (Control Group)

An example of this type of design is a study on improving the intellectual capability of chronically deprived children.[34] In this study, some chronically deprived children were randomly assigned to be treated to educational and health programs, whereas others were not. Measurements were taken before and after the treatment programs with the result that those children exposed to educational and health programs markedly improved their intellectual abilities over those not exposed to the treatment programs. Thus, the treatments were judged to be a success in improving children's cognitive (intellectual) abilities.

Quasi-Experimental Designs   The **quasi-experimental design** is similar in every respect to the classic experiment discussed above except that the cases (individuals, cities, organizations, etc.) in the program being evaluated (the experimental group) and the comparison group are not randomly assigned. Thus, the comparison group (sometimes called the control group) is "non-equivalent" to those in the experimental (program) group. This potential problem in the research design can be alleviated through a process called "matching," in which the researcher attempts to identify a group that is comparable in essential respects to those in the treatment (experimental) group. The validity of the quasi-experimental design depends in large part on how closely the comparison group resembles the experimental group in all essential respects.[35]

The Nonequivalent Control Group Design

0   X   0   (Experimental Group)
0   0   (Comparison Group)

An example of this type of design is a study that attempted to evaluate the effects of energy conservation programs on utility costs.[36] Because the energy conservation program was voluntary, the researcher could not use an experimental design and randomly assign customers into program and control groups. Nevertheless, he found a comparison group that did not participate in the energy conservation program and compared the energy consumption of both groups before and after the introduction of the energy conservation programs.

Essentially, he found that there was no significant difference between the energy consumption of the two groups in the pretest period, but after the homes of the experimental group had been weatherized, there was a significant difference in energy consumption. That is, the experimental group used much less energy than the nonexperimental group, which showed that the energy conservation program worked as expected.

Causal Modeling   Another approach often used in evaluation research is **causal modeling** or the use of statistical controls through regression analysis. In this approach, one constructs a mathematical model of the program and its intended effects. This model incorporates the assumptions built into the policy or program and includes program outputs or outcomes as well as the factors presumed to "cause" these outcomes. Although this approach is often very appropriate, and at times the only approach available, it carries certain limitations as well. For example, if the original theory behind the program is flawed, then the results may be meaningless as well. In addition, extraneous variables not included in the model may well be affecting the program outcome. This approach will produce satisfactory results only when the theory behind the model is sound and all the relevant causal variables are included in the model.

An example of this approach is the evaluation of the effect of educational expenditures on student performance. An increase in per pupil expenditures was supposed to produce improved student performance by raising teacher quality, providing better facilities, and improving the curriculum. The model is presented below:

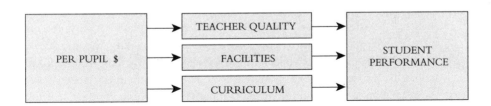

In certain circumstances, such as when only aggregate data are available for evaluation, this approach may be the most appropriate method, but its limitations should be kept in mind when interpreting the results.[37] No matter which research design is used, there are problems that affect evaluation. That is the subject of the following discussion.

Problems in Evaluating the Impact of Public Policy

Evaluating the impacts of programs or policies is very difficult, even under the best of conditions. Hogwood and Gunn identify several factors that pose severe problems for evaluating public policies or programs. These problems include:

1. *Objectives.* Nothing illustrates more clearly the problems of doing policy evaluation than the way in which policy objectives shape evaluation. If the

policy objectives are unclear or they are not specified in any measurable form, then the criteria for a policy's success are unclear.[38] However, vagueness in goals can often be a consequence of differences in points of view about policy objectives. Even when there is a clear statement of goals, problems remain. For example, how important are goals relative to each other when more than one is specified?[39]

2. *Defining the criteria for success.* Even when objectives are clearly stated, there is the question of how the success of the objective will be measured. For example, let us say that the objective is to produce an improvement in student performance in math using microcomputers. Even this specific objective is clouded by whether we want to assess student improvement in enjoyment of math using computers, or an improvement in understanding math itself, or an ability to apply this improvement to other areas, or a combination of all these.[40]

3. *Side effects.* Sometimes impacts from other policies or programs affect the policy or program under evaluation. Difficulties can be presented when we try to identify and measure side effects and separate these side effects from the policy or program being evaluated. Thus, there is the problem of how other factors (both adverse and beneficial) should be brought into the evaluation and how much these factors should be weighted relative to the central objectives.[41] For example, in attempting to evaluate the effects of the 55-mile-per-hour speed limit in reducing traffic fatalities, there is the complicating factor of seat-belt use. To what extent is the reduced speed a factor relative to the use of seat belts?

4. *Data problems.* Quite often the information necessary to assess the impact of a policy or program may not be available or may be available in an unsuitable form.[42] For example, if we were interested in evaluating the impacts of President Reagan's "new federalism" on state environmental protection, we would like to have data on the extent to which the individual states replaced the federal budget cuts with their own-source funds. However, not all the fifty states (or even very few of them) have kept careful records of the extent to which they replaced federal funds with state funds for environmental protection, and how much the states provided in this category of expenditure that was unique to the states as opposed to local governments.

5. *Methodological problems.* It is also common for a single problem or group of the population to be the target of several programs with the same or related objectives. For example, several policies are directed to the problem of poverty. In such cases, assessing the impact of a single program is difficult. For example, if crime rates go down, is this due to better policing, better education, welfare assistance, or employment opportunities? Big problems tend to have a lot of programs directed toward them, which makes it difficult to assess which, if any, are producing an effect.[43]

6. *Political problems.* Evaluation is very threatening to some people. What is being evaluated is the success or failure of a policy or program to which

politicians or bureaucrats have committed their personal reputations and careers, and from which clientele groups are receiving benefits. Evaluation may be seen as a threat to the continuation of a policy or program in which a number of people have an important stake. These considerations will obviously affect both how evaluation results are utilized and the ease with which the evaluation can be conducted, as the cooperation of public officials and clients is often required in the evaluation.[44]

7. *Cost.* It is not uncommon for evaluation to cost as much as 1 percent of the total program cost.[45] This is especially the case when more sophisticated methods are used in evaluation studies, such as experimental designs. Such costs are a diversion from the delivery of the policy or program.

These are just a few of the difficulties posed in the evaluation of public policies and programs. Simply because we have these problems in the process of evaluation, we should not be unduly discouraged from conducting evaluation activities. Rather than seeing these difficulties as insurmountable obstacles, we should see them as challenges for designing effective evaluations. In the following case study, we discuss an example of evaluation research—the impact of school spending on student performance.

CASE STUDY

Compensatory Education

One of the most interesting examples of evaluation research is that of **compensatory education**. In the Elementary and Secondary Education Act of 1965 (ESEA), "poverty-impacted" schools were the beneficiaries of increased federal aid to education programs. ESEA provided for federal financial assistance to "local educational agencies serving areas with concentrations of children from low-income families" for programs that contribute "to meeting the special needs of educationally deprived children."[46] Grants were made to public and private elementary and secondary schools for the acquisition of school library resources, textbooks, and other instructional materials. The logic embodied in ESEA was that an increase in per pupil expenditures (especially to students from poorer school districts) would allow these schools to purchase better educational materials, hire better teachers, and improve the curriculum. As a consequence, student performance would improve, thus allowing the poorer students to be more competitive in the marketplace after graduation. Ultimately, this would help to alleviate the disparities in income and thus reduce poverty in America. Indeed, ESEA was an important component of President Johnson's War on Poverty in the 1960s.

James Coleman, a Harvard sociologist, conducted an evaluation of the logic embodied in ESEA, producing what is popularly known as the Coleman Report.[47] Although his report was strongly criticized,[48] it undermined much of the conventional logic about the impact of increased expenditures on student performance. Prior to his study, legislators, teachers, school administrators, school board members, and the general public assumed that factors such as the number of pupils in the classroom, the amount of money spent on each pupil, library and laboratory facilities, teachers' salaries, the quality of the curriculum, and other characteristics of the school affected student performance (and hence educational opportunity). However, Coleman's analysis revealed that these factors had no significant effect on student learning or achievement. Rather, the only factors that had a significant effect were family background of the students themselves and the family background of their classmates. Family background factors affected the students' verbal abilities and attitudes toward education; both of the latter were strongly related to student performance.[49]

Although the Coleman Report made no policy recommendations, it nevertheless implied that compensatory education had very little educational value. If his report was correct, it seemed pointless to raise per pupil expenditures, increase teachers' salaries, lower the number of pupils per classroom, provide better libraries or laboratories, or adopt any curricular innovations. The reaction of professional educators to the Coleman Report was predictable. Perhaps they hoped that the report would not affect longstanding assumptions about the importance of money, facilities, classroom size, teacher quality, and curricula.[50] The reaction of the educational community points out the difficulties associated with the utilization of public policy analysis. Although the utilization of policy analysis is the subject of Chapter 14, we briefly describe some of the obstacles to the utilization of evaluation research in the following section.

SOME OBSTACLES TO UTILIZATION OF EVALUATION RESEARCH

A naive policy analyst would logically assume that once the evaluation was completed and the findings communicated to those who sponsored the study, the policy recommendations would be utilized by decision makers. Unfortunately, that is not often the case. A number of recent studies have identified obstacles to the more complete use of policy analyses in making public policy. These obstacles may be categorized into three groups of factors: (1) **contextual factors**, or factors having to do with the political environment within which the policy analysis took place; (2) **technical factors**, or factors having to do with the methodology employed in the policy analysis; and (3) **human factors**, or factors having to do with the psychological makeup of the users of the policy analysis.

Contextual Factors

Some scholars have suggested that the research utilization literature needs to include the political context into which analytic projects enter as a key set of variables that affect utilization.[51] An examination of the context in which policy research use takes place permits a more complete appreciation of the causes of research utilization.[52] These factors are especially concerned with the political environment within which policy analysis takes place. One of these factors concerns the nature of the problem itself. For example, what exactly are the intended effects of a policy? Rossi and Wright suggest that "the intended effects of a social policy are often so vaguely stated that almost any evaluation of it may be regarded as irrelevant because it missed the problem toward which the policy was directed."[53] Thus, the goals of the policy to be analyzed must be clearly stated so that an effective evaluation of its intended effects can be carried out.

Second, policymaking often involves the weighing of competing claims on communal resources. Achieving a balance among various claims may be more important to policymakers than enacting an effective social policy. Thus, the "political feasibility" of different courses of action is a constraint on utilization of policy analysis.[54] Furthermore, to be useful in policymaking, research has to occur in a timely manner; research is more likely to be used, for example, when an immediate decision is needed to resolve a specific problem and technical advice is provided early in the process.[55]

In addition, the amount of group conflict generated by the policy problem and the issue salience of the problem are factors that affect use. More specifically, greater use follows greater conflict and greater salience.[56] Lehne and Fisk point out several other factors that tend to influence utilization, including whether the issue under analysis is a single agency issue, whether a funding change is proposed, or whether (or not) an immediate decision is needed.[57] Others propose that centralized decision making is crucial to use.[58]

Technical Factors

Scholars have often argued that one of the major constraints on the application of social research to policymaking is methodological in character. For example, Meltzner highlights the problems associated with designing research capable of answering the questions posed by policymakers.[59] Indeed, "serious difficulties exist in the design and implementation of each evaluation research study."[60] One of the earliest studies of the impact of policy analysis on decision making identified several technical variables affecting use. These variables included study size (small, medium, large), study timing (good to poor), and methodological adequacy (superior to poor).[61] These authors discovered that one of the strongest factors influencing use was whether or not there was good timing in performing the analysis, as well as a narrow focus.[62]

Moreover, evaluation research often produces findings that are ambiguous or equivocal and, hence, of little apparent use to policymakers.[63] Thus, the more unequivocal the results, the greater the use. Finally, another factor influencing utilization of the findings is the credibility of the analysis itself and the analyst's organization.[64]

Human Factors

A number of other scholars have found knowledge utilization to be related to some of the personal characteristics of the users. For example, utilization has been found to be related to the cognitive skills of users, their ability to understand the findings, and the socioeconomic background of users.[65] Moreover, others have identified a number of personal motivations in decision makers (such as interest, enthusiasm, commitment, caring, or determination) as crucial to successful utilization.

One of the most salient variables believed to influence policymakers' use of policy analysis is the decision-making style adopted by the decision maker. Webber identifies three styles of decision making: the arbitrators, the messengers, and the evaluators. He concludes that arbitrators and messengers may be enlightened by policy research, but it is only the evaluator who will actively send for it.[66] Still others suggest that interest and participation by the decision maker in the policy analysis are crucial factors affecting use as well as the policymaker's worldview and the resultant commitment to specific solutions to policy problems. Finally, Rein and White suggest that use depends on a clear definition of objectives by policymakers.[67]

In summary, all of these factors influence the utilization of policy evaluations by decision makers. Policy analysts should not be discouraged if their evaluation is not used by decision makers, because most of the variables influencing use are beyond the control of the analyst himself or herself. Evaluators must simply do the best job they can and hope that their results will ultimately make a difference in the policy process.

SUMMARY

In this chapter, we have discussed policy evaluation, identified some of the ways in which policy evaluation is carried out, and discussed problems in the evaluation of public policy as well as obstacles to the utilization of evaluations in the redesign of policy.

Public policy is expected to remedy such problems as crime, poverty, educational failures, and environmental pollution, to name but a few of our concerns. Yet there are limitations of policy itself in affecting societal problems. Thomas Dye identifies a number of these limitations.

1. Some societal problems are incapable of solution due to the way in which they are defined. For example, if poverty is defined in *relative* terms, it may never be remedied by public policy, because there will always be those that are less well off than are others.[68]
2. Expectations may always outrun the capabilities of governments to remedy the problem. For example, there are high levels of concern over racism in the United States today even though affirmative action programs have done a great deal to equalize hiring and promotion of minorities in government and elsewhere.

3. Policies that solve the problems of one group in society may create problems for other groups. For example, policies that protect an endangered species may promote unemployment among certain sets of workers. As Thomas Dye argues, "there are *no* policies which can simultaneously attain mutually exclusive ends."[69]

4. Some societal forces quite possibly cannot be remedied by governmental action programs, no matter how desirable it is to do so. For example, some individuals may not succeed in school no matter how much money is spent or how well they are taught. For reasons having to do with the person himself or herself, some individuals may be beyond the ability of government to help.

5. Sometimes, people adapt themselves to public policies in ways that render the governmental policy useless in affecting the problem. For example, efforts to help the homeless in Portland, Oregon, by providing food and shelter ultimately failed because even more homeless individuals migrated there in search of these policies. Ultimately, the resources of the local government were exhausted by the "success" of the program in helping the homeless.

6. Some societal problems may have multiple causes, and a specific policy may not be able to alleviate the problem. For example, efforts to improve student performance by a more "inclusive" curriculum that includes more works by minorities may fail to improve student performance because the difficulties experienced by the students may have more to do with their innate intelligence than with their curriculum at school.[70]

7. The solution to some problems may require policies that are more costly than the problem itself.[71] Efforts to control public disorders, such as riots, civil disturbances, and violence, may entail the adoption of repressive policies that would prove to be too costly in terms of democratic values. Thus, a certain level of disorder may be more desirable than the alternative, which would result in a decrease in freedoms associated with rights of assembly and the like.

8. The political system is not structured to allow for completely rational decision making. Public policies are often formulated on the basis of political considerations rather than the most rational response to a particular problem. Sometimes policies are promoted that are the result of responses to group pressures, even when these policies make the problem worse than before the policy was adopted. In our next chapter on policy termination and change, we discuss the tendency in American politics to promote policies that favor some groups and hurt others. This tendency has been going on for a long time and illustrates how policies change over time as various groups gain influence in American politics. Public policy in America is never finished in the sense that we are always "fixing" public policy on the basis of some group's interest. Rationality is implied in systematic policy evaluation, but we must keep in mind that not all policies are determined on the basis of a particular kind of rationality.

NOTES

1. Melvin J. Dubnick and Barbara A. Bardes, *Thinking About Public Policy* (New York: Wiley, 1983), p. 203.
2. Robert Haveman, "Policy Evaluation Research After Twenty Years," *Policy Studies Journal* 16, no. 2 (Winter 1987), pp. 191–218.
3. Joseph S. Wholey et al., *Federal Evaluation Policy* (Washington, D.C.: The Urban Institute, 1970), p. 15.
4. Richard D. Bingham and Claire L. Felbinger, *Evaluation in Practice: A Methodological Approach* (New York: Longman, 1989), p. 3.
5. Some useful studies of policy evaluation include Carol Weiss, *Evaluation Research: Methods of Assessing Program Effectiveness* (Englewood Cliffs, NJ: Prentice-Hall, 1972); and David Nachmias, *Public Policy Evaluation: Approaches and Methods* (New York: St. Martin's Press, 1979).
6. Francis G. Caro, ed., *Readings in Evaluation Research*, 2d ed. (New York: Russell Sage Foundation, 1977), p. 6.
7. Ibid.
8. Ibid.
9. Haveman, "Policy Evaluation," p. 195.
10. Ibid., p. 196.
11. Ronald Lippitt, *Studies in Experimentally Created Autocratic and Democratic Groups* (Iowa City: University of Iowa, 1940).
12. Kurt Lewin, *Resolving Social Conflicts* (New York: Harper and Brothers, 1948).
13. Haveman, "Policy Evaluation," p. 196.
14. Ibid., p. 191.
15. Ibid.
16. Ibid., p. 200.
17. Dubnick and Bardes, *Public Policy*, p. 207.
18. Ibid.
19. Ibid.
20. Ibid.
21. Bingham and Felbinger, *Evaluation in Practice*, p. 4.
22. Ibid.
23. Ibid., p. 5.
24. Ibid., p. 6.
25. Ibid.
26. Laurence J. O'Toole, Jr., "Policy Recommendations for Multi-Actor Implementation: An Assessment of the Field," *Journal of Public Policy* (1986), pp. 181–210.
27. Garry D. Brewer and Peter DeLeon, *The Foundations of Policy Analysis* (Homewood, IL: Dorsey Press, 1983), pp. 320–321.
28. Brian W. Hogwood and Lewis A. Gunn, *Policy Analysis for the Real World* (New York: Oxford University Press, 1984), p. 234.
29. Ibid., p. 235.
30. Haveman, "Policy Evaluation," pp. 200–202.
31. James Q. Wilson, "On Pettigrew and Armor," *The Public Interest* 30 (Winter 1973), pp. 132–134.

32. Martha Derthick, "Defeat at Ft. Lincoln," *The Public Interest* 20 (Summer 1970), pp. 3–39.

33. Thomas R. Dye, *Understanding Public Policy*, 7th ed. (Englewood Cliffs, NJ: Prentice-Hall, 1991), pp. 357–358.

34. Harrison McKay et al., "Improving Cognitive Ability in Chronically Deprived Children," *Science*, 21 April 1987, pp. 270–278.

35. Bingham and Felbinger, *Evaluation in Practice*, p. 97.

36. Tim Newcomb, "Conservation Program Evaluations: The Control of Self Selection Bias," *Evaluation Review* 8, no. 3 (June 1984), pp. 425–440.

37. Hogwood and Gunn, *Policy Analysis* p. 230.

38. Ibid., p. 222.

39. Ibid., p. 223.

40. Ibid., p. 224.

41. Ibid., p. 225.

42. Ibid., p. 226.

43. Ibid.

44. Ibid., p. 227.

45. M. C. Aitken and L. G. Salmon, eds., *The Costs of Evaluation* (Beverly Hills, CA: Sage, 1983).

46. Dye, *Understanding Public Policy*, p. 9.

47. James S. Coleman, *Equality of Educational Opportunity* (Washington, D.C.: U.S. Government Printing Office, 1966).

48. We discuss some of these criticisms in Chapter 10.

49. Coleman, *Equality*.

50. Dye, *Understanding Public Policy*, p. 10.

51. Ibid.

52. To the contrary, one study found state contextual factors, such as population, mean family income, percent of labor force in agriculture, percent urban and so on, not to be associated with the use of policy analyses. See Robert D. Lee and R. J. Staffeldt, "Executive and Legislative Use of Policy Analysis in the State Budgetary Process," *Policy Analysis* 3, no. 3 (Summer 1977), pp. 395–406.

53. Peter Rossi and Sonia Wright, "Evaluation Research: An Assessment of Theory, Politics and Practice," *Evaluation Quarterly* 1, no. 1 (February 1977), pp. 5–51.

54. Arnold Meltzner, "Political Feasibility and Policy Analysis," *Public Administration Review* 32, no. 6 (December 1972), pp. 859–867.

55. Edward Suchman, "Action for What: A Critique of Evaluation Research," in *Evaluating Action Programs*, ed. Carol Weiss (Boston: Allyn and Bacon, 1972).

56. D. Whiteman, "The Fate of Policy Analysis in Congressional Decisionmaking," *Western Political Quarterly* 38 (1985), pp. 294–311.

57. Richard Lehne and D. M. Fisk, "The Impact of Urban Policy Analysis," *Urban Affairs Quarterly* 10, no. 2 (December 1974), pp. 115–138.

58. See Jerry Mitchell, "The Utilization of Policy-Relevant Information in State Government" (paper presented at the annual meeting of the Southern Political Science Association, Atlanta, Georgia, 1986); and Martin Rein and Sheldon White, "Can Policy Research Help Policy," *The Public Interest* 49 (Fall 1977), pp. 119–136.

59. Meltzner, "Political Feasibility."

60. Rossi and Wright, "Evaluation Research."

61. Not all researchers agree that methodological sophistication leads to greater use. On this point, see Peter DeLeon, "The Influence of Policy Analysis on U.S. Defense Policy," *Policy Sciences* 20, no. 2 (1987), pp. 105–128.

62. Lehne and Fisk, "Urban Policy Analysis."

63. Rossi and Wright, "Evaluation Research."

64. Barry Bozeman, "The Credibility of Policy Analysis: Between Method and Use," *Policy Studies Review* 14 (June 1986), pp. 51–57.

65. David J. Webber, "Legislators' Use of Policy Information," *American Behavioral Scientist* 30 (1987), pp. 612–631.

66. Ibid.

67. Rein and White, "Can Policy Research Help."

68. Dye, *Understanding Public Policy*, pp. 372–373.

69. Ibid., p. 372.

70. See Richard Herrnstein and Charles Murray, *The Bell Curve* (New York: Basic Books, 1994).

71. Ibid., p. 373.

POLICY CHANGE AND TERMINATION

"Policy entrepreneurs have a responsibility not only to the integrity of the political process, however, but also to the consequences of their actions, an obligation to see that ineffective and inefficient policies are either changed or eliminated."

ROBERT D. BEHN

One might think that once we reach policy evaluation, we have reached the end of the policy cycle. However, such a viewpoint would neglect the **consequences** of policy evaluation and how the old policy often leads into a new policy cycle. After evaluation, the next stages of the policy cycle are **policy change** and then **policy termination**. In these two stages, policies are reviewed, sometimes terminated, sometimes changed drastically, and then the entire cycle begins again as policies are reformulated and reimplemented. One might think of this aspect of the policy cycle as a further extension of our thinking about the public policy process (i.e., from the initiation of policy proposals to coming full circle and beginning the agenda-setting process all over). Political scientists have traditionally perceived policymaking as primarily the result of a power struggle among various interest groups with different resources and interests operating within a given institutional structure and a changing socioeconomic environment.[1] Yet, the implications of policy or program termination and changes in public policy have only recently begun to be explored.[2]

Sometimes, policies are not completely terminated. Rather they are changed in some form. In practice, most policies are changed as a result of the legislative oversight process in which policies are reviewed for their effectiveness from time to time. At other times, the desire for change originates within the bureaucracy. Regardless of whether policy changes originate in the legislature or in the bureaucracy, policy change is much more common than policy termination.[3]

THE CONCEPT OF POLICY CHANGE

By the concept of **policy change**, we mean the replacement of one or more existing policies by one or more other policies. It may mean both the adoption of new policies and the modification or repeal of existing ones. Essentially, policy change can take any one of three forms: (1) incremental changes in existing policies; (2) the enactment of new statutes in particular policy areas; or (3) major shifts in public policy as a consequence of realigning elections.[4] For example, the reauthorization of the Resource Conservation and Recovery Act of 1976 (RCRA) resulted in changing the scope of those affected by this policy. Originally, any company producing at least 1,000 kilograms of toxic waste per month was within the regulatory framework. In the 1984 revision of this act, all companies producing at least 100 kilograms were covered by the new regulations. This change substantially increased the number of firms that the EPA would have to monitor for compliance.

Rarely are policies maintained in the same form as when they were initially adopted; instead, they are constantly evolving. The revision of existing policies will depend on such factors as the extent to which the original policy is judged to "solve" the problem at which it was directed, the skill with which such policies are administered, the defects or shortcomings that may be revealed during policy implementation, or the political power and awareness of concerned or affected groups where the policy is delivered.[5] Also, problems themselves will change over time as well as the conventional wisdom about how to address these problems.[6] Thus, public policies evolve after their initial formulation and implementation to begin the policy process all over again. The evolution of public policy is really a cycle in which policies are formulated, implemented, evaluated, and then reformulated and reimplemented on the basis of legislative review of the extent to which these policies achieved their initial objectives. For example, the conventional wisdom about punishment for criminals changed in the 1950s from a harsh approach to a more lenient and rehabilitative one.[7] Educational policy changed in the 1980s from a liberal approach that emphasized innovations in curricula and open classrooms to a back-to-basics approach that stressed reading, writing, and arithmetic. Welfare policy also underwent major changes in the 1980s and 1990s as a conservative approach seemed to replace a more liberal one that was prevalent in the 1960s. Thus, the entire cycle of public policy is really a continuous loop over time.

Some Reasons for Change

Hogwood and Gunn suggest three reasons for expecting policy change to be an increasingly common feature of policy formulation in contemporary Western political systems, and therefore a candidate for greater attention by policy analysts.

1. Governments have over the years gradually expanded their activities in particular fields of policy, so that there are relatively few completely new activities in which they could be involved. Proposals for new policies are likely to overlap at least in part with existing programs.

2. Existing policies themselves may create conditions requiring changes in policies because of inadequacies or adverse side effects. Legislative oversight may be grounds for changing policies so that they "work better."

3. The relative rates of sustainable economic growth and the financial implications of existing policy commitments imply that the latitude for avoiding the problems of policy termination or policy change by instituting a new program without cutting the old one is considerably unlikely.[8] Although most of us can identify a number of public policies that we consider unnecessary, wasteful, or inappropriate, there will always be those who consider them to be useful and worth keeping.[9] Changing policies is always easier than terminating them.

In any case, policy change takes a variety of forms, as discussed in the following section.

Types of Policy Change

Given the likelihood of more policy change in the future, what forms may policy change take? Policy change, according to Peters, may take several forms:[10]

1. *Linear.* Linear policy change involves the direct replacement of one policy by another or the simple change of an existing policy. For example, the replacement of personnnel programs by the Comprehensive Employment and Training Act is an example of a linear policy change.

2. *Consolidation.* Some policy changes involve merging previous policies into a new single policy. For example, the rolling together of several health and welfare programs into a few programs is an example of consolidation.

3. *Splitting.* Some programs (and hence eventual policies from these agencies) are split into two or more individual components. For example, the Atomic Energy Commission (AEC) was split into the Nuclear Regulatory Commission (NRC) and the Energy Research and Development Administration (ERDA) in 1974, reflecting the contradictory programs of regulation and support of nuclear energy that had existed in the earlier organization of the AEC.

4. *Nonlinear.* Some policy changes are complex and involve elements of other kinds of changes. The complex changes involved in creating the Department of Energy (DOE) from existing programs is an example of nonlinear changes. An entirely new policy, program, or organization is created in the wake of former policies or programs or organizations.

In addition to various types of policy change, there are several models of policy change. These models help us to understand why major changes in policy occur in the United States.

Models of Policy Change

The concept of policy change, although new and little researched, is nevertheless a crucial aspect of the policy cycle. It is safe to assume that much policy analysis in the future will be directed toward an analysis of policy change over time. To do so, however, requires that we understand the process of policy change and develop some theoretical explanations about why policies evolve as they do. To date, at least three theories have been developed to explain why public policies evolve as they do. In the following sections, we review three extant theories of policy change over time. Each of these explanations attempts to describe and explain why American public policies evolve as they do over several decades or more. Some of these explanations are more developed than are others, but all of them are directed toward an explanation of policy change over time.

The Cyclical Thesis   The first explanation is the **cyclical thesis** offered by Arthur Schlesinger in which he argues that there is a continuing shift in national involvement between public purpose and private interest.[11] More specifically, he argues that American politics follows a fairly regular cyclical alternation between conservatism and liberalism in our national moods. That is, there are swings back and forth between eras when the national commitment is to private interest as the best means of meeting our national problems and eras when the national commitment is to public purpose. At roughly thirty-year intervals, Schlesinger argues, the nation turns to reform and affirmative government as the best way of dealing with our troubles. For example, Theodore Roosevelt ushered in the Progressive period in 1901, Franklin Roosevelt brought in the New Deal in the 1930s, and John Kennedy the New Frontier in the 1960s. Alternatively, Ronald Reagan ushered in a conservative era in the 1980s, which was a replay of the conservative 1950s, and the Harding-Coolidge era of the 1920s.

He claims that there is nothing mystical about the thirty-year cycle. Thirty years is the span of a generation. People tend to be formed politically by the ideals that are dominant in the years during which they attain political consciousness. When their own generation's turn in power comes thirty years later, they tend to carry forward the ideals they imbibed when young. Over time, each phase tends to run its natural course. The season of idealism and reform, when strong presidents call for active public interest in national affairs and invoke government as a means of promoting the general welfare, eventually leaves an electorate exhausted by the process and disenchanted by the results. People eventually become attuned to a "new" message that tells them that private action and self-interest in an unregulated market will solve our problems. This mood eventually runs its course as problems become acute, threaten to become unmanageable, and demand remedies by governmental actors. This change in the public mood thus ushers in a new era of reform and governmental intervention.

According to Schlesinger, then, a major proposition about the evolution of American public policy over the past hundred years would suggest the following:

Proposition 1: The evolution of public policy follows a fairly predictable pattern in which a period of private remedies (and minimal governmental intervention) will be followed by a period of significant governmental intervention and reform. A period of liberalism will be followed by a period of conservatism before the entire cycle repeats itself.

Figure 9-1 illustrates Schlesinger's cyclical thesis by suggesting that a thirty-year cycle produces alternate periods of liberalism and conservatism.

Samuel Huntington's elaboration of the cyclical model also emphasizes the power of ideas in shaping public policy and institutions. He argues that periods of "creedal passion," or intense and widespread debate over the gap between the ideals and the actual performance of the American government, lead to major bursts of institutional reform. The enactment and implementation of the reforms serves to channel and control the debate over fundamental values and ushers in an era of relative calm. In time, the shortcomings of the reforms will become increasingly obvious, triggering another period of controversy and another attempt to bring America's political system closer to its mythical ideals. Paradoxically, the reforms of one generation create the vested interests of the next generation.[12]

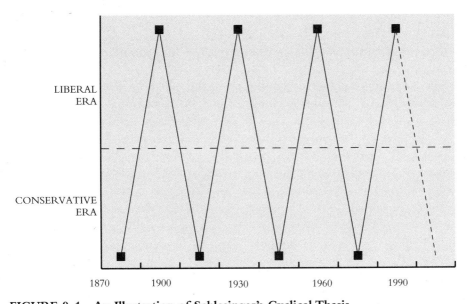

FIGURE 9–1   An Illustration of Schlesinger's Cyclical Thesis

Source: Adapted from *The Cycles of American History* by Arthur M. Schlesinger, Copyright © 1986 by Arthur M. Schlesinger. Reprinted by permission of Houghton Mifflin Company. All rights reserved.

The Evolutionary or Policy-Learning Thesis   A second explanation, the **policy-learning thesis**, comes from recent work by Paul Sabatier and his associates.[13] He has developed a conceptual framework of the policy process that views policy change as a function of three sets of factors: (1) the interaction of competing "advocacy coalitions" within a policy subsystem/community; (2) changes external to the subsystem; and (3) the effects of stable system parameters. The framework has at least three basic premises: first, that understanding the process of policy change—and the role of policy learning therein—requires a time perspective of a decade or more. This is so we can observe a more complete policy cycle, (i.e., from policy formation to implementation to evaluation and change). Second, that the most useful way to think about policy change over such a time span is through a focus on "policy subsystems," which are composed of "advocacy coalitions" (i.e., the interaction of actors from different institutions interested in a policy area). Third, that public policies can be conceptualized in the same manner as "belief systems" (i.e., sets of value priorities and causal assumptions about how to realize them).[14] Basically, policy change is viewed as the product of both changes in systemwide events, such as socioeconomic perturbations or outputs from other subsystems, and the striving of competing advocacy coalitions within the subsystem to realize their core beliefs over time as they seek to increase their resource bases, to respond to opportunities provided by external events, and to learn more about the policy problem(s) of interest to them.[15] Based on perceptions of the adequacy of governmental units and/or the resultant impacts, as well as new information arising from search processes and external dynamics, each advocacy coalition may revise its beliefs and/or alter its strategy. The latter may involve seeking major institutional revisions at the collective-choice level, making minor revisions at the operational level, or even going outside the subsystem, for example, by seeking changes in the dominant electoral coalition at the systemic level.[16]

   This framework has special significance for the study of policy-oriented learning (i.e., relatively enduring alterations of behavioral intentions that result from experience and that are concerned with the attainment or revision of public policy).[17] Specifically, the framework argues that the core aspects of a governmental action program—and the relative strength of competing advocacy coalitions within a policy subsystem—will typically remain rather stable over periods of a decade or more. Major alterations in the policy core will normally be the product of changes external to the subsystem—particularly large-scale socioeconomic conditions or changes in the systemwide governing coalition. Although changes in the policy core are usually the result of external perturbations, changes in the secondary aspects of a governmental action program are often the result of policy-oriented learning by various coalitions or policy brokers. Policy learning involves the feedback loops depicted in Figure 9–2, as well as increased knowledge of the problem and the factors affecting it. Figure 9–2 presents Sabatier's framework and the factors that condition public policy change over time.

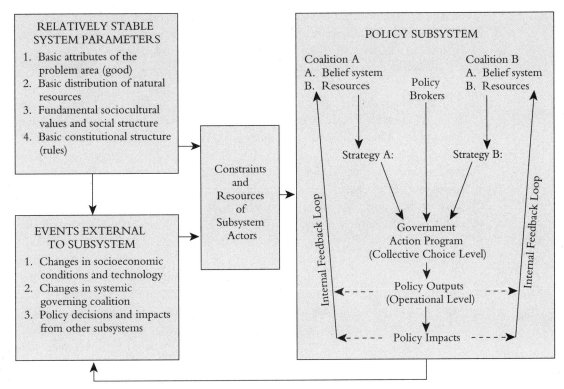

FIGURE 9–2   General Overview of Conceptual Framework of Policy Change
Source: Approximately one page from *Policy Change and Learning: An Advocacy Coalition Approach* by Paul A. Sabatier and Hank C. Jenkins-Smith (Boulder, CO: WestviewPress, 1993), p. 18. Copyright © 1993 by WestviewPress. Reprinted by permission of WestviewPress.

Proposition 2:   The evolution of public policy is explained by an extended period of policy change in which governmental actors repeatedly revise policy on the basis of "policy learning" brought on by events external to subsystem politics. More specifically:

Proposition 2a: Policy-oriented learning across belief systems is most likely when there is an intermediate level of informed conflict between the two. This requires that (1) each have the technical resources to engage in such a debate, and that (2) the conflict be between secondary aspects of one belief system and core elements of the other or, alternatively, between important secondary aspects of the two belief systems.

Proposition 2b: Policy-oriented learning across belief systems is most likely when there exists a forum that is (1) prestigious enough to force professionals from different coalitions to participate and (2) dominated by professional norms.

This framework has been tested in a very preliminary way by Sabatier and his colleagues in a number of policy areas, primarily dealing with energy and environmental policy. Thus far, the arguments concerning coalition stability and the prevalence of advocacy analysis have been confirmed, although much work remains for this model to be validated fully as an adequate explanation of policy change over periods of a decade or more.[18]

The Backlash or Zigzag Thesis   Still another explanation of changes in public policy over time is the **zigzag thesis**, which comes from the work of Edwin Amenta and Theda Skocpol.[19] They argue that there is an erratic pattern in the history of American public policies. It is characterized by a "zigzag effect" or a stimulus and response (or backlash). It is not so much a shift from liberal to conservative as from policy that first benefits one group, then another as a backlash to the first group. The concept of "class struggle" or competing societal coalitions comes to mind as a useful way to explain the above shifts. For example, the late nineteenth century was characterized by high levels of spending and for the distributive character and patronage for *white men*. Specifically, it was devised by the "radical Republicans" and included the Civil War pension system in which benefits were distributed in a partisan way. Benefits went to Northerners who could make a plausible case for their role in preserving the Union. Political affiliation to Republicans was a major criterion for the pension. This led to a backlash against the radical Republicans in the Southern states. There were also federal jobs for those with suitable party connections. The federal bureaucracy can be seen as largely an employment program for the "right people" (i.e., northern and midwestern Republicans).

This was followed by the Progressive Era (1900–1930), in which there was an attempt to eliminate political machines and patronage from the previous era. Civil-service reforms, including the merit hiring system, were instituted. There was a movement away from direct election of administrative officials. There were child-labor laws and legislation limiting women's working hours. A variety of public health and safety laws were passed as was worker's compensation. Gradually, Democrats became more powerful due to their Southern and Western bases of support. Individual and corporate income taxes were established. Democrats became known as the reform party due to their attempt to replace the radical Republicans with their own members. By the end of the 1920s, Democrats allied with the labor movement and threw their support behind social spending. Essentially, the Democrats almost established themselves as a "social democratic" party at this time.

This was followed by the New Deal period (1930–1950), in which many of the social insurance programs and welfare programs were enacted. These initiatives were propelled by the Great Depression, and Democrats continued their domination of the public policy debate. Legislation included the 1935 Social Security Act (the centerpiece of the New Deal). According to this model, we adopted Keynesian economics and used the federal government as an agency for massive redistribution of wealth through the creation of large social spending programs and direct intervention in the economy. Politically this encouraged deficit spending and not balanced budgets. As for social spending policy, veterans of World War II and retired veterans of wage-earning employment and their survivors were advantaged relative to other social groups.

Finally, the authors see a postwar period (1950–1980s), in which there was a reaction to the free-spending ways of the previous period of Democratic administrations. In particular, the "new federalism" of the 1970s and 1980s represented a backlash against large federal welfare programs. Later cuts deeply reduced the growth in Great Society programs enacted in the late 1960s. Recent economic policies have relied on fiscal stimulation rather than New Deal liberalism, such as tax reduction rather than spending programs to stimulate the economy. There were heavy investments in military spending (jobs in the military have been the counterpart to employment in the civilian bureaucracy in the late nineteenth century). Patronage today exits in terms of military employment and old-age assistance. This model finds, in effect, policies today are very similar to the first period of the late nineteenth century.

Thus, the arguments of Amenta and Skocpol suggest that there is a pattern in the history of American public policies. It is a zigzag effect or a stimulus and response (backlash) that is not so much a shift from liberal to conservative as from a policy that benefits one group, then another as a backlash to the first group. The following proposition is derived from their argument:

Proposition 3:   The evolution of public policy during the period 1890–1990 is best explained by a "zigzag pattern" in which the public policies of one era provide the stimulus for a reaction in the next era. Thus, policies undergo drastic changes as a reaction to a previous policy; for example, policies that favor one group (e.g., citizen interests) in one era are replaced by policies that favor other groups (e.g., the corporate sector) in the next era.

All of these explanations may be used to analyze policy change over long periods of time. Although none of them has gained widespread acceptance in the policy literature, all three are potentially very useful. In the following brief case study, we explore some examples of policy change by focusing on the area of oceans policy.

CASE STUDY
Intergovernmental Relations and Ocean Policy Change

Federal ocean policy, according to many analysts, is in transition.[20] A debate has now developed between those who argue on the one hand that the oceans are sacrosanct and that any entry of polluting substances is undesirable and, on the other hand, that the oceans have an almost infinite capacity to receive societal wastes. Moreover, it was the position of the Reagan administration that, in general, our environmental laws and regulations needed careful review and modification. More specifically, the Reagan administration was concerned that the benefits to be derived from rigid environmental regulations might not be justified in terms of economic costs.[21] These developments led some observers in the 1980s to believe that the United States was undergoing a policy change from an "ocean protection" strategy that was characteristic of the 1970s to an "ocean management" strategy that was characteristic of the 1980s.[22] It was argued that we would probably observe the evolution of an overarching philosophy for the management of ocean space and resources that would resemble the evolution of policies for the management of our public lands. Essentially, it was argued that ocean policy changed from "strict protection" to something akin to "management flexibility."

Changes in Ocean Dumping Policy   The first concerted effort to control ocean dumping began in the early 1970s at a time when many environmental protection laws were passed. President Nixon, in his address of February 8, 1971, to Congress announced that the nation's policy should be "to ban unregulated ocean dumping of all material and to place strict limits on ocean disposal of any materials harmful to the environment."[23] The EPA transmitted to Congress two days later a bill that eventually became the Marine Protection, Research, and Sanctuaries Act of 1972 (MPRSA). This bill dictated the strictest possible standards in existence at the time for any continued dumping. Indeed, the research program created by this act had the explicit purpose of "determining the means of minimizing or ending all dumping of materials within five years of the effective date of the act."[24] In addition, this act established a permit system under which ocean dumping was regulated jointly by the EPA and the Army Corps of Engineers. The EPA set criteria for evaluation of all permit applications and issued permits for dumping of all materials except dredged spoils; the Army Corps then issued permits for dumping of dredged spoils using the EPA's criteria.[25]

On October 15, 1973, the EPA promulgated its final regulations and criteria in which it took a strict, highly restrictive approach toward applying the criteria embodied in the act.[26] In these regulations, the EPA intended to terminate all harmful ocean dumping, regardless of whether the permit applicant could demonstrate that its dumping would not unreasonably degrade the marine environment. In effect, the EPA established a policy of phasing out all ocean dumping of sewage sludge. In doing so, the EPA assumed a highly protective approach to ocean dumping.

In 1980, when the city of New York applied for a permit to continue dumping sewage sludge, the EPA refused to permit this activity after December 31, 1981. The city of New York brought suit in a federal district court in New York. The court endorsed the arguments by the city and limited the ability of the EPA to terminate ocean dumping of sewage sludge. By the time this decision was issued on April 14, 1981, a new president had assumed office who was significantly less enthusiastic about environmental regulations. By 1981, a significant change had taken place in ocean dumping policy.

In the aftermath of *City of New York* v. *EPA*, it became apparent that the EPA was shifting its policy toward ocean dumping. The agency soon stated that in the future it would be more "flexible" about ocean dumping and would now view the oceans as a legitimate disposal option. In sum, the EPA moved from strict, confrontational protection of the oceans toward a more flexible, accommodating posture during the period 1971–1985.

Several factors affected this change in ocean dumping policy: (1) The status of knowledge about the oceans' vulnerability to environmental contamination was changing. During the period 1971–1985, scientific data accumulated that suggested that ocean dumping posed only modest environmental risk as compared to other threats to the oceans' environment. (2) Fundamental sociocultural attitudes during the late 1970s and early 1980s were changing as a result of the oil embargo and the subsequent energy dislocations. Specifically, the "zeal which attended the movement to clean up the environment became tempered by the growing burden of inflation, increased energy consumption, and public discontent with government spending and regulation".[27] (3) The systemic governing coalition changed with the election of Ronald Reagan as president. This administrative change may partially account for the EPA's movement away from confrontational intergovernmental relations to a more accommodating federal stance toward municipal sludge dumping, evident perhaps in the agency's decision not to appeal the lower court decision in *City of New York* v. *EPA*.

Applying These Explanations to the Evolution of Ocean Policy   The three potential explanations of policy change described earlier may be used to analyze the evolution of ocean policies in the United States during the period 1975–1990. Based on the brief description of ocean policy change, the policy-learning thesis offers the best fit between theory and practice. In the case described above, the EPA seemed to have "learned" from its experiences. A fundamental change in ocean dumping policy took place between 1971 and 1981. The cyclical thesis and the zigzag thesis do not seem to apply to this area of policy change. The change in policy did not reflect a turn from liberalism to conservatism; nor does this policy area suggest that policy first favored one group, then another, as the zigzag thesis would predict. Rather, public policy in this area reflects the kind of policy learning that the Sabatier and Jenkins–Smith model would suggest.

Sometimes policies or programs are not merely changed, but instead terminated. During the 1990s, it is expected that many policies, programs, and organizations will be terminated.

THE CONCEPT OF POLICY TERMINATION

The term **policy termination** refers to agency termination, basic policy redirections, program eliminations, partial terminations, and fiscal retrenchments.[28] As a concept, it became the object of study in the mid-1970s when scholars focused on the termination of organizations as a means of ending out-worn or inadequate policies or programs.[29] For several reasons, it is perhaps the most difficult phase of the policy cycle. Once started, policies, programs, and agencies have a life of their own with substantial momemtum. In addition, there is no incentive to admit past mistakes. A political reluctance against termination often exists, because vested interests will fight to keep the program because of "sunk costs." Moreover, antitermination coalitions will mobilize and use all their resources to retain the policy, program, or organization. Finally, the costs of ter-mination activities are high; considerable resources will have to be mobilized to counter antitermination coalitions, and organizations are reluctant to terminate their own programs for this reason.[30]

Since the 1970s, interest in termination has significantly increased for several reasons. First, some policies and programs are simply not effective and need to be abolished. Second, a political climate of fiscal retrenchment that began in the late 1970s and early 1980s has led to substantial budgetary cutbacks in the 1980s and 1990s. Moreover, in Washington, D.C., today, there is a strong desire to ter-minate many programs that are deemed to be unnecessary and expensive. The recent change to a Republican Congress has increased the likelihood that many programs will, in fact, be terminated. For example, there is much talk about clos-ing many military bases, cutting NASA's space budget significantly, terminating the Fulbright Scholars program, and terminating (or significantly modifying) affirmative action policies. Finally, termination is a part of the policy cycle that calls for additional study—we simply need to understand the politics of policy termination to effectively implement termination or to prevent termination. Unfortunately, very little policy research on the termination process has been reported since the late 1970s.[31] Despite universal recognition that termination is a vital component of policy studies, it remains the "neglected butt of the pol-icy process."[32] Thus, this is an appropriate time to focus on policy or program termination.

Types of Termination

There are several types of termination, including functional termination, organi-zational termination, policy termination, or program termination.

Functional Termination   This type of termination refers to the termination of an entire area (e.g., health care). This type covers many organizations and poli-cies, and it is a very rare phenomenon. Privatization of trash collection would be an example of this type of termination.

Organizational Termination   This type of termination refers to the elimination of an entire organization. During the 1980s, the Departments of Energy and Education were targeted by the Reagan administration for elimination. However, organizations generally will be reorganized, rather than completely eliminated. For example, in 1974, the Atomic Energy Commission (AEC) was split into the Energy Research and Development Administration (ERDA) and the Nuclear Regulatory Commission (NRC). ERDA was responsible for the development of energy sources, and the NRC was primarily responsible for regulating nuclear energy. This reorganization was believed to be necessary to avoid conflicts of interest.

Policy Termination   This type of termination refers to the elimination of a policy when the underlying theory or approach is no longer needed or believed to be correct. For example, the Fair Trade Legislation was terminated in 1975. This legislation was originally adopted in the 1930s to permit manufacturers of trademarked or brand-name products to set mandatory minimum resale prices for their products. Over the years, however, fair trade became a tired, worn-out policy with little congressional support.[33]

Program Termination   This refers to the elimination of specific measures designed to implement a policy. This is the most common type of termination because limited constituencies characterize specific programs. Eliminating a specific program with a relatively smaller constituency is always easier than eliminating a policy or organization with a much larger constituency. An example of program termination would be the federal revenue sharing program that was begun in 1972 during the Nixon administration. This program channeled billions of dollars to state and local governments with few strings attached. It was terminated in 1986 due to large federal budget deficits, although there was always considerable congressional opposition to revenue sharing.[34]

Approaches to Termination

Termination can be approached in generally two basic ways. The first approach is called the **"big bang"** termination.[35] This approach usually occurs with a single authoritative decision or one decisive stroke at a single point in time. With this type of termination, the opposition has no time to organize against the termination. Rather, the termination is a swift and closed issue that occurs with a shattering force. Such a termination is usually the product of a long political struggle involving many participants. It is the most common approach to termination. An example of this type of termination was the proposal to terminate the Department of Energy during the Reagan administration in the early 1980s. However, it was not terminated.

The second type of termination is called the **"long whimper"** approach.[36] This type of termination comes about through a long-term decline in the resources by which a policy or organization is sustained. It is a moderately paced and deliberate phasing-out of a policy, program, or organization. It is sometimes called "decrementalism," by which the budget of an organization is slowly reduced or positions are slowly eliminated. Finally, the organization (or program) can no longer function effectively.

The major disadvantage of this type of termination, from the perspective of those trying to terminate the program, is that the opposition can organize to fight the termination. An example of this type of termination is the decision to terminate the Comprehensive Employment and Training Act (CETA) program of the 1970s and replace it with the Job Training and Partnership Act (JTPA) program in 1983.

Reasons for Termination and Types of Terminators

Termination decisions are made for various reasons. Both DeLeon and Cameron hypothesize that political values and ideology play the key role in these decisions.[37] Citing many instances of termination during the Reagan administration, DeLeon argues that "it is ideological stance rather than rigorous analysis or evaluation that (drove) the . . . termination activities."[38] Similarly, Cameron summarizes his points about the role of ideology in terminations:

> Legitimizing the proposal involves a systematic effort to delegitimize the policy it is designed to supplant. This frequently takes the simplistic form of "the right and the good" versus the "wrong and immoral." . . . But the simplistic approach that gives ideology its coalescing force results in ill-considered policy choices: data that are inconsistent with the ideology are ignored or explained away; rigid adherence to credo becomes more important than inquiry into the potential risks attending the prospect of contingencies.[39]

Based on their analyses of policy and program termination, *political* considerations, rather than evaluative elegance, are at the basis of most termination decisions. This observation, argues Peter DeLeon, suggests that termination researchers should look beyond the straightforward issues of economics and efficiencies as the basis for termination decisions. "If one wishes to operate effectively in the termination arena, one needs to address the ideological motivations."[40]

Nevertheless, several types of terminators exist. Bardach has identified three types: the *oppositionists*, the *economizers*, and the *reformers*.[41] The oppositionists are those who dislike the policy or program because they feel that it is a bad policy. It is a challenge to their sense of values or offends their social, economic, or political interests. The economizers are those who see a need to economize. Thus, they favor termination as a means of reducing expenditure outlays; at other times they are simply more interested in reprogramming expenditures. Finally, the reformers are those who see the termination as essential to the development of a substitute policy or program or organization that they believe will be more useful.[42] Bardach argues that ideological or political considerations are usually the motive behind reformers and oppositionists, whereas programmatic considerations (i.e., economics and efficiency) are usually the motive behind the behavior of the economizers. In any case, sometimes programmatic reasons are used for convenience when in reality they are attempts to mask what are essentially ideological or political motivations.

Some Rules for Would-Be Terminators

Robert Behn suggests the following political strategies that may help policy terminators achieve their objectives.

1. *Don't float trial ballons.* A termination trial balloon will allow the opposition to organize supporters. Therefore, terminators need to prevent information leaks until they have formalized comprehensive justifications for their termination decision.
2. *Enlarge the policy's constituency.* Organized constituencies often determine whether a policy is continued or terminated; consequently, terminators are more successful in eliminating a policy if they can enlarge the termination constituency body beyond the policy's original clientele base.
3. *Focus attention on the policy's harm.* Eliminating policies that can be shown to have a particularly harmful effect is easier than eliminating policies that have general effects or ineffectiveness or inefficiency.
4. *Take advantage of ideological shifts to demonstrate harm.* Policies are often evaluated on the basis of an ideological framework. Terminators can utilize or create ideological shifts that would create a new perspective that an established policy is actually harmful.
5. *Inhibit compromise.* Political supporters of a policy make compromises to maintain the policy. By making compromises impossible, terminators prevent the possibility that this will be chosen instead of termination.
6. *Recruit an outsider as a terminator.* This facilitates termination because the agency must renounce its programmatic philosophy and disrupt its administrative procedures. The current administration may be reluctant to adopt a negative view of the agency's past behavior and make unpopular statements and directives necessary for termination.
7. *Avoid legislative votes.* Because legislators try to avoid making enemies, they may not be willing to force an unpopular termination. Legislators are interested more in compromise than in asymetrical decisions.
8. *Don't encroach upon legislative prerogatives.* Executive branch terminators should avoid conflict between constitutional powers of the president and the Congress.
9. *Accept short-term cost increases.* Terminating a policy can often cost more in the short-term than continuing it due to severance payments and the costs of initiating a replacement policy.
10. *Put off the beneficiaries.* Offer new jobs for the employees of terminated programs and make severance payments to the policy's clientele.
11. *Advocate adoption, not termination.* Make the case that the adoption of policy B necessitates the termination of policy A rather than advocating termination of policy A.
12. *Terminate only what is necessary.* Terminators should be aware of their motivation. Is the target of termination really a harmful or ineffective policy or an expensive agency? Be judicious in deciding what to terminate.[43]

Behn cautions that not all these suggestions will be appropriate for every ter-mination effort. In addition, his suggestions are more relevant to "big bang" ter-minations than to the "long whimper" variety. Nevertheless, they are useful bits of advice for would-be terminators.

In the next section of this book, we describe the evolution of several domes-tic policies and examine the extent to which our theories of policy change explain these phenomena. In Chapters 10 through 13, the evolution of educa-tional policy, welfare policy, crime policy, and environmental policy is discussed during the period from the early 1960s to the present.

NOTES

1. See David B. Truman, *The Governmental Process* (New York: Alfred Knopf, 1951); and David B. Easton, *A Systems Analysis of Political Life* (New York: Wiley, 1965).
2. Peter DeLeon, "A Theory of Policy Termination," in *The Policy Cycle*, ed. J. V. May and Aaron Wildavsky (Beverly Hills, CA: Sage, 1978), pp. 279–300; Brian W. Hogwood and B. G. Peters, *Policy Dynamics* (New York: St. Martin's Press, 1983); Brian W. Hogwood and Lewis A. Gunn, *Policy Analysis for the Real World* (Oxford: Oxford University Press, 1984), pp. 241–260; and Paul A. Sabatier, "Top-Down and Bottom-Up Approaches to Implementation Research: A Critical Analysis and Suggested Synthesis," *Journal of Public Policy* 6, no. 1 (1986), pp. 21–47.
3. James E. Anderson, *Public Policymaking: An Introduction* (Boston: Houghton Mifflin, 1990), p. 257.
4. Ibid., p. 402.
5. Ibid., p. 250.
6. Hogwood and Gunn, *Policy Analysis*, p. 251.
7. Ibid.
8. Ibid., p. 242.
9. Anderson, *Public Policymaking*, p. 255.
10. B. Guy Peters, *American Public Policy: Promise and Performance* (Chatham, NJ: Chatham House, 1986), pp. 143–144.
11. See Arthur Schlesinger, Jr., *The Cycles of American History* (Boston: Houghton Mifflin, 1986); and Arthur Schlesinger, Jr., "America's Political Cycle Turns Again," *Wall Street Journal*, 10 December 1987. See also Walter Dean Burnham, *Critical Elections and the Mainsprings of American Politics* (New York: Norton, 1970).
12. Samuel P. Huntington, *American Politics: The Promise of Disharmony* (Cambridge, MA: Belknap/Harvard University Press, 1981), p. 284.
13. See Paul A. Sabatier, "Knowledge, Policy-Oriented Learning and Policy Change: An Advocacy Coalition Framework," *Knowledge: Creation, Utilization, Diffusion* 3, no. 4 (June 1987), pp. 649–692; see also Paul A. Sabatier and Hank Jenkins-Smith, eds., *Policy Change and Learning: An Advocacy Coalition Approach* (Boulder: WestviewPress, 1993).
14. Paul A. Sabatier, "An Advocacy Coalition Framework of Policy Change and the Role of Policy-Oriented Learning Therein," *Policy Sciences* 21, nos. 2–3 (1988), pp. 129–168.
15. Ibid.

16. Sabatier, "Knowledge, Policy-Oriented Learning, and Policy Change," p. 653.

17. See Hugh Heclo, *Social Policy in Britain and Sweden* (New Haven: Yale University Press, 1974), p. 306.

18. See Paul A. Sabatier and Hank C. Jenkins-Smith, "Policy Change and Policy-Oriented Learning: Exploring an Advocacy Coalition Framework," *Policy Sciences* 21, nos. 2–3 (1988), pp. 123–278; see also Paul A. Sabatier, "Toward Better Theories of the Policy Process," *PS: Political Science and Politics* 24, no. 2 (June 1991), pp. 147–156; and Sabatier and Jenkins-Smith, *Policy Change and Learning*. Sabatier and Jenkins-Smith argue that the "stages heuristic" (agenda setting to policy termination) has outlived its usefulness for teaching and research purposes; however, we feel that the stages heuristic continues to be useful for pedagogical purposes. Indeed, it has provided an organizing framework for this book. We present the policy change model by Sabatier and Jenkins-Smith as yet another phase or stage in the policy process rather than as a replacement for the policy process model.

19. See Edwin Amenta and Theda Skocpol, "Taking Exception: Explaining the Distinctiveness of American Public Policies in the Last Century," in *The Comparative History of Public Policy*, ed. F. G. Castles (New York: Oxford University Press, 1989).

20. Maynard Silva, ed., *Ocean Resources and U.S. Intergovernmental Relations in the 1980s* (Boulder: WestviewPress, 1986).

21. R. L. Swanson and M. Devine, "Ocean Dumping Policy: The Pendulum Swings Again," *Environment* 24, no. 5 (June 1982), pp. 15–20.

22. James W. Curlin, "Ocean Policy Comes of Age: The End of the Beginning or the Beginning of the End," *Sea Technology* 21, no. 1 (1980), pp. 23–28.

23. Alan Bakalian, "Regulation and Control of U.S. Ocean Dumping: A Decade of Progress, An Appraisal for the Future," *Harvard Environmental Law Review* (1984), pp. 193–256.

24. Julian H. Spirer, "The Ocean Dumping Deadline: Easing the Mandate Millstone," *Fordham Urban Law Journal* 11, no. 1 (1982/1983), pp. 1–49.

25. William H. Lahey, "Ocean Dumping of Sewage Sludge: The Tide Turns from Protection to Management," *Harvard Environmental Law Review* (1982), pp. 395–431.

26. Spirer, "Ocean Dumping Deadline."

27. Ibid., p. 36.

28. Peter DeLeon, "Policy Termination as a Political Process," in *The Politics of Program Evaluation*, ed. Dennis Palumbo (Beverly Hills, CA: Sage, 1987), p. 194.

29. Garry D. Brewer, "Termination: Hard Choices, Harder Questions," *Public Administration Review* 38, no. 4 (July/August 1978), pp. 338–344; and Herbert Kaufman, *Are Government Organizations Immortal?* (Washington, D.C.: Brookings Institution, 1976.

30. Hogwood and Gunn, *Policy Analysis*, pp. 247–248.

31. Janet E. Frantz, "Reviving and Revising a Termination Model," *Policy Sciences* 25 (May 1992), pp. 175–189.

32. Robert Behn, "How To Terminate a Public Policy: A Dozen Hints for the Would-Be Terminator," *Policy Analysis* 4, no. 3 (Summer 1978), pp. 393–413.

33. Anderson, *Public Policymaking*, p. 256.

34. Ibid.

35. Eugene Bardach, "Policy Termination as a Political Process," *Policy Sciences* 7, no. 2 (June 1976), pp. 123–132.

36. Ibid.

37. DeLeon, "Policy Termination," pp. 173–194; James M. Cameron, "Ideology and Policy Termination: Restructuring California's Mental Health Systems," in *The Policy Cycle*, ed. Judith May and Aaron Wildavsky (Newbury Park, CA: Sage, 1978), pp. 301–328.
38. DeLeon, "Policy Termination," p. 185.
39. Cameron, "Ideology and Policy Termination," p. 306.
40. DeLeon, "Policy Termination," p. 194.
41. Bardach, "Policy Termination," p. 126.
42. Ibid., p. 127.
43. Behn, "Terminate a Public Policy," pp. 393–413.

ANALYZING PUBLIC POLICY CHOICES

CHAPTER   TEN

EDUCATIONAL POLICY

"The poorest states, if left to their own resources, have no reasonable prospect of raising the funds to provide adequate education. Some form of equalization is needed, because it is vital to the nation that the children in the poorest states also be well educated. Therefore, Federal participation in the financing of their schools is essential."
EDUCATIONAL POLICIES
COMMISSION (1962)

"Our nation is at risk. Our once unchallenged pre-eminence in commerce, industry, science and technological innovation is being overtaken by competitors throughout the world. . . . The educational foundations of our society are presently being eroded by a rising tide of mediocrity that threatens our very future as a nation and a people. . . . We have, in effect, been committing an act of unthinking, unilateral educational disarmament."
NATIONAL COMMISSION ON
EXCELLENCE IN EDUCATION (1983)

"Each student will develop the ability to understand, respect, and accept people of different races, sex, cultural heritage, national origin, religion, and political, economic, and social background, and their values, beliefs, and attitudes."
NEW YORK STATE BOARD OF
REGENTS (1990)

These three quotes from different decades reflect different emphases at different times on issues that have been omnipresent in U.S. educational policy. How public schools should be funded, what should be included in the curriculum, how equal educational opportunities can best be defined, and how educational services are best delivered are issues that have been contested throughout American history and have galvanized both conservative and liberal forces. Today, educational institutions, from elementary schools to universities, are under attack from many directions.[1] As we move into the next century, the conflicts in funding redistribution, financial aid to poor children, taxpayer support for all public education, "tracking" of students into different curricula, bilingual education, equal opportunities for racial minorities, testing of students, school choice, community control of schools, and countless other manifestations will continue.

In this chapter we examine some of these concerns. We first provide a brief sketch of the scope of public education in the United States. Second, we examine where educational policy is made, highlighting the intergovernmental structure inherent in all policymaking in America. Next, we discuss the major issues mentioned above, including alternative views of various educational practices and the evolution of these practices over time. Finally, we evaluate some of the reforms in educational policy over this time and discuss the future of educational policy in the next century.

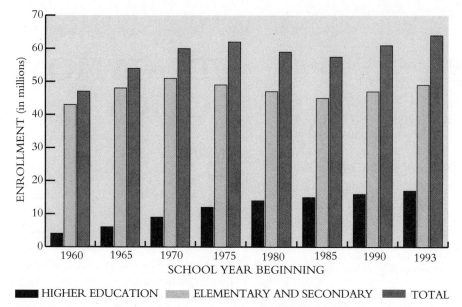

FIGURE 10-1   Enrollments in Elementary, Secondary, and Higher Education, 1960–1993

Source: U.S. Department of Education, National Center for Education Statistics, *Statistics of State School Systems; Statistics of Public Elementary and Secondary School Systems; Statistics of Nonpublic Secondary School Systems; Statistics of Nonpublic Elementary and Secondary Schools; Revenues and Expenditures for Public Elementary and Secondary Education; Fall Enrollment in Institutions of Higher Education; Financial Statistics of Institutions of Higher Education;* Common Core of Data Surveys; and Integrated Postsecondary Education Data System surveys.

EDUCATION IN AMERICA

In the 1993–1994 school year, almost sixty-five million students were enrolled in educational institutions at all levels.[2] Figure 10-1 illustrates the enrollment levels in the United States from 1960 to 1993. Current data indicate that enrollments in elementary and secondary education as well as higher education are expected to increase slightly by 2000.[3] In addition, expenditures for education have more than tripled from 1960 to 1993. The biggest increase in school expenditures has been at the college level, where expenditures have increased almost five and one-half times since 1960. Figure 10-2 presents data on school expenditures from 1960 to 1993.

At the same time school expenditures were increasing, student performance was declining. Figure 10-3 illustrates the decline in SAT scores from 1960 to 1993. The data show that although expenditures on elementary and secondary schools have increased more than 200 percent since 1960, average SAT scores have declined 73 points. This decline is probably the most commonly cited statistic to support the argument that the educational system is failing.[4]

However, another possible reason for this decline lies in the changing composition of the students taking the exam. Since the mid-1970s, more students who rank below the top one-fifth of their high school classes, more students for whom English is a second language, and more racial and ethnic minorities—who tend to score lower on standardized achievement tests—have been taking the

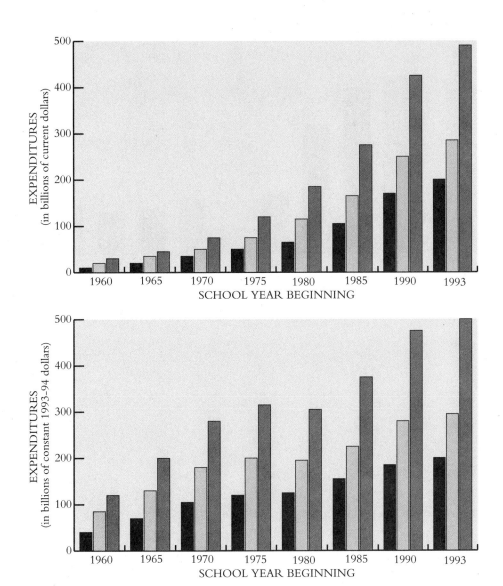

FIGURE 10-2   Educational Expenditures, 1960–1993

Source: U.S. Department of Education, National Center for Education Statistics, *Statistics of State School Systems; Statistics of Public Elementary and Secondary School Systems; Statistics of Nonpublic Secondary School Systems; Statistics of Nonpublic Elementary and Secondary Schools; Revenues and Expenditures for Public Elementary and Secondary Education; Fall Enrollment in Institutions of Higher Education; Financial Statistics of Institutions of Higher Education;* Common Core of Data Surveys; and Integrated Postsecondary Education Data System surveys.

SAT. In fact, most of the decline occurred by 1975, after which the scores have remained relatively stable. Average scores for white students are remarkably stable after 1975, and scores for black and Mexican-American test takers have risen. Analysts at the Sandia National Laboratories estimate that if one takes into account the changing demographic composition of the test takers, the 1990 SAT scores are actually 30 points better than the 1975 test scores.[5]

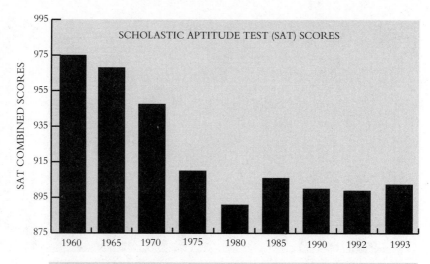

SCHOLASTIC APTITUDE TEST (SAT) SCORES			
YEAR	VERBAL	MATHEMATICAL	COMBINED
1960	477	498	975
1965	473	496	969
1970	460	488	948
1975	437	473	910
1980	424	466	890
1985	431	475	906
1990	424	476	900
1992	423	476	899
1993	424	478	902

FIGURE 10-3   SAT Scores, 1960–1993.

Note: Scholastic Aptitude test scores among all students have dropped 73 points from 1960 to 1993.
Source: William J. Bennett, *The Index of Leading Cultural Indicators* (New York: Simon and Schuster, 1994), p. 82.

Regardless of the reasons, the decline in performance scores has clearly fueled a perception that the educational system is in crisis and has encouraged educational reform movements throughout the period 1960 to 1990. Furthermore, citizens often blame schools for problems in society—ranging from perpetuating the income inequalities in society to the "moral collapse" of society as manifested by drug and alcohol abuse and lack of discipline to the declining international competitiveness of American business.[6] To understand how educational policies are produced and evolve, we must understand the locus of educational policymaking.

THE LOCUS OF EDUCATIONAL POLICYMAKING

Federal Government

Although the federal government has never assumed a large role in funding public elementary and secondary schools—its contribution has never exceeded 10 percent of total expenditures—its interest in education is a longstanding one. Congress offered land for public schools in the new territories in the famous Northwest Ordinance of 1787 and provided grants of federal land to each state for the establishment of colleges under the Morrill Land Grant Act of 1862. The Smith-Hughes Act of 1917 set up the first program of federal grants-in-aid to promote vocational education, which enabled schools to provide training in agriculture, home economics, trades, and industries.[7] Beginning in 1946, the federal government supported the National School Lunch and Milk programs in which federal grants and commodity donations were the basis for low-cost lunches and milk served in both public and private schools.

After World War II, the federal government increased its involvement in public education through the Federal Impacted Areas Aid program in which federal aid was authorized for areas of the country in which federal activities (such as a military base) created a substantial increase in school enrollments or a reduction in taxable resources because of a federally owned facility. In the National Defense Education Act of 1958, Congress provided financial aid to the states and public school districts to improve instruction in science, math, and foreign languages. This was largely in response to the Soviet Union's launch of the first satellite in space and the belief that American education might not be competitive with other nations' success in science and technology.[8]

Beginning with the Elementary and Secondary Education Act (ESEA) of 1965, the federal government began to play an even larger role. This act established the single, largest federal aid to education program, in which poverty-impacted schools were the beneficiaries of aid for instructional materials and educational research and training. ESEA provided for federal financial assistance to local educational agencies that served areas with concentrations of children from low-income families for programs that were targeted to meeting the needs of educationally deprived children.[9] Federal aid was substantially increased during this period. This program continued through the 1960s and the 1970s.

This perceived decline in student performance prompted further federal action. In 1983, the National Commission on Excellence in Education recommended a series of reforms in American education that began the back-to-basics movement that persisted through the 1980s. Federal aid to education declined in the 1980s as the Congress and the public began to question the relationship between expenditures and student performance. There seemed to be no corresponding increase in performance with an increase in support; in fact, the relationship was inversely related. Figure 10-4 illustrates this relationship. A sort of educational "backlash" developed in which the federal government, state legislatures, and the public favored reducing financial support to schools.

During the Bush presidency, the proposed national goals of the White House and the National Governors' Association assumed that schools would improve if standards were set and incentives created to force school professionals to pay attention to those standards. This theory of educational policy was the basis for President Bush's "America 2000" plan for national educational reform.

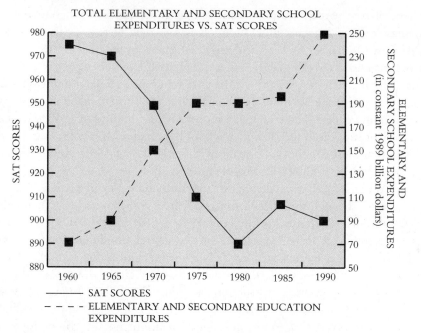

FIGURE 10-4   School Expenditures versus SAT Scores

Note:While expenditures on elementary and secondary education have increased more than 200 percent since 1960, SAT scores have declined 73 points.

Source:William J. Bennett, *The Index of Leading Cultural Indicators* (New York: Simon and Schuster, 1994), p. 82.

State Governments

As a power not granted to the national government, either expressly or by implication, establishing, supporting, and overseeing public education is a power reserved to the states under the Tenth Amendment to the U.S. Constitution. States vary in terms of how much they have centralized and bureaucratized the provision of educational services. Joseph McGivney, building on the earlier work of Lawrence Iannaccone, argues that state educational politics takes one of four forms.[10] In some states, educators, state education agencies, and legislatures try to maintain local control. In a second set of states, the education advocacy coalitions are concerned with issues broader than those defined by local interests, but the relationships between the actors remain cooperative. In yet other states, educational policymaking is more centralized, and different educational interests compete for the establishment or maintenance of a particular set of programs or funds. In a final set of states, educational policymaking is highly centralized, and educational politics may take the form of "iron triangles" of interest groups, state legislators, and agency officials cooperating with each other in competition with other policy subsystems to pursue their goals. McGivney sees a tendency to move to more centralization over time. Political scientist Fred Wirt agrees that the most important issues in educational policymaking are decided at the state, not local, level and that even in the most decentralized states, key functions such as teacher certification, accreditation, and minimum attendance policies are performed at the state level.[11]

Beginning in the 1930s, the states have steadily increased their financial involvement in the public schools, as citizens and policymakers have lost confidence in the schools' ability to provide a quality education.[12] The cornerstone of state educational policymaking is the State Educational Agency (SEA). The SEA is composed of a state board of education, a chief state school official (usually called the commissioner or superintendant of education), and a department of education. The state board of education is ordinarily concerned with the overall educational policies for the state, including minimum high school graduation requirements.[13] It also legitimizes decisions made by the state department of education, and it appoints the chief school officer.

Moreover, the influence of the SEAs has grown over the years as the local school districts look to the SEA to provide educational leadership for the state.[14] The SEA distributes state educational funds to local school districts and provides basic research and information to legislative committees that investigate school problems. Some of the most visible educational reforms in the 1980s, including teacher testing and tightening graduation requirements, were forced on local school districts by governors and state legislatures.[15] The back-to-basics movement of the 1980s was, in large part, a movement that was spearheaded by the state government.

The Local Role

Local influence in education has traditionally been thought of as being exercised primarily through financing schools via the property tax. However, the percentage of total school revenues provided by local governments has been declining since the 1930s. Moreover, the taxpayer revolts of the 1970s and the 1980s have caused a severe erosion of local property tax dollars for public education. For example, in California, the local share of school funding dropped from 70 percent in 1970 to 20 percent in 1982.[16] Figure 10-5 illustrates the relative contribution of federal, state, and local government to educational revenue from 1970 to 1992.

What has often been ignored is the local politics of education. The progressive reformers of the early twentieth century went to great lengths to remove educational systems from partisan politics and to create the illusion that educational systems were apolitical. All they did, in fact, was change the nature of the politics.

Educational researcher Joel Spring paints a richly textured picture in which the community power structure, the educational needs of the local labor market, the governing style of the local school board, the personal style of the superintendent, and the power of both the educational bureaucracy and the teachers' unions are all factors in local education politics.[17] But even he acknowledges

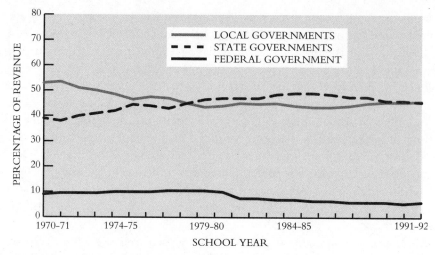

FIGURE 10-5   Sources of Revenue for Public Elementary and Secondary Schools: 1970–71 to 1991–92

Source: U.S. Department of Education, National Center for Education Statistics, *Digest of Education Statistics, 1994* (Washington, D.C.: U.S. Government Printing Office, 1994), p. 49.

that, "one can argue that local political battles are of little importance when compared to those that occur in state and federal politics."[18]

OTHER ACTORS IN EDUCATIONAL POLICY

Teachers

Aside from parents, teachers are perhaps the most important influence on students' intellectual and emotional development. Yet many often argue that the quality of individuals who choose to enter the teaching profession has declined over the years.[19] This is true for a number of reasons. First, this decline in quality over the past twenty-five years is due to changes in the workforce. Highly qualified women, who previously found teaching one of the few professions open to them, began to enter traditionally male-dominated jobs between 1965 and 1990. These new jobs offered better pay and more prestige than the teaching profession. Those that entered the teaching profession in the 1980s had lower average SAT scores than did their predecessors of the 1960s.[20]

In addition, part of the blame for declining quality of teachers rests with the educational programs of colleges and universities, which emphasized "educational methodology," rather than knowledge of their subject matter.[21] Teachers were given much more training in how to teach than in what to teach.

These problems in teacher quality led Albert Shanker, the president of the American Federation of Teachers, to say: "For the most part you are getting illiterate, incompetent people who cannot go into any other field."[22] Moreover, there is a growing shortage of teachers, especially in math, science, and foreign languages. Between 1989 and 1994, the United States required over a million new teachers while it is estimated that only about 625,000 were available.[23] These developments affecting teachers during the period 1965–1990 have led to the various state efforts to reform education in the 1980s and early 1990s. The movement for "teacher accountability" and "minimum competency testing" for teachers led by many state legislatures and some governors is directly related to the decline in teacher quality. Teachers have become objects of more scrutiny than ever before as state legislatures have become concerned over the decline in teacher quality during the past twenty-five years.

The Courts

The courts are also important actors affecting all areas of educational policy-making. Litigation by disabled, language, racial, and religious minorities has sought to affect how schools operate and has often been successful. Examples range from cases affecting minority group representation on school boards to those attempting to insure equality of educational funding to cases mandating racial and ethnic desegregation to those attempting to ban prayers in public schools. At times, these cases have led the courts to fashion remedies affecting school budgets, teacher and pupil assignments, the curriculum, transportation, textbooks, and administrative organization.[24]

At times, though, courts have refused to get involved. For example, some argue that the vast differences in the amounts of per pupil spending in various school districts violate the equal protection clause of the Fourteenth Amendment of the U.S. Constitution. But, in *Rodriguez* v. *San Antonio Independent School District*, the U.S. Supreme Court ruled that equalization of school financing was an issue that "must come from the lawmakers and from the democratic pressures of those who elect them."[25] With this decision, the issue of fiscal disparities between school districts was left to the various states to work out.

In summary, we can see how various actors, including the federal government, state and local governments, teachers, and the courts, have affected the evolution of educational policy. Before discussing this evolution, let us first discuss alternative perspectives on educational policy.

APPROACHES TO EDUCATIONAL POLICY

Why do some students fail? Policymakers have long debated the causes of educational failures in our schools. Basically, there are two major perspectives on the causes of failure, and each view carries with it a set of policies that would remedy the cause of failure. We briefly explore these two perspectives.

The Liberal (Structural) View

The liberal view begins with an optimistic view of human nature. Much like Thomas Sowell's "unconstrained vision," the liberal believes that all of us can succeed in the educational realm if given the chance and not shackled by an envi-

ronment that is not conducive to success. Within this perspective, the failures that
do occur are the result of the school system itself or the instructional environment, rather than the individual. The liberal believes that, with the exception of
mentally handicapped children, everyone has the potential to acquire knowledge
and develop employable skills.[26] Liberals advocate moving beyond simply acquiring basic skills. They have promoted such innovations as the open classroom and
individualized learning, which were characteristic of educational reforms in the
1960s and the 1970s. They are opposed to expelling disruptive students; rather
they favor keeping such students in the classroom, because they believe that all
students can succeed in education. When there are failures in student performance, then that is the fault of the school environment rather than the individual. In the 1960s, this perspective saw segregation and the lack of adequate
resources as the primary cause of failures in the classroom. They have promoted
such policies as mandatory racial desegregation, community control, and the
equalization of school funding by school districts. They are committed to the
principle of *equity* in that they feel that inequities in funding and/or the curriculum offerings produce a hostile learning environment.[27]

   The most recent manifestation of this view is that minority students have not
performed as well as they could have because of the "hegemony of Western culture and institutions" in the curriculum. Because schools have emphasized
Western European culture, institutions, and values and, at the same time,
neglected the culture, literature, and institutions of Third World cultures, minority students' self-esteem has been adversely affected. What is needed then,
according to the **multiculturalists** is an infusion of Third World cultures, institutions, and values into the curriculum at every level to help build the self-
esteem of minority students. By enhancing their self-esteem, it is argued, their
scholastic performance will eventually improve as well.

The Conservative (Individualist) View

Conservatives begin with a more pessimistic view of human nature, much like
Thomas Sowell's "constrained vision" of human nature. That is, they believe that
not all of us can succeed in the educational arena due to constraints within ourselves. Perhaps due to a lack of talent, intelligence, motivation, and/or what it
takes to succeed, there will inevitably be a certain percentage of failures in the
educational system. For example, Edward Banfield argues that "there will be *some*
number of students who are simply not capable of doing high school work."[28]
The fact that these failures tend to be concentrated in the lower socioeconomic
classes and the racial minorities is said to be a function of their "culture of
poverty," which inhibits the desire for self-improvement and deferred gratification. Other writers within this perspective attribute poor educational achievement to genetic factors, such as IQ.[29] For example, in their recent book, *The Bell
Curve*, Richard Herrnstein and Charles Murray argue that IQ is more important
than socioeconomic status in predicting which white youths will never complete

a high school education; moreover, the probability of getting a college degree increases as IQ goes from low to high.[30] One of the most controversial scholars, Arthur Jensen, suggests that education for "low-IQ disadvantaged" students should be directed to rote memory learning versus conceptual or cognitive learning.[31] These authors have recently come under much criticism for their views on IQ and scholastic performance.[32]

The conservative tends to stress *individual* reasons for failure to perform well. This failure is said to be the result of a present-oriented mind-set or perhaps genetic imbalances (i.e., IQ deficiencies) within the student population and/or a poor family background. The policies favored by conservatives include a back-to-basics approach; an emphasis on reading, writing, and mathematical skills; rote learning; the voucher system; an opposition to mandatory desegregation; parental choice in schools; and minimum competency testing for students and teachers.

Table 10-1 provides a comparison of the liberal and conservative perspectives on educational policy.[33]

In the following discussion, we see how these alternative approaches to educational policy have guided different periods of educational reform from the 1960s to the 1990s. At any given time, one of these approaches seemed to occupy the intellectual high ground and formed a basis for the policies being promoted at that particular time. For example, in the 1960s and the 1970s, the emphasis on compensatory education reflected the liberal view, whereas the back-to-basics

TABLE 10-1   Conflicting Views of Public Education

	Liberals	Conservatives
View of human nature	Optimistic	Pessimistic
Function of education	Promote social and economic mobility	Promote social and economic mobility
View of education curriculum	Advocate reform in education; emphasis on experimentation; "open classroom"	Back-to-the-basics; emphasis on the Three Rs; rote learning
View of discipline	Opposed to expelling students; keep disruptive students in the classroom	Emphasis on rigid discipline; favor right to suspend and expel troublesome students
Reasons for failures in education	Stress failure of the school system itself (e.g., segregation and/or a lack of adequate school resources)	Stress individual failure of the student (e.g., culture of poverty, genetic imbalances within student population, poor family background)
Preferred policy solution	Involuntary busing; community control; citizen participation; desegregation; multiculturalism	Educational vouchers; opposed to busing; minimum competency testing for students

Source: Adapted from *Politics and Policy in States and Communities,* 5th ed. by John J. Harrigan (New York: HarperCollins, 1994), pp. 392–394. Copyright © 1994 by HarperCollins College Publishers. Reprinted by permission.

movement of the 1980s reflected the conservative view. Currently, one can find each approach being emphasized in different locales.

THE EVOLUTION OF EDUCATIONAL POLICY

The 1960s and 1970s: Inadequate Resources and Compensatory Education

As noted above, education is the single biggest expenditure of state and local governments, yet spending for education varies a great deal. Table 10-2 illustrates the per pupil expenditures among the states for elementary and secondary education in 1992. Expenditures range from $9,549 per pupil in the District of Columbia to $3,040 in the state of Utah. Moreover, the amount of spending per pupil is largely explained by state wealth; the wealthier states spend more than the poorer ones. In the 1960s (and even today) many believed that wealthy states could provide better education for their children with less economic sacrifice than poor states. This relationship between state wealth and state spending for education suggested the need for federal aid to education. It was argued then that federal aid would help to equalize educational opportunities throughout the nation. Thus, the Elementary and Secondary Education Act of 1965 doubled federal contributions to education and targeted aid for poverty-impacted schools. A large part of the efforts of the Great Society programs of the 1960s were devoted to equalizing educational resources across the states. Moreover, in the 1970s, this point was argued at the level of the local school district by several court cases. Because of the heavy reliance on local property taxes and the resultant inequities in per pupil expenditures among school districts, some claimed that students from poor districts were being denied equal protection of the law under the Fourteenth Amendment of the U. S. Constitution. For example, in *Serrano* v. *Priest*, the Supreme Court of California ordered that action be taken to equalize school expenditures throughout the state.

Thus, the problem in education was seen as a lack of resources among poorer school districts as well as the inequities associated with school district financing of public schools. The remedy was some attempt to equalize per pupil expenditures in the hope that these expenditures would allow the school to do a number of things better. The logic embodied in the notion of "compensatory education" in the Elementary and Secondary Education Act of 1965 was that an increase in school expenditures would allow the student–teacher ratios to drop to a more acceptable level, that better teachers could be hired with better salaries, and that the physical facilities could be improved with this infusion of resources. Consequently, students' performance would improve after these conditions were improved.

However, this was not the case. In the 1980s, another problem surfaced that called into question the relationship between school spending and student performance.

TABLE 10-2   Public Elementary and Secondary School Expenditures by State, 1992

| State | Average Expenditure per Pupil | |
	Amount	Rank
U.S. Average	$5,421	
Alabama	3,616	48
Alaska	8,450	4
Arizona	4,381	40
Arkansas	4,031	45
California	4,746	34
Colorado	5,172	26
Connecticut	8,017	5
Delaware	6,093	13
District of Columbia	9,549	1
Florida	5,243	25
Georgia	4,375	41
Hawaii	5,420	21
Idaho	3,556	49
Illinois	5,670	18
Indiana	5,074	29
Iowa	5,096	28
Kansas	5,007	30
Kentucky	4,719	35
Louisiana	4,354	42
Maine	5,652	19
Maryland	6,679	7
Massachusetts	6,408	10
Michigan	6,268	11
Minnesota	5,409	22
Mississippi	3,245	50
Missouri	4,830	33
Montana	5,423	20
Nebraska	5,263	24
Nevada	4,926	31
New Hampshire	5,790	16
New Jersey	9,317	2
New Mexico	3,765	46
New York	8,527	3
North Carolina	4,555	37
North Dakota	4,441	38
Ohio	5,694	17
Oklahoma	4,078	44
Oregon	5,913	14
Pennsylvania	6,613	8
Rhode Island	6,546	9
South Carolina	4,436	39
South Dakota	4,173	43
Tennessee	3,692	47
Texas	4,632	36
Utah	3,040	51
Vermont	6,944	6
Virginia	4,880	32
Washington	5,271	23
West Virginia	5,109	27
Wisconsin	6,139	12
Wyoming	5,812	15

Source: U.S. Department of Education, Center for Statistics, *Digest of Education Statistics,* 1994 (Washington, D.C.: U.S. Government Printing Office, 1994), p. 165.

The 1980s: Poor Student Performance and Back to Basics

In the 1980s, the problems of education were defined not as a lack of resources, as they were in the 1960s and the 1970s, but rather as poor student performance stemming partly from poorly conceived reforms of the earlier era. Specifically, it was argued that educational permissiveness had allowed the school to drift away from the basics of education, which focused on reading, writing, and mathematical skills. Many criticisms were directed to the "open classroom" and "making learning fun" approaches that were characteristic of the 1960s and the early 1970s.

Moreover, in 1983, a blue-ribbon national educational commission declared a "crisis in education," with its often-cited report, *A Nation at Risk*. According to the report, ". . . our nation is at risk. Our once unchallenged pre-eminence in commerce, industry, science and technological innovation is being overtaken by competitors throughout the world. . . . The educational foundations of our society are presently being eroded by a rising tide of mediocrity that threatens our very future as a nation and a people. . . . We have, in effect, been committing an act of unthinking, unilateral educational disarmament."[34] The authors of *A Nation at Risk* advocated a restructuring of the curriculum requirements for all secondary school students to include four years of English; three years of science, math, and social studies; and at least one-half year of computer science. College-bound students would be expected to take two years of a foreign language. Essentially, the report advocated a back-to-basics approach, with an emphasis on curriculum reform. The report pointed out that about twenty-three million Americans were functionally illiterate or unable to perform the simple tasks of reading, writing, and comprehension. About two-thirds of all students lacked the ability to solve a math problem involving several steps, 80 percent could not write an effective essay, and 40% were "unable to draw inferences from written material."[35] In summary, the report emphasized the need to reform the curriculum. This contrasts sharply with the earlier reform period during the 1960s and the 1970s when the emphasis was on increasing the level of school expenditures.

The second wave of reform took place between 1986 and 1990 and moved beyond setting standards to improving the quality of teaching and learning at the school site. This second wave of reforms has been labeled the "restructuring movement." Although this term means different things to many people, it calls for the reorganization of instruction so that students could truly understand the material presented to them, the provision of more in-depth learning as opposed to covering a great amount of content, and student engagement in higher-order thinking. This wave of reform was oriented around restructuring strategies that emphasize variation in teaching approaches, empowerment of teachers and students, and bottom-up decision making.[36] Thus, the failure of our public schools was seen (mostly) as a failure of the schools themselves and partly as a failure of the individual students.

The 1990s: Cultural Hegemony and Multiculturalism

In the late 1980s and early 1990s, a view has developed that the poor performance of minority students in our public schools is a function of **cultural bias**. Specifically, the existing curriculum in the schools stresses the accomplishments of white male, Western thinkers and ignores the contributions of blacks, women, and other minorities. This, it is argued, produces an intellectual climate in which minorities are excluded from the intellectual life of the educational process. The argument is that our schools have been guided by a "Eurocentric bias," which has alienated blacks, women, and other minorities and left them with an incomplete view of their own history and contributions. Thus, the remedy for this occurrence is that a "restructuring" must take place to replace the long-reigning intellectual "colonization, distortion, and oppression" that is now said to taint the entire curriculum. In effect, this means that there needs to be a process of infusing race, ethnicity, and gender across the curriculum and making sure that every student's studies include "multicultural" aspects.

In the elementary schools, this revision is known as restructuring; in the secondary schools, this revision is known as globalism; and in the colleges and universities, it is known as multiculturalism and/or cultural diversity. In every instance, however, the process is the same in that it is intended to make minorities more comfortable with the curriculum by including more contributions from Third World countries and women. Presumably, this would result in an improvement in the self-esteem of women and minorities and thus improve their well-being as well as their academic performance. For the nonminorities, such as white males, it would help them appreciate cultures other than their own.

Table 10-3 illustrates the evolution of educational policy from the 1960s to the 1990s.

EVALUATING EDUCATIONAL REFORMS

Compensatory Education

One of the most interesting examples of evaluation research is that of compensatory education. In the Elementary and Secondary Education Act of 1965

TABLE 10-3   The Evolution of Educational Policy, 1960–1990

	1960–1970s	1980s	1990s
Nature of problem	Unequal resources	Poor performance	Cultural hegemony
Reason for failure	Lack of resources	Lack of skills	Lack of self-esteem
Reform proposed	Compensatory education	Back-to basics	Multicultural curriculum
Specifics	ESEA, 1965 busing	Rote learning	Cultural diversity
	Community control	Minimum competency testing	Affirmative action
			Minority incentives

(ESEA), poverty-impacted schools were the beneficiaries of the increased federal aid to education programs. ESEA provided for federal financial assistance to "local educational agencies serving areas with concentrations of children from low-income families" for programs that contribute "to meeting the special needs of educationally deprived children."[37] Grants were made to public and private elementary and secondary schools for the acquisition of school library resources, textbooks, and other instructional materials. The logic embodied in the ESEA was that an increase in per pupil expenditures (especially to students from poorer school districts) would allow these schools to purchase better educational materials, hire better teachers, and improve the curriculum. As a consequence, student performance would improve, thus allowing the poorer students to be more competitive in the marketplace after graduation. Ultimately, this would help to alleviate the disparities in income and thus reduce poverty in America. Indeed, the ESEA was an important component of President Johnson's War on Poverty in the 1960s.

Professor James Coleman, a Harvard sociologist, conducted an evaluation of the logic embodied in the ESEA, producing what is popularly known as the Coleman Report.[38] Although his report was criticized, it undermined much of the conventional logic about the impact of increased expenditures on student performance. Prior to his study, legislators, teachers, school administrators, school board members, and the general public assumed that factors such as the number of pupils in the classroom, the amount of money spent on each pupil, library and laboratory facilities, teachers' salaries, the quality of the curriculum, and other characteristics of the school affected student performance (and hence educational opportunity). However, Coleman's analysis revealed that these factors had no significant effect on student learning or achievement. Rather, the only factors that had a significant effect were family background of the students themselves and the family background of their classmates. Family background factors affected the students' verbal abilities and attitudes toward education; both of the latter were strongly related to student performance.

Although the Coleman Report made no policy recommendations, it nevertheless implied that compensatory education had very little educational value. If his report was correct, one inference that could be and was drawn was that it seemed pointless to raise per pupil expenditures, increase teachers' salaries, lower the number of pupils per classroom, provide better libraries or laboratories, or adopt any curricular innovations.[39] Moreover, Coleman's conclusions have been reexamined in more than 150 studies. A review of 120 of these studies found that only 18 found a statistically significant positive relationship between school expenditures and student performance and concluded that no strong, systematic relationship exits.[40] Indeed, since the 1960s, there have been around 200 studies that examine the relationship among the inputs to schools, the resources spent on schools, and the performance of students. These studies tell a consistent story that "there is no systematic relationship between expenditures on schools and student performance."[41]

In 1972, Christopher Jencks sought to examine the relationships between education and mobility or success, as measured by income. He questioned whether schools were performing a redistributive function in society by helping individuals to move from lower classes to middle- and upper-income classes on the basis of their education. Essentially, he found that there was little correlation between income and the quality of schooling. Therefore, educational reforms (especially compensatory educational reforms) could no longer be regarded as an effective means of equalizing income.[42] Neither family background, cognitive skills, educational attainment, nor occupational status explained much of the variation in men's incomes. Income differences seemed to be better explained by the values held by the individuals themselves, their skills, and simply luck.[43]

In his later research, Jencks further examined the relationships among values held by the individual, educational attainment, family background, and economic success.[44] He found that family background (especially the father's education), personality characteristics of the students (e.g., dependability, industriousness, perseverance, and leadership ability), and years of school completed had the strongest effects on men's earnings. However, the "best readily observable predictor of a young man's eventual status or earnings is the amount of schooling he has had."[45] His findings pointed up the need for effective education and the importance of reducing drop-out rates. Moreover, his findings, along with *A Nation at Risk*, called into question the adequacy of our public educational system.

Back to Basics and Accountability

In the 1980s, state legislators introduced more education-related bills than ever before. Nearly every state joined in a national movement to address the concerns expressed in 1983's *A Nation at Risk*. What effect, if any, did this educational reform have on student performance? In a report aimed at appraising state educational initiatives during this period, Firestone, Fuhrman, and Kirst identified several areas of reform.[46] The first wave of reform took place between 1982 and 1986 and involved establishing minimum competency standards for students and teachers. The highest level of state activity was in mandating more academic courses and upgrading teaching through changes in certification and compensation.[47] Within two years after the publication of *A Nation at Risk*, forty-seven states had raised or proposed raising graduation requirements, forty-four had implemented minimum competency testing of their students, forty-nine had raised teacher preparation standards, and thirty-four states had increased the amount of instructional time.[48] In addition, teachers' salaries increased 22 percent in real terms between 1980 and 1988, with most of the growth occurring between 1983 and 1988.

What effect, if any, did this educational reform have on student performance? In the first half of the 1980s, SAT scores began to climb. Thus, there is some evidence that these reforms had positive effects. On the other hand, some argue that states have met with only modest success the educational goals expressed in *A Nation at Risk*. It is true that high school curricula are more academically oriented, standards for entering the teaching profession are more selective, teacher salaries are higher, and state and local governments have boosted educational funding, but there are still doubts about the rigor of these reforms.[49]

Multiculturalism

It is probably too soon to fully evaluate the impact of the current emphasis on multiculturalism in the schools. Yet the current emphasis on multicultural education clearly has produced a backlash among many conservatives and produced a literature that is strongly critical of this approach to education. Some argue that multicultural education teaches students not to make moral judgments about customs, laws, or cultures other than their own.[50] This can lead to a mindless acceptance of practices that would not be tolerated in a democracy and the "closing" of the students' minds to moral scrutiny.[51]

EDUCATIONAL POLICY IN THE FUTURE

As noted above, the proposed national goals of the Bush White House and the National Governors' Association assumed that schools would improve if standards were set and incentives created to force school professionals to pay attention to those standards. This theory of educational policy was the basis for President Bush's "America 2000" plan for national education reform. Thus, his plan emphasized choice through the voucher plan and national testing with school scores triggering the allocation of some federal funds. Financial support to the schools would to be tied to performance by the schools and students.

During the 1992 presidential campaign, the "Clinton/Gore Plan for Education" stressed funding for Head Start, support for Chapter One funding for low-income students, a system of national standards for students, public school choice programs such as those in Arkansas, and bilingual education, among others.[52] In 1993, the Clinton plan for education emerged as the "Goals 2000: Educate America Act." It included items that the president wanted written into law such as national goals, standards, and tests for elementary and secondary educational systems. More specifically, the goals prescribed that by the year 2000:

1. All children would start school ready to learn.
2. At least 90 percent of students would finish high school.
3. Students would leave grades four, eight, and twelve with demonstrated competence in English, math, science, foreign languages, arts, history, and geography.
4. The United States would be first in the world in math and science achievement.

5. Every adult American would be literate and possess the skills necessary to compete in a global economy.
6. Every school would be free of drugs and violence.
7. More parents would participate in their children's schooling.
8. All teachers would have access to good teacher training.[53]

In April 1993, President Clinton proposed a "national service program" that was designed to make a college education available to all students, regardless of their financial situation. Under this proposal, students could acquire college loans and repay them through automatic deductions from future earnings or by performing community service jobs, such as working as teachers, police officers, or social workers after graduation. In 1993, Congress passed the National Service Bill, which provided up to $9,450 in education grants to volunteers when they completed their community service.[54] Clearly, educational policy is likely to be a priority for President Clinton in the coming years, as it was during his tenure as governor of Arkansas.

In any case, the current movement for accountability is based on a marketlike view that schools need to be run much like a business, with rewards (more money) for performance and punishments (less money) for failures. Yet critics argue that making schools "compete" with each other without investing more to improve them means greater segregation and inequality for many, with improved education for a few.[55] Indeed, political scientists Kevin Smith and Kenneth Meier charge that the "coin of the realm" in an educational marketplace is not educational quality, but racial, religious, and socioeconomic segregation.[56]

Taken together, these findings suggest a more focused role for government as far as its efforts to improve student performance. Perhaps a more effective role for government than increasing school expenditures might be to decrease the number of children living in poverty. Thus, our educational policies are inevitably bound up with our welfare policies (not to mention our policies for economic development). In any case, we need to reexamine our assumptions about why students succeed or fail in various educational contexts. We have assumed that the financial environment in the schools themselves, what we teach, or how we teach what we teach are the reasons for student failures. Perhaps we need to take a hard look at *individual*-level factors and do what we can to enhance those individual traits that are associated with improved student performance. In addition, health considerations, such as prenatal health care, and the living conditions within the student population are clearly important to the success of students. Perhaps we should offer courses that increase individual motivation and assist students in developing the values needed to succeed in schools. Educational policy in the future will need to be innovative and not bound to assumptions that have been called into question by the extant public policy research in this area over the past thirty years.

NOTES

1. See, for example, John E. Chubb and Terry M. Moe, *Politics, Markets, and America's Schools* (Washington, D.C.: Brookings Institution, 1990).
2. U.S. Department of Education, National Center for Education Statistics, *Digest of Education Statistics* (Washington, D.C.: U.S. Government Printing Office, 1994), p. 8.
3. Ibid., p. 12.
4. Jeffrey R. Henig, *Rethinking School Choice* (Princeton: Princeton University Press), p. 27.
5. Sandia National Laboratories, "Perspectives on Education in America: An Annotated Briefing," *Journal of Educational Research* 86 (1993), pp. 267–270.
6. Ann O'M. Bowman and Richard Kearney, *State and Local Government* (Boston: Houghton Mifflin, 1990), p. 426.
7. Thomas R. Dye, *Politics in States and Communities*, 7th ed. (Englewood Cliffs: Prentice Hall, 1991), p. 419.
8. Ibid., p. 172.
9. Ibid., p. 173.
10. Joseph H. McGivney, "State Educational Governance Patterns," *Educational Administration Quarterly* 20 (Spring 1984), pp. 43–63; Lawrence Iannaccone, *Politics in Education* (New York: Center for Applied Research in Education, 1967).
11. Frederick Wirt, "School Policy Culture and State Decentralization," in *The Politics of Education*, ed. Jay D. Scribner (Chicago: University of Chicago Press, 1977), pp. 186–187.
12. Bowman and Kearney, *State and Local Government*, p. 432.
13. John J. Harrigan, *Politics in States and Communities* (New York: HarperCollins, 1991), p. 391.
14. Ibid.
15. Ibid.
16. Robert B. Hawkins, "Education Reform California Style," *Publius* 14 (Summer 1984), p. 100.
17. Joel Spring, *Conflicts of Interests: The Politics of American Education* (New York: Longman, 1988), pp. 93–124.
18. Ibid., p. 120.
19. Bowman and Kearney, *State and Local Government*, p. 430.
20. Ibid.
21. Ibid.
22. David Savage, "Teaching: The Heart of the Problem," *State Legislatures* 9 (October 1983), pp. 212–224.
23. William E. Blundell, "A Certified Need: Teachers," *Wall Street Journal*, 19 May 1989, p. 1.
24. Michael Rebell and Arthur Block, *Educational Policy Making and the Courts* (Chicago: University of Chicago Press, 1982).
25. *Rodriguez* v. *San Antonio School District*, 411 U.S. 59 (1973).
26. John J. Harrigan, *Politics and Policy in States and Communities* (New York: HarperCollins, 1991), p. 396.
27. Ibid., pp. 395–397.
28. Edward Banfield, *The Unheavenly City* (Boston: Little, Brown, 1970), p. 134.

29. See, for example, Arthur Jensen, "How Much Can We Boost IQ and Scholastic Achievement," *Harvard Educational Review* 39 (Winter 1969), pp. 1–123.

30. See Richard J. Herrnstein and Charles Murray, *The Bell Curve: Intelligence and Class Structure in American Life* (New York: Free Press, 1994), pp. 143–154.

31. Jensen, "How Much Can We Boost IQ."

32. See, for example, James J. Heckman, "Cracked Bell," *Reason* (March 1995), pp. 49–55; and Arthur S. Goldberger and Charles F. Manski, "Review Article: *The Bell Curve* by Herrnstein and Murray," *Journal of Economic Literature* 33 (June 1995), pp. 762–776.

33. See Harrigan, *Politics*, pp. 392–394.

34. National Commission on Excellence in Education, *A Nation at Risk: The Imperative for Educational Reform* (Washington, D.C.: U.S. Government Printing Office, 1983), p. 1.

35. Ibid., pp. 4–5.

36. Theodore Sizer, *Horace's Compromise: The Dilemma of the American High School* (Boston: Houghton Mifflin, 1984).

37. Thomas R. Dye, *Understanding Public Policy*, 7th ed. (Englewood Cliffs; Prentice Hall, 1991), p. 9.

38. James S. Coleman, *Equality of Educational Opportunity* (Washington, D.C.: U.S. Government Printing Office, 1966).

39. Dye, *Understanding Public Policy*, p. 10.

40. Eric Hanushek, "Throwing Money at Schools," *Journal of Policy Analysis and Management* 1, no. 1 (Fall 1981), pp. 19–41; and "The Economics of Schooling: Production and Efficiency in Public Schools," *Journal of Economic Literature* 24 (September 1986), 1141–1177.

41. See Eric Hanushek, "How Business Can Save Education: A State Agenda for Reform" (paper presented at the Heritage Foundation Conference, April 24. 1991.

42. Christopher Jencks et al., *Inequality: A Reassessment of the Effect of Family and Schooling in America* (New York: Basic Books, 1972).

43. Ibid., p. 219.

44. Christopher Jencks, *Who Gets Ahead? The Determinants of Economic Success in America* (New York: Basic Books, 1979).

45. Ibid., p. 230.

46. William Firestone, Susan H. Fuhrman, and Michael W. Kirst, "Implementation Effects of State Education Reform in the 1980s," *NASSP Bulletin* 74 (February 1990), pp. 75–84.

47. Ibid., p. 76.

48. D. Doyle and T. Hartle, *Excellence in Education* (Washington, D.C.: American Enterprise Institute, 1985), p. 18.

49. Firestone, Fuhrman, and Kirst, "Implementation Effects," p. 81.

50. Albert Shanker, "The Pitfalls of Multicultural Education," *The Education Digest* 57 (December 1991), pp. 5–6; see also, David P. Bryden, "It Ain't What They Teach, It's the Way That They Teach It," *Public Interest* 103 (Spring 1991), pp. 38–53.

51. Allan Bloom, *The Closing of the American Mind* (New York: Simon and Schuster, 1987).

52. See Bill Clinton, "Putting People First: A National Economic Strategy for America;" 1992 Democratic Platform, "A New Covenant with the American People;" and "Clinton/Gore on Education," a position paper distributed by the Democratic Party, November 1992.

53. See *1993 Congressional Quarterly Almanac* (Washington, D.C.: Congressional Quarterly Press, 1993), p. 404.

54. See Stephen J. Wayne, G. Calvin Mackenzie, David O'Brien, and Richard L. Cole, *The Politics of American Government* (New York: St. Martin's Press, 1995), p. 625.

55. Linda Darling-Hammond, "National Goals and America 2000: Of Carrots, Sticks, and False Assumptions," *The Education Digest* 57 (December 1991), pp. 25–27.

56. Kevin B. Smith and Kenneth J. Meier, *The Case Against School Choice: Politics, Markets, and Fools* (Armonk: M. E. Sharpe, 1995). See also, Jeffrey R. Henig, *Rethinking School Choice: The Limits of the Market Metaphor* (Princeton: Princeton University Press, 1994). For a contrasting view, see Chubb and Moe, *Politics*.

WELFARE POLICY

"The poor are still there. Two decades after the President of the United States declared an 'unconditional' war on poverty, poverty does not simply continue to exist; worse, we must deal with structures of misery, with a new poverty much more tenacious than the old."

MICHAEL HARRINGTON

"What emerged in the 1960s was an almost unbroken intellectual consensus that the individualist explanation of poverty was altogether outmoded and reactionary."

CHARLES MURRAY

"The best hope is to understand the real causes of poverty and to address them directly."

DAVID T. ELLWOOD

"The poverty of today's underclass differs appreciably from poverty in the past: underclass poverty stems less from the absence of opportunity than from the inability or reluctance to take advantage of opportunity."

LAWRENCE M. MEAD

The problem of poverty is a highly charged issue today, as it has been for the past four hundred years. Even after centuries of public and private attention to this problem, we still do not fully understand the real causes of poverty. These four quotations illustrate various perspectives about the most appropriate welfare policy for the 1990s and beyond. In the 1930s and again in the 1960s, we expanded our social welfare programs to provide for the poor in America. However, these efforts were judged to be a failure by policy analysts in the 1980s. Some argued that the programs actually did harm, developing a **welfare dependency** among the poor.[1] In the 1980s and early 1990s, we went through another round of welfare reform as decision makers tried to develop a better social welfare system. Beginning in 1981, individual states (such as Wisconsin) have tried to develop innovative ways to combine work with welfare. By 1987, twenty-six states had implemented some degree of workfare programs, though many of the "statewide" programs were tested or implemented in only a few counties.[2] Low rates of workfare implementation greatly limited the effectiveness of these programs in reducing welfare caseloads in the 1980s.[3] Thus, it seems that workfare programs are not working as well as anticipated in these states.[4]

In short, there is much disagreement about the causes of poverty and, consequently, much disagreement about the most appropriate welfare policy. **Welfare policy** refers to a variety of social services including income assistance, child and family services, vocational rehabilitation, day care, some aspects of primary health care, and in some states, care for prisoners in penal institutions.[5] In this chapter, we discuss poverty in America, paying particular attention to alternative conceptions of the poverty problem and to the attendant solutions (welfare policies) derived from these alternative conceptions of the problem.

POVERTY IN AMERICA

Defining Poverty

The first step in constructing appropriate policy solutions is to try to understand the scope and nature of this public policy problem. Thus, we need to measure the extent of poverty in the United States, which can be done in several ways. These alternative measures of poverty include both *quantitative* and *qualitative* indices. For example, the official definition of poverty developed by the U.S. Social Security Administration is a quantitative index. An individual or family is defined as "poor" if their income is below a certain level. This level is adjusted for the size of the family and for changes in prices each year. It is usually defined as three times the amount of income needed to eat according to a modest food plan. For 1992, the poverty line for a nonfarm family of four was $14,335. By this definition, about thirty-seven million Americans or 14.5 percent of the U.S. population was classified as poor.[6] Table 11-1 illustrates the amount of poverty in America from 1960 to 1992.

This official definition of poverty has been criticized on many grounds. For example, liberal critics argue that this definition of poverty does not take into account regional differences in the costs of living, climate, or accepted styles of living.[7] Moreover, the "thrifty" food budget on which the poverty level is based is too low for good nutrition and health, and this defintion of poverty does not consider what poor people actually think they need to live. Conservative critics also challenge this definition of poverty on the grounds that it does not consider the value of family assets, such as homes owned, furniture, and automobiles. Moreover, this index contains many individuals who do not consider themselves poor, such as students or the elderly. Finally, this index excludes in-kind benefits given to the poor by governments, such as food stamps, free medical care, public housing, and school lunches.[8]

Other definitions of poverty include those reported by Charles Murray in his book *Losing Ground*.[9] He distinguishes among *official poverty*, which is based on cash income only, *latent poverty*, which is based on the number of people who would be considered poor without the assistance they receive from federal programs, and *net poverty*, which refers to people who remain poor even after counting their in-kind government benefits. Murray considers the latent poverty figure as the most damning statistic because it counts the number of people in our society who are economically dependent and could not exist on their own.[10] Figure 11-1 illustrates his three types of poverty.

TABLE 11–1   Persons Below Poverty Level and Below 125 Percent of Poverty Level, 1960 to 1992

Year	Number Below Poverty Level (millions)				Percent Below Poverty Level				Below 125 Percent of Poverty Level		Average Income Cutoffs for Nonfarm Family of Four[3]	
	All races[1]	White	Black	Hispanic[2]	All races[1]	White	Black	Hispanic[2]	Number (millions)	Percent of total population	At poverty level	At 125 percent of poverty level
1960	39.9	28.3	(NA)	(NA)	22.2	17.8	(NA)	(NA)	54.6	30.4	3,022	3,778
1966	28.5	20.8	8.9	(NA)	14.7	11.3	41.8	(NA)	41.3	21.3	3,317	4,146
1969	24.1	16.7	7.1	(NA)	12.1	9.5	32.2	(NA)	34.7	17.4	3,743	4,679
1970	25.4	17.5	7.5	(NA)	12.6	9.9	33.5	(NA)	35.6	17.6	3,968	4,960
1975	25.9	17.8	7.5	3.0	12.3	9.7	31.3	26.9	37.2	17.6	5,500	6,875
1976	25.0	16.7	7.6	2.8	11.8	9.1	31.1	24.7	35.5	16.7	5,815	7,269
1977	24.7	16.4	7.7	2.7	11.6	8.9	31.3	22.4	35.7	16.7	6,191	7,739
1978	24.5	16.3	7.6	2.6	11.4	8.7	30.6	21.6	34.2	15.8	6,662	8,328
1979[4]	26.1	17.2	8.1	2.9	11.7	9.0	31.0	21.8	36.6	16.4	7,412	9,265
1980	29.3	19.7	8.6	3.5	13.0	10.2	32.5	25.7	40.7	18.1	8,414	10,518
1981	31.8	21.6	9.2	3.7	14.0	11.1	34.2	26.5	43.7	19.3	9,287	11,609
1982	34.4	23.5	9.7	4.3	15.0	12.0	35.6	29.9	46.5	20.3	9,862	12,328
1983[5]	35.3	24.0	9.9	4.6	15.2	12.1	35.7	28.0	47.2	20.3	10,178	12,723
1984	33.7	23.0	9.5	4.8	14.4	11.5	33.8	28.4	45.3	19.4	10,609	13,261
1985	33.1	22.9	8.9	5.2	14.0	11.4	31.3	29.0	44.2	18.7	10,989	13,736
1986	32.4	22.2	9.0	5.1	13.6	11.0	31.1	27.3	43.5	18.2	11,203	14,004
1987[6]	32.2	21.2	9.5	5.4	13.4	10.4	32.4	28.0	43.0	17.8	11,611	14,514
1988	31.7	20.7	9.4	5.4	13.0	10.1	31.3	26.7	42.6	17.5	12,092	15,115
1989	31.5	20.8	9.3	5.4	12.8	10.0	30.7	26.2	42.7	17.3	12,674	15,843
1990	33.6	22.3	9.8	6.0	13.5	10.7	31.9	28.1	44.8	18.0	13,359	16,699
1991	35.7	23.7	10.2	6.3	14.2	11.3	32.7	28.7	47.5	18.9	13,924	17,405
1992	36.9	24.5	10.6	6.7	14.5	11.6	33.3	29.3	49.2	19.4	14,335	17,919

NA Not available. [1]Includes other races not shown separately. [2]Persons of Hispanic origin may be of any race. [3]Beginning 1981, income cutoffs for nonfarm families are applied to all families, both farm and nonfarm. [4]Population controls based on 1980 census. [5]Beginning 1983, data based on revised Hispanic population controls and not directly comparable with prior years. [6]Beginning 1987, data based on revised processing procedures and not directly comparable with prior years.

Source: U.S. Bureau of the Census, *Current Population Reports,* P60-185 (Washington, D.C.: U.S. Government Printing Office, 1994), p. 475.

Another definition of poverty is based on the distribution of wealth in America. This definition of poverty is based on the concept of relative deprivation, or the amount of income inequality in America. Figure 11-2 divides all American families into three groups—from the poorest two-fifths of the population to the wealthiest two-fifths of the population—from 1929 to 1990. From this table we can see that income distribution has changed relatively little over the past sixty years. Moreover, the gap between the richest two-fifths and the poorest two-fifths has widened. Liberal critics of our welfare system point to these data in defining the scope of the poverty problem.

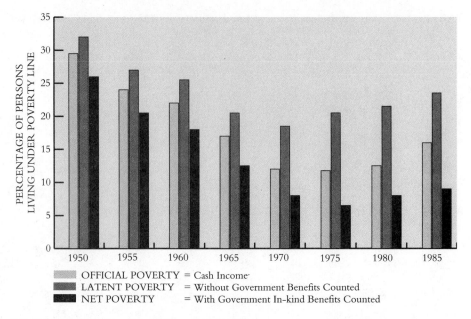

FIGURE 11-1   Three Definitions of Poverty

Source: Figure 4-5 on p. 65: "Three Views of Poverty" from *Losing Ground: American Social Policy 1950–1980* by Charles Murray (New York: BasicBooks, 1984). Copyright © 1984 by Charles Murray. Reprinted by permission of BasicBooks, a division of HarperCollins Publishers, Inc.

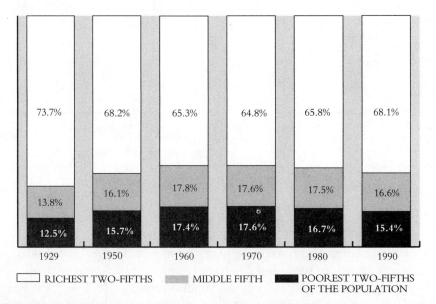

FIGURE 11-2   Trends in Income Inequality, 1929–1990: Percentage of the National Income Earned by Each of Three Income Groups

Sources: For 1970 thru 1988, Bureau of the Census, *Current Population Reports: Trends in Income by Selected Characteristics: 1947 to 1988* (Washington, D.C.: U.S. Government Printing Office, 1990), p. 9. For earlier data, *Statistical Abstract of the United States*, various years. For 1990, *Statisical Abstract: 1992, p. 450*.

Finally, Edward Banfield in *Unheavenly City Revisited* used a qualitative index whereby poverty was described in four stages or levels of poverty. The most severe stage was described as *destitution*, in which there was a lack of sufficient income to prevent starvation. The second level of poverty was described as *want*, or lack of enough income to support essential welfare, including food, clothing, and shelter. The third level of poverty was described as *hardship*, or a lack of sufficient income to prevent acute discomfort, including food, clothing, shelter, health, and transportation needs. The least severe level of poverty was called *relative deprivation*, or a lack of enough income to prevent one from feeling poor. He argued that poverty in America was typified by the third and fourth levels, rather than the first two. Moreover, he argued that poverty by this definition was in decline.[11]

In sum, the extent of poverty in America can be measured in numerous ways. Quite often, the measure of poverty used is related to the orientation of the analyst. That is, liberals like to use the distribution of wealth as their measure, whereas conservatives like to use the official index or qualitative indices, such as Edward Banfield's levels of poverty. Using their respective measures of poverty, liberals conclude that the extent of poverty in America has remained pretty much the same for the past sixty years, whereas conservatives argue that poverty in America has significantly declined over this same period.

Who Are the Poor?

Table 11-2 presents a comparative profile of those considered poor by the U.S. government's definition. Poverty occurs most commonly among female-headed families, blacks, Hispanics, and children. Poverty is also more likely in large families and for families headed by a high school dropout or an unemployed person. The aged in America, on the other hand, experience less poverty than the nonaged. The elderly are generally *not* poor because they typically own their homes and have paid-up mortgages, receive Medicare and Social Security, and have fewer living expenses. Thus, even with reduced incomes, the aged are much less likely to be poor than younger, female-headed families.

An Illustration in Welfare Assistance   An illustration of the dilemma of poverty and the need for welfare assistance is provided by the case of Josie Hill of Larimer County, Colorado. Ms. Hill was married for ten years to her former husband, Tom, a construction worker. Tom lost his job and began to drink heavily. It was not long before Ms. Hill decided to divorce her husband. At the time of the divorce trial her husband was unemployed and, consequently, the judge in the trial awarded no alimony and only minimal child support payments to Ms. Hill. Although she was employed as a hairdresser, she only earned about $400 a month even though she worked full time. In short, she was a member of the "working poor." To meet her living expenses for herself and two young girls, she decided to apply for food stamps. Her rent alone was $550 monthly and food for

182   ANALYZING PUBLIC POLICY CHOICES

TABLE 11–2 People Likely to Be Poor

Characteristics	Percentage Below the Poverty Line, 1990
All Persons	*13.5%*
By race and marital status	
Whites	
All whites	10.7%
Whites living alone or with unrelated individuals	18.6
In married couple families	5.1
In male-headed households, no wife present	9.9
In female-headed households, no husband present	26.8
Blacks	
All blacks	29.3%
Blacks living alone or with unrelated individuals	35.1
In married couple families	12.6
In male-headed households, no wife present	20.4
In female-headed households, no husband present	48.1
Hispanics	
All Hispanics	28.1%
Hispanics living alone or with unrelated individuals	34.3
In married couple families	17.5
In male-headed households, no wife present	19.4
In female-headed households, no husband present	48.3
Children under age 18, by family type and race	
In married couple families	
All children	8.9%
White children	7.9
Black children	16.0
Hispanic children	22.6
In female-headed households, no husband present	
All children	53.4%
White children	45.9
Black children	64.8
Hispanic children	68.5

Source: From *Politics and Policy in States and Communities,* 5th ed. by John J. Harrigan (New York: HarperCollins, 1994) Table 13–2, p. 348. Copyright © 1994 by HarperCollins College Publishers. Reprinted with permission.

herself and her two daughters came to about $450 a month. She moved in with her father-in-law to reduce her living expenses. Yet she still needed some form of welfare assistance to meet her costs of living. With the food stamps, help from her father-in-law, some child support, and her monthly income of $400, she was able to survive, albeit modestly.

After a period of time with this arrangement, the beauty shop where she worked had to close when one of the owners decided to sell the shop. Josie was soon out of work altogether. She then decided to enter another career that would provide more income for herself and her two young daughters; however, she will need some help with retraining for a new career. Finally, she applied to the welfare assistance office for a workfare program that will allow her to enter a new career and, hopefully, get off welfare altogether.

This case illustrates how easily people can become "welfare cases" through little fault of their own. An unemployed husband, a divorce, and a shop closing have conspired to make Josie Hill a welfare recipient. Even though she is a hardworking individual, is motivated to produce more income, and is dedicated to providing a better life for herself and her children, she needs help temporarily.

Some Myths About Poor Americans One of the welfare myths is that welfare recipients are lazy and that they make welfare a way of life. The case above, to the contrary, suggests that welfare recipients are sometimes highly motivated, energetic people who encounter difficulties that make welfare a temporary necessity. Moreover, most welfare recipients are either over 65 or under 18.

A second myth is that welfare recipients are mostly able-bodied men. This is completely wrong. Males generally cannot obtain welfare assistance. Only about twenty-eight states allow Aid to Families with Dependent Children (AFDC) for men. In addition, single males, or couples without children, cannot qualify for AFDC in any of the fifty states.

Another myth is that the poor squander their money. In fact, the poor spend most of their money on food, housing, transportation, and medical expenses, much like the average American. Studies suggest that no more than 5 percent of the poor's money goes toward recreation, compared to about 8 percent for the average American.

Yet another myth states that it is easy to get on welfare. Welfare recipients must fill out long forms to qualify for assistance. In addition, they must submit to home visits, and they must submit to an audit of their income and living expenses.

In addition to these myths, there is the myth that the poor are "welfare cheats." No study has found more than 1 to 3 percent of welfare program funds going to ineligible persons because of fraud. Thus, the claim that welfare recipients are mostly cheats is grossly exaggerated.

Finally, there is the myth that "once on welfare, always on welfare," or that welfare assistance becomes a way of life rather than a second chance. Actually, welfare recipients are a rather fluid group; the average welfare recipient receives AFDC for about twenty months. The poor tend to be those who temporarily need help, much like the case of Josie Hill discussed above.

Although these myths persist in the public's mind, the root causes of poverty are not completely understood. One of the most heavily debated issues is the question of why the poor are poor. It is that question to which we now turn.

ALTERNATIVE PERSPECTIVES ON WELFARE POLICY

Why are the poor poor? As we saw in the earlier discussion, policymakers cannot agree on the scope of poverty in America or on how it should be measured.

Not surprisingly, then, they cannot agree on the root causes of poverty and how to solve the problem. In any case, there are two major perspectives or approaches concerning the causes and cures of poverty.

The Liberal (Structural) View

Liberal theories of poverty argue that poverty is caused by structural or environmental conditions. Thus, poverty results from such conditions as economic stagnation, unemployment, discrimination, or in the most extreme case, "capitalist exploitation."[12] For example, Michael Harrington argues that poverty results from "structural economic change" in that a lack of employment opportunities for the poor were brought about in the last two decades by automation (and the loss of manufacturing jobs) and the importation of cheap (foreign) labor.[13] Marxists, representing a more extreme argument, stress that poverty is maintained by the ruling class to serve their self-interests. Thus, the poor are utilized by the affluent as a source of cheap labor, and welfare policy will be designed to maintain poverty. Welfare programs will not be designed to alleviate poverty or end poverty but to "regulate" the poor.[14] For example, Piven and Cloward argue that the minimal level of welfare in the United States is designed not to help but to maintain the legitimacy and support for the political system. In the absence of welfare aid, the argument goes, the poor would be inclined toward rioting, violence, or revolution. Welfare thus creates a calming effect on the poor, and they are less inclined to threaten the political system.

The Conservative (Individualist) View

The conservative view argues that poverty results from conditions within the individual himself or herself. For example, many economists suggest that the poor are poor because their economic productivity is low. They simply do not have the motivation, intelligence, skills, training, or work habits to sell to employers in a free market. For example, authors Richard Herrnstein and Charles Murray suggest that poverty is related to intelligence or IQ; they argue that 57 percent of chronic welfare recipients are in the bottom 20 percent of intelligence.[15] Others, such as Edward Banfield, argue that a "culture of poverty" exists in which poverty is a way of life that is learned by the poor. This culture of poverty is based on indifference, apathy, irresponsibility, and "present-orientedness," rather than "future-orientedness." These attitudes prevent the poor from taking advantages of opportunities that are available to them.[16]

In its most extreme form, the conservative explanation for poverty is **social Darwinism**. Social Darwinists, such as Herbert Spencer, argue that poverty is a mechanism for the survival of the fittest in the economic arena. Poverty sorts out the weak from the strong. Those who are able to overcome poverty are the strongest members of the society, and this process results in an overall

TABLE 11–3 Overview of Alternative Perspectives on Poverty

	Structural View (Liberal)	Individual View (Conservative)
Views on human nature	1. Optimistic view of human nature 2. The individual is shaped by his or her environment	1. Pessimistic view of human nature 2. The individual is master of his or her fate
Underlying cause of poverty	1. Poverty arises from accidents of birth or social injustice 2. Poverty can be adjusted by a redistribution of resources	1. There is a natural distribution of talents, abilities, faculties 2. Nothing can be done; poverty is inevitable, a state of mind
Measure of poverty	1. Emphasize relative deprivation 2. The level of poverty is quite significant	1. Emphasize absolute deprivation 2. The level of poverty is insignificant and/or declining
Role of government	1. Government should guarantee some level of substantive equality 2. Make people free and equal; equality should be mandated and results achieved	1. Government has no real responsibility or should only provide opportunities for the poor 2. Government should stop at procedural level; results are not to be mandated
Preferred policy solution	1. Government should create jobs and/or train poor 2. Government should provide direct benefits to the poor (income subsidies, services-in-kind)	1. Government should pursue a laissez-faire policy or encourage private sector to create jobs 2. Government should encourage trickle-down economics

healthier society. Some carry this argument to its logical extreme and argue that the government has no role in this area at all. An illustration of this argument is provided in the recent book by Charles Murray.[17] In his book, he argues that the present welfare system itself is to blame for poverty. That is, the welfare system of the last thirty years encouraged the view that the individual was *blameless* for his or her condition of poverty.[18] Although Murray's thesis has been criticized on a number of grounds, it has been thought-provoking on the subject of welfare.[19]

Table 11-3 illustrates the liberal and the conservative views on poverty.

INTERGOVERNMENTAL ROLES IN WELFARE POLICY

The liberal and conservative perspectives on welfare have influenced the evolution of welfare policy in the United States over the past two hundred years. At first, welfare policy was pretty much the domain of state and local governments. However, after the depression of the 1930s, all three levels of government became involved in the delivery of our welfare system. Welfare policy today is truly intergovernmental in nature. In the following sections, we discuss the role of each level of government.

The Federal Role

The federal government is involved in the welfare system in several distinct ways. First, through intergovernmental grants-in-aid, the federal government provides financial support to the states for a variety of welfare programs. These programs include, for example, Aid to Families with Dependent Children (AFDC) and unemployment compensation. Second, the federal government establishes minimum payment levels for the welfare programs that are administered by the states. In addition, the federal government decides which poverty programs will be tackled and what kinds of programs will be developed to tackle them. Finally, the federal government operates a number of programs, such as Medicare, that are run exclusively by the federal government.[20]

State Roles

The states are left to implement many of the welfare policies that are set by the federal government. For example, the state welfare departments oversee the implementation of the AFDC program, including drawing up the rules and regulations for eligibility. State legislatures are also involved in that they supplement the minimum payment levels for AFDC. This causes some states to pay more for AFDC benefits than other states. In addition, the amount of AFDC benefits paid to individuals is very much a function of the level of state affluence. Figure 11-3 shows the relationship between state affluence and AFDC benefits.

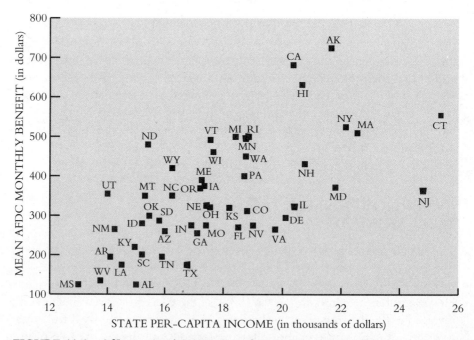

FIGURE 11-3   Affluence and AFDC Benefit Levels by State, 1990

Source: Bureau of the Census, *Statistical Abstract of the United States: 1992* (Washington, D.C.: U.S. Government Printing Office, 1992), pp. 371, 439.

States also provide supplemental welfare assistance through their general assistance programs, which is assistance given to needy individuals who do not qualify for categorical assistance (meaning categories including the aged, the blind, the disabled, or AFDC). States also maintain institutions to care for individuals who are so destitute, alone, or ill that financial assistance alone cannot help. Such institutions include state orphanages, homes for the aged, and homes for the mentally ill.[21]

Local Roles

Local welfare departments are heavily involved in the administration of various welfare programs, such as AFDC. Local welfare officials determine eligibility of the recipients and what level of benefits the applicant will receive. Local officials also try to find jobs for welfare recipients through the Work Incentive (WIN) program and help with enforcement of child support payments.[22]

THE EVOLUTION OF WELFARE POLICY

In the following discussion of welfare policy in America, we see how these alternative perspectives on poverty were the basis for welfare policies in different eras. We began our welfare policies with the individualist assumptions that gave rise to a more austere policy in the early history of our country. Then, beginning in the 1930s and continuing through the 1970s, the structuralist assumptions guided our welfare policies. Most recently, we seem to have reached somewhat of a consensus that combines both liberal and conservative assumptions about poverty in America.

The Elizabethan Poor Laws

The first recognizable welfare policy may be traced back to the Poor Relief Act of 1601 established by the English Parliament. Prior to the 1930s, this Poor Relief Act was a model for American welfare policy. This early act tended to view poverty as the product of moral or character deficiencies in individuals. Care for destitute persons was to be minimal to discourage all but the most desperate of the poor from seeking aid. It differentiated between the "worthy poor" (including widows, the aged, orphans, and the handicapped) and the "able-bodied poor" (including the unemployed). The former were sent to so-called poor-houses, whereas the latter were sent to county workhouses. Whatever relief was provided by the public could never exceed the value of the income of the lowest paid person in the community who was not on relief. Poor rolls were made public, and relief was provided only if no living relative could be legally required to support a destitute member of their family. Under Elizabethan law, the care of the poor was the responsibility of the local government rather than the state government. Residency requirements were established for welfare care so that local governments could make certain that they were not caring for the poor of other communities. Support was limited to those who had been born in the area or who had lived there for some time.[23]

The Political Machine

From 1870 to 1920, a number of institutions provided what was, in effect, welfare. The political machine, for example, provided baskets of food, bushels of coal, small loans, jobs, and other favors to those who supported the machine. The political machine essentially traded votes for political favoritism and provided a welfare function for the newly arrived immigrants to the United States in this period.

In addition, private philanthropers, such as the Rockefeller family, provided funds for the poor. State almshouses were set up as well. In short, this period in welfare assistance relied on political machines and private philanthropy to take care of the poor in the United States.

The Great Depression of 1929

The Great Depression brought about significant changes in attitudes toward public welfare and in the policies and administration of welfare programs. No longer were many people willing to believe that poverty was a product of the individual's moral or character faults. Millions who had previously considered welfare recipients to be unworthy of public concern now joined in the breadlines themselves. One out of four Americans was unemployed, and one out of six was receiving some sort of welfare assistance. This widespread experience with poverty changed public attitudes toward welfare and lead to a change away from an Elizabethan-based policy in the United States. In short, welfare was now considered to be a societal and governmental concern, rather than an individual one.

In 1935, the Social Security Act was passed, which provided the basic framework for welfare policies for all levels of government. The act placed great reliance on a program of social insurance as well as a public assistance program.[24]

Welfare Reforms, 1960–1990

The 1960s: The Great Society and the War on Poverty   President Lyndon Johnson (1963–1969) undertook a war on poverty itself as his Great Society expanded social service programs. The cornerstone of his program was the Economic Opportunity Act of 1965. This act created the Office of Economic Opportunity to conduct experiments in social services and to coordinate all the poverty programs of the agencies in the federal government. In addition, new programs were begun, such as Medicare, Medicaid, and legal services. In 1966, the Model Cities program was created to target federal aid in specific neighborhoods of 150 selected major cities. Community Action Agencies (CAA) were set up in all communities that received federal funds so that people affected by the programs could participate in designing program plans. These efforts stimulated community organizing efforts in poor neighborhoods and attempted to develop community leadership in black neighborhoods, provided jobs for poor and middle-class blacks, and organized residents of those neighborhoods to pressure local governments for better services.

The social programs of the War on Poverty came under rather severe criticism in the 1980s as conservative scholars suggested that these programs did not end poverty, may have brought about the urban riots of the late 1960s, and developed welfare dependency among the poor.[25]

The 1970s: Income Maintenance President Nixon proposed the Family Assistance Plan (FAP), which featured a federally funded minimum-income guarantee to all Americans. A four-person family with no other income would receive $1,600. For each dollar earned beyond this amount, the government's payment would decrease by fifty cents. When the family's income reached $3,920, the government's benefits would be phased out completely. However, this proposal failed for a number of reasons. First, liberals feared that the FAP would eliminate other programs, such as food stamps. Conservatives felt that FAP would reward poor families for not working. Moreover, the majority of public opinion was opposed to the FAP and the idea of a guaranteed minimum income. Finally, Nixon himself grew cool to the idea when he could not build necessary public support.

President Carter tried to resurrect the idea in the late 1970s by proposing a work benefit and income support program to replace the existing AFDC, SSI, and food stamp programs.[26] Under his plan, a family of four would receive a cash payment of $2,300 as long as its earned income was less than $3,800. For each dollar earned above that amount, the cash supplement would be reduced by fifty cents until it was completely phased out at $8,400. Thus, every four-person family in the country would be guaranteed a minimum income of $8,400. Carter's proposal faced the same kind of opposition as President Nixon's plan.

The 1980s: The Reagan Revolution Following the failure of guaranteed income plans in the 1970s, welfare reform in the 1980s shifted toward reducing the welfare rolls and making the welfare recipients work to earn their grants. President Reagan's approach was to force welfare recipients into the job market by reducing expenditures for most social welfare programs and by tightening up eligibility requirements for the programs.[27]

In 1988, Congress passed the Family Support Act, which had four main components:

1. *The JOBS program.* To qualify for federal AFDC grants, all states will be required by 1995 to enroll at least 20 percent of their AFDC cases into a program that will develop an employability plan for each participant.

2. *Child support enforcement.* States are now required to provide for automatic withholding of court-ordered child support payments from the wages of noncustodial parents whose children are on AFDC. States are also required to set up regular reviews of child support agreements in AFDC cases, so that the payments can be adjusted upward with inflation and the changing circumstances of the noncustodial parent.

3. *Transitional benefits.* Both Medicaid and child-care benefits will be provided while the participant is in the JOBS program and for a transitional period of up to a year when the participant leaves the JOBS program and enters the workforce.

4. *Special provisions for minor parents.* Because some have argued that traditional AFDC allows a teenage mother to set up a household of her own once her child was born and to raise that child in circumstances that were believed to be dysfunctional, the new law permits states to allow minors to live with their parents and still qualify for AFDC benefits.

This new workfare program is being implemented during the 1990s, and it will be closely observed to see whether it reduces welfare expenditures and helps AFDC recipients become financially independent.

STRUCTURES OF WELFARE POLICY

The Social Security Act of 1935 (and subsequent amendments) constitutes the basic structure of welfare policy in America at both national and state levels.[28] This act promotes two structures of relief for the poor. The first type is more appropriately called **social insurance**, because it is not really based on need. It is provided to everyone who qualifies, regardless of need. It was originally set up to prevent individuals from being poor. The second type is appropriately called **welfare assistance**, because it is need-based. Both of these forms of assistance are described below.

Preventive Strategy: Social Insurance

Social insurance includes the following types of assistance:

1. Old Age Survivors Disability and Health Insurance (OASDHI) is given to retired people and/or the survivors of workers who died. This is commonly known as Social Security. It is available to people over 65 who have contributed to the system and to all those over 72, regardless of their contributions and income. It is an entitlement program in that recipients have a vested right to benefits, usually because of their contributions to the system through compulsory payroll taxes authorized by the Federal Insurance Contributions Act (FICA).

2. Medicare is given to the aged in all income categories after age 65.

3. Unemployment compensation is given to the temporarily unemployed.

Reliance on funding benefits from current contributors to the program means that the Social Security system represents income transfers from younger, employed members of society to the elderly and disabled, whether rich or poor. In 1984, Congress increased program revenues by raising FICA payroll taxes and included federal employees as contributors. This insured the fiscal solvency of Social Security through the year 2010.[29]

Alleviative Strategy: Welfare Assistance

In contrast to the entitlement programs above, welfare is organized as a public charity. The poor have no entitlement to public assistance; rather, access to benefits is based on qualifications and specific needs of the recipients. Welfare requires the application of a means test, in which the poor must prove that they have no income or that their income is insufficient to meet their needs. Welfare assistance includes the following types of programs, which were a part of the Social Security Act of 1935 and the Great Society programs of the 1960s:

1. Aid to Families with Dependent Children (AFDC) is given to the non-working poor who have children. This includes mostly single, divorced, or widowed mothers and their children.
2. Food stamps are given to the bottom 40 percent of income recipients, which includes both the working and nonworking poor.
3. Supplemental Security Income (SSI) is given to the aged, the blind, and the disabled.
4. General public assistance (excluding AFDC and SSI) is given to mostly destitute and homeless people who do not qualify for AFDC, SSI, or unemployment compensation.
5. In-kind assistance includes housing assistance, Medicaid and other health programs, legal services, employment programs, and other social services, such as child care and family planning.

Welfare recipients can receive assistance from more than one source. For example, a working mother (without a husband) could receive AFDC, food stamps, and in-kind assistance, such as day care for her children. Table 11-4 illustrates the major federal social welfare programs as of 1992.

What difference have these various programs of welfare made on the poor? Has poverty been reduced? Have the poor benefited from the various welfare programs of the 1930s and the 1960s? These questions have been put to the test by various policy analysts over the past three decades.

EVALUATING THE IMPACT OF SOCIAL WELFARE PROGRAMS

What has been the effect of our various welfare programs over the past sixty years? Broadly speaking, there are two types of recent research on the welfare

TABLE 11–4   Major Federal Social Welfare Programs

Social Insurance Programs	Beneficiaries (millions)
Social Security	
Total	39.8
Retirement	28.4
Survivors	7.1
Disabled	4.3
Unemployment Compensation	
Total	8.6

Public Assistance Programs	Beneficiaries (millions)
Cash Aid	
AFDC	12.1
SSI	4.9
Needy veterans	1.1
General assistance	1.2
Income tax credit	33.7
Medical Care	
Medicaid	25.3
Veterans	0.6
Indians	1.1
Community health centers	5.3
Food Benefits	
Food stamps	21.5
School lunches	11.6
Women, infants, children	4.5
Nutrition program	3.5
Housing Benefits	
Total	3.9
Education Aid	
Stafford Loans	3.6
Pell Grants	3.4
Head Start	0.5
Work study	0.8
Educational opportunity grants	0.6
Job Training	
Total	1.5
Energy Assistance	
Total	5.8

Source: U.S. Bureau of the Census, *Statistical Abstract of the United States, 1992* (Washington, D.C.: U.S. Government Printing Office, 1992), pp. 356, 361.

system by researchers in think tanks, other research organizations, universities, and government policy analysts. Policy analysts recognize that the welfare programs of the past have failed to end poverty, but some credit the social programs of the 1960s with some important successes. At best, we can say that it has been a record with mixed success. For example, John Donovan argues that the Great Society programs created hopes for winning the War on Poverty without developing and adequately supporting a program for that purpose.[30] Others, such as Senator Daniel P. Moynihan, argue that there were at least four distinct (and incompatible) "understandings" of what community action programs intended. The Bureau of the Budget (now OMB) concept was concerned with efficiency and administrative coordination. Others, such as community organizers, were concerned with conflict and empowering the poor so that they could push for additional benefits. Still others were imbued with youthful idealism about "doing good" for the poor, much like the Peace Corps concept abroad. Finally, others were concerned with political effectiveness. Essentially, argues Moynihan, the U.S. government did not know what it was doing. As a result, those involved in community action programs (especially blacks and middle-class whites) were left confused at best or frustrated and angry at worst.[31]

More recent critics of the social programs of the 1960s include Edward Banfield and Charles Murray. Banfield argues that the social programs of the 1960s may have promoted (rather than helped) urban decline by encouraging dispersion of the urban population to the suburbs by subsidized housing and FHA and VA loans.[32] Similarly Murray argues that the government welfare programs of the period 1950–1980 have only made problems worse by sapping poor people of their initiative and making them dependent on the welfare system.[33]

On the other hand, some argue that the welfare programs of the 1960s produced some positive benefits for the poor. Levitan and Taggart, for example, argue that the Great Society did indeed succeed.[34] Moreover, John Schwarz argues that the welfare programs of the last twenty years had some important successes.[35] For the elderly, the welfare programs seemed to have made a positive difference. For others, such as women, blacks, Hispanics, and children, the various programs do not seemed to have worked well.

In sum, the most positive view of the Great Society programs suggests several advantages:

1. The welfare programs of the 1960s stimulated the states and cities to spend considerable amounts of money on urban problems that they would not have spent without these programs, such as Model Cities and Community Action Programs (CAP).
2. These programs provided some badly needed services with some positive results in income redistribution and increases in educational attainments.
3. These programs provided paths to future funds by establishing relationships among federal, state, and local governments.
4. These programs stimulated the local economy through jobs and money.
5. These programs provided a mechanism for the federal government to deal with what are national problems that cannot be adequately dealt with at the local level, such as poverty and transportation.

Passage of the Family Support Act of 1988 has brought welfare reform to the attention of state and local policymakers once again. Evaluations of the effects of this act should provide important new information about how our current welfare programs are working.

Since 1981, the states have begun to experiment with workfare programs that offer job training with child care and transportation or opportunities to return to school. By 1988, however, fewer than 5 percent of welfare recipients were participating in workfare programs.[36] At the present time, the evidence on workfare is that "there is no clear-cut agreement on what types of work-welfare programs work best."[37]

Some evidence suggests that because of the way Aid to Families with Dependent Children (AFDC) has been implemented it has had a deleterious effect on family structure by discouraging first marriages, encouraging marital breakup, and delaying remarriage.[38] In summary, we know that some welfare programs worked and some did not.[39]

WELFARE POLICY FOR THE 1990s

America's welfare system needs to be reformed. However, liberals and conservatives can agree on little else. Most agree that some have become dependent on welfare.[40] Both agree that this state of welfare dependency must (and can) be broken by getting these individuals into the workforce. Conservatives would correct the long-term dependence on welfare by abolishing the welfare system or by replacing it with **workfare**. For them, some form of transitional aid (such as education, job training, continued health care, and day care for children) is necessary so that these individuals can return to the workplace. Liberals, on the other hand, want to make major investments in people, to break down discriminatory barriers, to humanize the welfare system, to offer government jobs, and to reform the economy.[41]

The Clinton plan incorporates elements of both liberal and conservative views. The Clinton administration promises to "scrap the current welfare system and make welfare a second chance, not a way of life."[42] His plan calls for increased support for education, child care, and an expansion of the earned income tax credit as well as enforcement of child support obligations for deadbeat parents.[43] The underlying purpose of Clinton's proposal is to transform welfare from a permanent way of life into a temporary safety net. His plan is expected to offer more education, training, and social services to beneficiaries to prepare them for entry into the workforce, while at the same time imposing a two-year limit on welfare payments to the most able-bodied recipients of AFDC. As part of his plan, Clinton succeeded in 1993 in pushing through an increase in the earned income tax credit for low-income families.[44]

Regardless of the particular approach adopted, some argue that we could go a long way toward improving the plight of the poor by creating a system that encourages and rewards work and responsibility. What is needed in welfare reform is a program that reinforces (rather than dissolves) basic values about independence, work, family, merit, and community. Recently, a number of authors have begun to question whether our uncritical acceptance of the structural basis of poverty and solutions based on high welfare expenditures and welfare dependency among the poor is the best long-run approach. Charles Murray, for example, argues that "The proposed program . . . consists of scrapping the entire welfare and income-support structure for working-aged persons, including AFDC, Medicaid, Food Stamps, Unemployment Insurance, Worker's Compensation, subsidized housing, disability insurance, and the rest. It would leave the working-aged person with no recourse whatsoever except the job market, family members, friends, and public or private locally funded services."[45]

Others, such as David Ellwood, are less draconian in their preferred approaches. Toward the same end, he recommends that we undertake five significant reforms: (1) ensure that everyone has medical attention; (2) make work pay so that working families are not poor by raising the minimum wage; (3) adopt a uniform child support assurance system; (4) convert welfare into a transitional system designed to provide serious but short-term financial, educational, and social support for people who are trying to cope with a temporary setback; and (5) provide minimum-wage jobs to persons who have exhausted their transitional support.[46]

Finally, both liberals and conservatives agree that the states should be free to experiment and develop innovative responses to welfare reform. One of the major objectives for welfare policy in the 1990s will be to fine-tune the 1988 reforms as states encounter problems trying to implement the legislation's child support and work components.[47] Most agree that child support programs need strengthening along the lines of increasing the rate of child support awards, increasing payment levels, and enforcing payments.[48]

Whatever welfare policy ultimately emerges in the 1990s, it will be a better policy if it recognizes the validity of both structural (liberal) and individualist (conservative) explanations. That is, "liberals need to show why poor people are blameless, therefore still deserving; conservatives need to show how the poor are competent and why they need to be held accountable, in spite of dysfunction."[49] There will always be those who need help because of conditions beyond their immediate control; however, we must also recognize that a workable welfare system must be one that reinforces a sense of individual responsibility and one that respects basic values about independence, work, merit, the importance of keeping families together, and community. A synthesis of both liberal and conservative thought (combined with better policy analysis) in this area could provide the basis for powerful new doctrines of social welfare policy that could grapple with poverty more successfully than in the past.

NOTES

1. Lawrence M. Mead, "The New Politics of the New Poverty," *The Public Interest* 103 (Spring 1991), pp. 3–20.
2. Bradley R. Schiller and C. Nielson Brasher, "Workfare in the 1980s: Successes and Limits," *Policy Studies Review* 9 (Summer 1990), pp. 665–680.
3. Ibid., p. 676.

4. Mary Bryna Sanger, "The Inherent Contradiction of Welfare Reform," *Policy Studies Journal* 18 (Spring 1990), pp. 663–680.

5. Robert Albritton, "Social Services: Welfare and Health," in *Politics in the American States*, ed. Virginia Gray, Herbert Jacob, and Robert Albritton (Glenview, IL: Scott, Foresman/Little, Brown, 1990), p. 411.

6. See U.S. Department of Commerce, Bureau of the Census, *Statistical Abstract: 1994* (Washington, D.C.: U.S. Government Printing Office, 1994), p. 475; see also Stephen J. Wayne, G. Calvin Mackenzie, David O'Brien, and Richard L. Cole, *The Politics of American Government* (New York: St. Martin's Press, 1995), p. 625.

7. Thomas R. Dye, *Understanding Public Policy*, 7th ed. (Englewood Cliffs, NJ: Prentice-Hall, 1991), p. 110.

8. Ibid., p. 111.

9. Charles Murray, *Losing Ground* (New York: Basic Books, 1984).

10. Ibid.

11. Edward C. Banfield, *The Unheavenly City Revisited* (Prospect Heights, IL: Waveland Press, 1990).

12. Paul E. Peterson, "The Urban Underclass and the Poverty Paradox," *Political Science Quarterly* 106 (Winter 1991–1992), pp. 617–637.

13. Michael Harrington, *The New American Poverty* (New York: Viking Penguin, 1985).

14. Frances Fox Piven and Richard A. Cloward, *Regulating the Poor: The Functions of Public Welfare* (New York: Vintage Books, 1971).

15. See Richard J. Herrnstein and Charles Murray, *The Bell Curve: Intelligence and Class Structure in American Life* (New York: Free Press, 1994), pp. 127–142.

16. Banfield, *Unheavenly City*; and Mead, "New Politics."

17. Murray, *Losing Ground*.

18. Ibid.

19. Sheldon Danzinger and Peter Gottschalk, "The Poverty of Losing Ground," *Challenge* 28 (May–June 1985), pp. 32–38; and David Ellwood and Lawrence H. Summers, "Is Welfare Really the Problem?" *Public Interest* 83 (Spring 1986), pp. 57–78.

20. John J. Harrigan, *Politics and Policy in States and Communities* (New York: HarperCollins Publishers, 1991), pp. 358–359.

21. Ibid.

22. Ibid., p. 359.

23. Dye, *Understanding Public Policy*, p. 127.

24. Ibid., p. 468.

25. See, for example, Stuart Butler and Anne Kondratas, *Out of the Poverty Trap: A Conservative Strategy* (New York: Free Press, 1987); and Murray, *Losing Ground*.

26. See President Carter's message in the *New York Times* (7 August 1977), pp. 1, 40.

27. Harrigan, *Politics and Policy*, p. 376.

28. Albritton, "Social Services," p. 412.

29. Ibid., p. 413.

30. John C. Donovan, *The Politics of Poverty* (New York: Pegasus, 1967).

31. Daniel P. Moynihan, *Maximum Feasible Misunderstanding* (New York: Free Press, 1970).

32. Banfield, *Unheavenly City*.

33. Murray, *Losing Ground*.

34. Sar A. Levitan and Robert Taggart, "Great Society Did Succeed," *Political Science Quarterly* 91 (Winter 1976–1977), pp. 601–618.

35. John E. Schwarz, *America's Hidden Success: A Reassessment of Twenty Years of Public Policy* (New York: W. W. Norton, 1983), esp. pp. 57–59.

36. Thomas R. Dye, *Politics in States and Communities* (Englewood Cliffs, NJ: Prentice-Hall, 1991), p. 479.

37. Ibid., p. 32.

38. Robert Moffitt, "Welfare Reform in the 1990s: The Research View," *Intergovernmental Perspective* 17 (Spring 1991), pp. 31–33.

39. Sheldon H. Danzinger and Daniel H. Weinberg, *Fighting Poverty: What Works and What Doesn't* (Cambridge, MA: Harvard University Press, 1986).

40. Mead, "New Politics," pp. 3–20.

41. David T. Ellwood, *Poor Support* (New York: Basic Books, 1989), p. 236.

42. Bill Clinton and Al Gore, *Putting People First: A National Economic Strategy for America* (New York: Times Books, 1992), p. 12.

43. Ibid., pp. 12–13.

44. See *1993 Congressional Quarterly Almanac* (Washington, D.C.: Congressional Quarterly Press, 1993), p. 373.

45. Murray, *Losing Ground*, pp. 227–228.

46. Ellwood, *Poor Support*, p. 238.

47. Robert Reischauer, "The Welfare Reform Legislation: Directions for the Future," in *Welfare Policy for the 1990s*, ed. Phoebe H. Cottingham and David T. Ellwood (Cambridge, MA: Harvard University Press, 1989).

48. Moffitt, "Welfare Reform," p. 33.

49. Mead, "New Politics," p. 19.

CHAPTER TWELVE

CRIME POLICY

"The most important consequences of public policy toward crime may be their tutelary, not their direct, effects. How we spend money on schools, job training, or welfare programs may be less important than the message accompanying such expenditures: Do we appear to be rewarding the acceptance or the rejection of personal responsibility?"

JAMES Q. WILSON AND
RICHARD HERRNSTEIN

"We need a fundamental change of direction, towards proven programs and policies that work to reduce both imprisonment and crime."

MARC MAUER

"We've got to stop jailing and start rehabilitating. . . . We can build all the jails we think we need and slam the doors down on thousands of people, but it won't make a bit of difference until we address the fundamental causes of crime."

REP. JOHN CONYERS, DEMOCRAT
FROM MICHIGAN

"We need to put more police on the streets of our cities and more criminals behind bars."

CANDIDATE BILL CLINTON

The United States is often characterized as "the most violent and crime-ridden society in the industrialized world."[1] With more than two million people behind bars in a jail, police station, or penitentiary, the United States incarcerates a bigger share of its population than any other nation. This high incarceration rate results from increasingly harsh public attitudes toward dealing with lawbreakers. Yet, we still do not know precisely what causes criminal behavior. We have been debating alternative explanations of crime and their attendant solutions (e.g., imprisonment or rehabilitation) for many years, but even in the 1990s we are still searching for proven programs and policies that work.

In this chapter, we discuss the scope and nature of crime in the United States, alternative perspectives on crime, and an evaluation of these prescriptions for reducing crime rates. To begin our discussion, we establish some important definitions about what we mean by crime.

WHAT IS CRIME?

Crime is "all behaviors and acts for which a society provides formally sanctioned punishment."[2] In this chapter we are principally concerned with **crimes against property** and **crimes against persons**, rather than **victimless** crimes. Crimes against *property* include larceny of $50 or more, burglary, and auto theft. Crimes against *persons* include homicide, assault, robbery, and rape. Finally, *victimless* crimes include public drunkenness, gambling, prostitution, obscenity, and drug addiction.

In the United States, what is criminal is specified in the written law, although what is included in the definition of crime varies among federal, state, and local jurisdictions.[3] Criminologists devote a great deal of attention to defining crime because the definitional process is the first step toward the goal of attaining accurate crime statistics. Some types of crimes, such as murder, robbery, and burglary, have been defined as crimes for centuries, whereas other types of conduct have not been viewed as crimes. As social values change, society has increasingly codified some conduct as criminal (e.g., the criminalization of drunk driving), while decriminalizing other conduct (e.g., homosexuality). Table 12-1 lists several types of crimes and their definitions.

How much crime is there? According to the National Crime Victimization Survey (NCVS), in 1992 approximately 33.6 million "victimizations," or incidents of crime, occurred in the United States. This represents a noticeable drop from the estimated 41.4 million victimizations in 1981, but the overall decline in

TABLE 12–1 Definitions of Various Crimes

Crime	Definition
Homicide	Causing the death of another person without legal justification or excuse including *Uniform Crime Report* crimes of murder and nonnegligent manslaughter and negligent manslaughter.
Rape	Unlawful sexual intercourse with a female, by force or without legal or factual consent.
Robbery	The unlawful taking or attempted taking of property that is in the immediate possession of another, by force or threat of force.
Assault	Unlawful intentional inflicting, or attempted inflicting, or injury upon the person of another.
Burglary	Unlawful entry of any fixed structure, vehicle, or vessel used for regular residence, industry, or business, with or without force, with the intent to commit a felony or larceny.
Larceny	Unlawful taking or attempted taking of property other than a motor vehicle from the possession of another, by stealth, without force and without deceit, with intent to permanently deprive the owner of the property.
Arson	The intentional damaging or destruction or attempted damaging or destruction by means of fire or explosion of property without the consent of the owner, or of one's own property or that of another by fire or explosives with or without the intent to defraud.
Vandalism	Destroying or damaging, or attempting to destroy or damage, the property of another without his or her consent, or public property, except by burning, which is arson.

Source: Bureau of Justice Statistics, *Dictionary of Criminal Justice Data Terminology*, 2d ed. (Washington, D.C.: U.S. Government Printing Office, 1981).

crime masks annual fluctuations, differing trends by type of crime, and rising crime rates against certain segments of the population. The violent crime rate rose to an all-time high of 35.3 per 1,000 persons in 1981, after which it dropped, but began climbing again after 1989 until it reached 32.1 per 1,000 persons in 1992 (the latest year for which data are available). Personal theft victimization peaked in 1974 (95.1 thefts per 1,000 persons), remained high through 1978, declined significantly through 1985, after which it remained steady until significant drops in both 1991 and 1992. The personal theft victimization rate was a record low of 59.2 per 1,000 persons in 1992. Likewise, total household crime rates (burglary, larceny, and motor vehicle theft) dropped 30 percent from 1973 to 1992, reaching the level of 152 crimes per 1,000 households, the lowest rate recorded in the twenty-year history of the survey. But, the young, central city residents and blacks have increasingly been the victims of crime. For example, persons between 16 and 19 years of age were victims of rape, robbery, or assault at a rate of 68 per 1,000 persons in 1981. By 1992, that rate was almost 78 per 1,000 persons.[4]

The decline in crime rates is at odds with public perceptions about crime, and in making crime policy, these perceptions may be more important than reality. Although crime is seldom seen as the most important problem facing the country, depending on the wording of the question, it is often reported in public opinion polls to be among the most serious problems. Compounding these perceptions is a lack of confidence in the police as a source of protection from violent crime. A 1993 Gallup poll reported that 54 percent of the respondents had "not very much" or "no" confidence that the police could protect them from violent crime.[5] Thus, whether the data show that aggregate crime rates are rising or falling, if a person perceives that he or she could be a victim of a crime and that those in society who are charged with offering protection are incapable of doing so, crime becomes a salient public policy issue. Perhaps the best indicator of the public's feelings is its expression of willingness to spend money to address the problem. Since 1973, national public opinion polls consistently found at least 63 percent of the population express the opinion that as a nation we are spending "too little" to "halt the rising crime rate."[6]

Comparatively, crime rates are higher in the United States than any other advanced industrial democracy. Table 12-2 provides some comparative crime data for several European and Latin American countries. It shows that the United States leads many countries of the world in homicides, rape, and robbery for the year 1990. These statistics have led to the view that "crime in the United States is more common than in any other advanced industrial nation of the world."[7] In 1990 alone, the United States had nine times more homicides, 31 times more rapes, and over 200 times more robberies than Japan. New York City alone has twice as many homicides as Japan. In 1990, there were 277 robberies per 100,000 people in the United States compared with 64.2 in Italy and 1.3 in Japan. These figures are staggering and have led to greater efforts by all three levels of government to combat crime.

TABLE 12–2   Crime Rates in Selected Countries, 1990

Country	Number of Crimes per 100,000 Population				
	Homicide	*Rape*	*Robbery*	*Burglary*	*Auto Theft*
United States	9.4	41.2	277.0	1235.9	657.8
Austria	2.3	7.0	51.9	1151.6	26.7
Belgium	2.2	6.1	79.8	NA	281.0
Canada	5.6	NA	98.1	1331.7	382.6
Denmark	4.5	9.4	41.4	2382.9	575.9
Finland	.6	7.6	55.5	1436.6	364.8
France	4.5	8.1	106.3	711.9	519.6
Italy	6.4	NA	64.2	NA	546.0
Japan	1.0	1.3	1.3	184.3	27.6
Norway	2.6	9.0	23.7	116.4	608.7
Spain	2.4	4.5	270.6	1211.5	342.8
Sweden	7.0	16.4	69.4	1801.7	879.0
USSR	8.7	7.8	43.9	NA	46.7

NA = Not available.

Source: Interpol, *International Crime Statistics*, Vols. 1989–1990.

INTERGOVERNMENTAL ROLES IN CRIME POLICY

In 1990, national, state, and local police and correctional agencies had 1.6 million full-time employees, and expenditures for criminal justice exceeded 47 billion dollars.[8] Every level of government is involved even though primary responsibility for dealing with crime rests with state and local authorities.

The Federal Role

The Federal Bureau of Investigation (FBI) in the Department of Justice was created in the 1920s and charged with the enforcement of federal laws. The federal government employs fewer than 50,000 persons in all law enforcement activities. Federal crimes, such as treason, kidnapping, and counterfeiting are investigated by the FBI and processed through the federal courts and federal correctional facilities. Federal prisons contain about 26,000 inmates, compared with over 400,000 in state prisons.

In addition, the national government provides certain forms of direct financial assistance to states and localities. One of the biggest federal programs was the Law Enforcement Assistance Administration (LEAA). LEAA (now defunct) transferred millions of dollars to state and local police agencies during the 1970s for equipment and training. Other national efforts to assist states and cities include the Juvenile Delinquency Prevention and Control Act of 1968, the Organized Crime Control Act of 1970, and the Comprehensive

Crime Control Act of 1984. The latter provided limited funding for law enforcement projects, prison construction, and state victim-compensation programs.[9]

The State Role

The state attorney general formally heads the law enforcement function in most states. In addition, the state highway patrol and special state law enforcement are also important actors in law enforcement. The state courts decide the innocence or guilt of defendants brought before them. State prisons incarcerate those convicted of serious crimes and, in many instances, states carry out the death penalty. Several states voluntarily abolished capital punishment in the 1960s and the 1970s, but the majority of states rewrote their statutes to allow the death penalty in the last two decades after the Supreme Court struck down state and federal capital punishment laws that permitted wide discretion in the application of the death penalty. Thirty-seven states have death penalty laws in place today. Table 12-3 identifies those states that permit capital punishment. A total of 3,909 people have been executed since 1930, including 50 since 1977. In 1994, 2,848 inmates were on death row. Texas had 386 inmates awaiting execution, California had 383, Florida had 330, Pennsylvania had 170, and Illinois had 161.[10]

The Local Role

The local government is perhaps the most heavily involved in criminal justice policy. It includes sheriffs, city police, and other law enforcement officials who arrest those believed to be perpetrators of crimes or civil violations. It also includes county and district attorneys who prosecute those charged with crimes. Local courts decide the guilt or innocence of those charged with crimes, and jails are used to incarcerate those convicted of crimes or civil violations.

Municipal police departments carry most of the load of law enforcement, employing about 60 percent of all sworn police employees. Spending by local governments exceeds that of state governments because municipalities have the main responsibility for police protection, which accounts for 48 percent of all justice spending. In fact, municipal spending for police alone amounts to 27 percent of all justice spending in the country.[11] Since 1971, however, municipal spending for the justice system has been declining as a proportion, whereas the state and county shares have been increasing. This change is due primarily to state and county governments taking responsibility for justice functions that had been carried out by other levels of government. For example, several states have set up a system of state courts that replaced some county and municipal courts. The increased shares for states and counties also reflect large increases in correctional costs borne by those levels of government.[12]

TABLE 12–3   Prisoners on Death Row, by Race, Ethnicity, and Jurisdiction on April 20, 1994

		Race, Ethnicity					
Jurisdiction	Total	White	Black	Hispanic	Native American	Asian	Unknown
United States[a]	2,848	1,423	1,138	208	50	20	9
Federal statutes	5	1	3	1	0	0	0
U.S. military	8	1	6	0	0	1	0
Alabama	122	68[b,c]	52[b,d]	1	0	1	0
Arizona	119	80[d,e,f]	14[g]	20[d,f]	4	0	1
Arkansas	41	24	15[f]	1	1[f]	0	0
California	383	166[b,h]	143[e]	54[e]	13	6	1
Colorado	3	2	0	1	0	0	0
Connecticut	5	3	2	0	0	0	0
Delaware	15	7	8	0	0	0	0
Florida	330	184[g,i,j]	112[e]	32[e]	1	1	0
Georgia	109	60	49[k]	0	0	0	0
Idaho	23	21	0	2[f]	0	0	0
Illinois	161	52[e]	98[b,f]	8[e]	0	0	3
Indiana	51	31[f]	19[f,l]	1	0	0	0
Kansas	0	x	x	x	x	x	x
Kentucky	25	19[e]	6[d]	0	0	0	0
Louisiana	42	11	29	2	0	0	0
Maryland	14	3	11	0	0	0	0
Mississippi	52	21[d,e,f]	31[k]	0	0	0	0
Missouri	84	47[m]	33[f]	1[e]	1	1	1
Montana	8	6	0	0	2	0	0
Nebraska	10	6	3	0	1	0	0
Nevada	66	36	23[e,f]	7	0	0	0
New Hampshire	0	x	x	x	x	x	x
New Jersey	9	3[f]	5	1	0	0	0

Continued on next page

ALTERNATIVE PERSPECTIVES ON CRIME
The Conservative (Individualist) View

The conservative view sees crime as deviant behavior that is a product of genetic, moral, psychic, or cultural defects in the individual. There is not much hope for rehabilitation. Essentially, components of individual human nature dispose some to deviate from accepted rules of behavior.

Neoconservative theories of crime include those by James Q. Wilson and Edward Banfield. Banfield argues that poor children are socialized into a "culture of poverty," in which they learn to be more interested in immediate gratification than deferred gratification. That is, they are unable to plan for their future by

Continued from previous page

Jurisdiction	Total	White	Black	Hispanic	Native American	Asian	Unknown
New Mexico	1	1	0	0	0	0	0
North Carolina	132	71[l]	52[e]	1	4	1	3
Ohio	127	60	62	3	2	0	0
Oklahoma	118	72[d,f,m]	29[e]	2	13[f]	2	0
Oregon	14	12	0	1	1	0	0
Pennsylvania	170	60[e]	101[b,f,k]	7	0	2	0
South Carolina	55	27[d]	27[d]	0	1	0	0
South Dakota	1	1	0	0	0	0	0
Tennessee	100	65[e]	31[f]	1	2	1	0
Texas	386	167[d,m]	150[b,n]	60[j]	5	4	0
Utah	11	8	2	1	0	0	0
Virginia	46	24[d]	22[d]	0	0	0	0
Washington	13	9	3	0	0	1	0
Wyoming	0	x	x	x	x	x	x

Note: The NAACP Legal Defense and Educational Fund, Inc. periodically collects data on persons on death row. As of Apr. 20, 1994, 37 jurisdictions, the Federal Government, and the United States military had capital punishment laws: and 34 jurisdictions, the Federal Government, and the United States military had at least 1 prisoner under sentence of death. Between Jan. 1, 1973 and Apr. 20, 1994, an estimated 1,379 convictions or sentences have been reversed or vacated on grounds other than constitutional. Between Jan. 1, 1973 and May 30, 1990, an estimated 558 death sentences have been vacated as unconstitutional.

[a] Detail will not add to total because inmates sentenced to death in more than one State are listed in the respective State totals, but each is counted only once at the national level.

[b] Includes two females.

[c] Includes three males who were juveniles at the time of their offenses.

[d] Includes one male who was a juvenile at the time of his offense.

[e] Includes one female.

[f] Includes one male sentenced to death in the State but serving another sentence in another State.

[g] Includes two males sentenced to death in the State but serving another sentence in another State.

[h] Includes three males sentenced to death in the State but serving another sentence in another State.

[i] Includes four females.

[j] Includes four males who were juveniles at the time of their offenses.

[k] Includes two males who were juveniles at the time of their offenses.

[l] Includes one female sentenced to death in the State but serving another sentence in another State.

[m] Includes three females.

[n] Includes six males who were juveniles at the time of their offenses.

Source: Table constructed by SOURCEBOOK staff from data provided by the NAACP Legal Defense and Educational Fund, Inc.

investing in education; rather they turn to crime on the streets to reap immediate rewards.[13]

A variation of this perspective is social heterogeneity theory, which argues that the high crime rate in the United States is a product of its social heterogeneity— the multiethnic, multiracial character of the American population.[14] Low levels of crime in European countries, Japan, and China are often attributed to their homgeneous populations and common cultures. Blacks and Hispanics in the United States are both victims and perpetrators of various types of crime far more frequently than whites or Asians. Although blacks constitute only about 12 percent of the U.S. population, they account for almost 30 percent of all persons arrested for serious crimes; also blacks were almost 60 percent more likely to be the victim of a crime of violence in 1992 than was a white person.[15]

Finally, James Q. Wilson (writing with Richard Herrnstein) argues that criminals compare the costs (punishment) with the benefits (money) associated with crime and calculate that crime does indeed pay. Criminals are rational human beings who therefore consciously engage in criminal activity after considering the costs and benefits and conclude that the former exceed the latter.[16]

Following the logic embodied in these individualist theories of criminality, the criminal must be punished rather than rehabilitated. The punishment must therefore be harsh and certain to deter others from committing crimes. The policy prescriptions under this perspective focus on increasing the certainty that a crime will be followed by costly punishment by hiring additional police officers or by adding new hardware to the department to increase the chances of catching the criminal. In addition, the severity of the punishment must be increased. In other words, the punishment must be so certain, so extreme, and so unpleasant that crime will be deterred.

In the 1960s, an aversion to biological and/or cultural explanations developed, partly as the result of the rise of fascism in the 1930s and its vulgar and lethal perversion of the study of human biology. Instead, researchers in criminology turned to sociological (environmental) explanations of crime. Part of the reason is that people believe that it is easier to do something about an environmental cause of crime than a biological or cultural one.[17]

The Liberal (Structural) View

Under the liberal perspective, the prime determinants of criminal behavior are found in the social structure or the environment, as opposed to the individual himself or herself. The individual is constrained by his or her environment insofar as conditions such as low socioeconomic status, low education, and high levels of unemployment or poverty inhibit the individual's chances of acquiring success, money, and power. Individuals turn to crime out of frustration associated with the constraints imposed by their environment. For example, Cloward and Olin's theory of crime is that criminal acts are adaptations to an environment that blocks individual access to the legitimate reward structure.[18] They argue that ghetto youths have the same desires for success as do their peers, but born poor, often without a father as a role model, and failing in school, they turn to crime as the only path to success. Drug dealing, petty theft, prostitution, gambling, and other forms of criminal activity offer immediate routes to success that might not otherwise be available.[19]

The policy solutions under this perspective include using positive inducements to reduce crime. The goal of public policy from this point of view is to alleviate the environmental conditions that gave rise to crime in the first place. Programs intended to reduce poverty, eliminate racial discrimination, and provide employment are the liberals' program for dealing with crime. For example, the War on Poverty was largely an effort to reduce crime by eliminating or

TABLE 12–4   Overview of Theories of Crime and Punishment

	Liberal	Conservative
Major cause of crime	Social injustice	Individual defects
View of the criminal offender	Can be rehabilitated	Probably cannot be rehabilitated
View of punishment	No useful function	Deters others from committing crime
View of prisons	Reduce to the minimum needed to incarcerate dangerous criminals; prefer community corrections	Prisons preferred over community corrections
View of police	Skeptical	Positive
Preferred policy solutions	Make educational, employment, and social reforms to reduce the stimuli to crime	Make punishment more severe and increase the likelihood of getting caught and being punished

Source: From *Politics and Policy in States and Communities* by John J. Harrigan (New York: HarperCollins, 1994), Table 12–4, p. 329. Copyright © 1994 by HarperCollins College Publishers. Reprinted by permission.

reducing poverty. Similarly, the Comprehensive Employment and Training Act (CETA) and the Job Training Partnership Act (JTPA) were passed to help fight crime from the liberal point of view. Thus, an effective welfare policy is a good crime policy, according to liberals. The quote from Representative Conyers at the beginning of this chapter is illustrative of this point of view.

The liberal and conservative perspectives on crime are illustrated in Table 12-4.

A BRIEF HISTORY OF CRIME POLICY

Criminal justice was seen by the Founding Fathers as a function of the states, reflecting a fear of a central police authority in the national government. The only federal crime defined in the U.S. Constitution is treason against the United States. However, increasingly in the last sixty years, numerous acts of the Congress have cataloged more than three thousand crimes that can be prosecuted in the federal courts.[20] Until the 1930s, the dominant view of corrections policy was primarily punishment and deterrence, and it was believed that criminals could not be rehabilitated.[21] From the 1930s to the 1970s, an emphasis on rehabilitation came into greater favor.[22] In the 1970s and continuing to the present, the emphasis has been on a punishment and deterrence philosophy of corrections.[23] Nearly all candidates for public office in American cities had to demonstrate that they were "tough on crime" in the 1970s and 1980s to get elected. Thus, the tendency was to rely more on incarceration than

TABLE 12–5   Federal and State Prisoners, 1970 to 1992
(Based on Bureau of the Census estimated resident population, as of July 1. Prior to 1970, excludes State institutions in Alaska. Beginning 1980, includes all persons under jurisdiction of Federal and State authorities rather than those in the custody of such authorities. Represents inmates sentenced to maximum term of more than a year. See also *Historical Statistics, Colonial Times to 1970,* series H 1135-1140)

	Present at End of Year						Received from Courts					
	All Institutions		Federal		State		All Institutions		Federal		State	
Year	Number	Rate[1]	Number	Rate[1]	Number	Rate[1]	Number	Rate[1]	Number	Rate[1]	Number	Rate[1]
1970	196,429	96.7	20,038	9.8	176,391	86.8	79,351	39.1	12,047	5.9	67,304	33.1
1975	240,593	113.3	24,131	11.4	216,462	102.0	129,573	61.0	16,770	7.9	112,803	53.1
1980	315,974	139.2	20,611	9.1	295,363	130.1	142,122	62.7	10,907	4.8	131,215	57.9
1985	480,568	216.5	32,695	13.6	447,873	187.6	198,499	82.7	15,368	6.4	183,131	76.3
1986	522,084	230.4	36,531	15.0	485,553	201.4	219,382	91.0	16,067	7.0	203,315	84.0
1987	560,812	229.0	39,523	16.0	521,289	214.2	241,887	99.0	16,260	7.0	225,627	92.0
1988	603,732	244.0	42,738	17.0	560,994	227.0	261,242	106.0	15,932	6.4	245,310	99.3
1989	680,907	274.3	47,168	19.0	633,739	255.3	316,215	127.4	18,388	7.4	297,827	120.0
1990	739,980	295.0	50,403	20.1	689,577	274.9	(NA)	(NA)	(NA)	(NA)	323,069	128.8
1991	789,610	309.6	56,696	22.2	732,914	287.3	(NA)	(NA)	(NA)	(NA)	317,237	124.4
1992	847,271	330.2	65,706	25.6	781,565	304.6	(NA)	(NA)	(NA)	(NA)	334,301	130.3

NA-Not Available. [1]Rate per 100,000 estimated population.

Source: U.S. Bureau of Justice Statistics, *Prisoners in State and Federal Institutions on December 31,* annual, and *Correctional Populations in the United States,* annual (Washington, D.C.: U.S. Government Printing Office).

on a policy of rehabilitation. Table 12-5 illustrates the increase in federal and state prisoners from 1970 to 1992. These data show that there has been an increase in the incarceration strategy, even when controlling for population growth. Moreover, projections indicate that incarceration rates will increase in the 1990s.[24]

Thus, we see that just as in our other policy areas, both liberal and conservative perspectives have guided American public policy in this area since the 1930s. From the 1930s to the 1970s, the liberal point of view was the dominant perspective on crime. More recently, the conservative point of view has dominated crime policy as the public has become progressively more concerned about levels of crime.

EVALUATING CRIMINAL JUSTICE POLICY

Have our various crime policies reduced the rate of crimes or recidivism (i.e., criminals returning to prison) in the United States? Does punishment deter crime? Does rehabilitation work? These are difficult questions to answer due to the mixed findings on evaluations of crime policy.

The Conservative (Deterrence) Approach

Evaluations of the effects of deterrence have traditionally focused on the effects of either severity or certainty of punishment. Measures of certainty have typically been identified with three stages of the criminal justice system, including arrest, trial, and imprisonment.[25] Thus, ratios of the likelihood or probability of arrest, sentencing, or incarceration have been constructed as measures of certainty. Measures of severity are usually represented as the length of sentences or the actual amount of time served.[26]

Some evidence suggests that imprisonment and other legal sanctions have some deterrent effects, though the findings are ambiguous.[27] The economist Gordon Tullock, for example, argues that certainty of punishment and severity of punishment has a deterrent effect on crime rates.[28] On the other hand, there is no evidence that recidivism rates went down after the get-tough policies of the 1980s.[29] Thus, most social scientists argue that the system of criminal justice in America is *not* a serious deterrent to crime.

The Liberal (Rehabilitation) Approach

Evaluating the liberal approach typically focuses on the effects of rehabilitation on crime rates. A number of studies have examined the effects of rehabilitaion on recidivism. There is no strong evidence that rehabilitation programs produce lower recidivism rates.[30] As much as 80 percent of all felonies are committed by repeaters or individuals who have had prior contact with the criminal justice system and were not corrected by it.[31] In sum, there is no convincing evidence that rehabilitation works, no matter what is done. Even probation has been just as ineffective as prison in reducing crime.[32] Studies indicate that nearly two-thirds of probationers will be arrested, and over one-half will be convicted for a serious crime while they are on probation.[33]

The liberals respond that American prisons have never been fully committed to rehabilitation, that more often than not they have been little more than "schools for crime," or places where criminals learn new skills of their deviant subculture.[34]

THE FUTURE OF CRIMINAL JUSTICE POLICY

Designing a more effective crime policy for the 1990s is one of the most important challenges facing us today. Policy solutions aimed at reducing poverty and unemployment assume that criminals are rational, economically motivated beings. Yet, this assumption applies principally to property crimes. Crimes against persons are frequently acts of passion or anger that have very little to do with economic considerations. Moreover, given the ambiguous findings about the effects of various crime policies, it appears that nothing works.[35]

Nevertheless, a number of policy solutions have been offered to reduce crime rates. Policy prescriptions for reducing crime include the following:

1. Reduce unemployment and poverty.
2. Reduce drop-out rates.
3. Increase police staffing.
4. Provide more education and job training.

5. Increase sentence severity.
6. Use more vocational counseling.
7. Provide more rehabilitation programs.
8. Provide better police hardware.
9. Utilize media campaigns to change criminals' perceptions about the likelihood of punishment.

During the 1992 presidential campaign, the Clinton–Gore plan on crime and drugs stressed putting 100,000 more police on the streets, an expansion of federal crime assistance to include community-based policing, drug treatment on demand, drug education in the schools, and stricter gun control laws, among other measures. Essentially, the plan called for "putting more police on the streets and more criminals behind bars," a form of the get-tough policy discussed above. Opening his campaign to pass a crime bill in August 1993, President Clinton outlined a plan that would put more police officers on the streets, make it harder for inmates to appeal their death sentences, and require a waiting period for handgun purchases. Clinton also acted immediately on two gun control measures, issuing executive orders barring the import of certain semiautomatic assault weapons and tightening enforcement of federal gun dealer licenses.[36]

Yet we know from previous studies that a get-tough policy does not necessarily reduce crime rates. Perhaps the safest strategy for public policy in this area, given the tentative nature of the empirical findings on deterrence and rehabilitation on crime rates, is to employ a mixed strategy. That is, we might provide funds for both policing and social services, along with increased sentence severity and media campaigns to change criminals' perceptions about the likelihood of conviction and punishment.

In addition to these strategies, we will need to better understand the real causes of crime. There is evidence, for example, of a relationship between drug use and crime. A recent study by the Justice Department found that 78 percent of prison inmates used some type of drug, including alcohol, compared with 37 percent for the general population of the United States.[37] Moreover, a high proportion of offenders grew up in homes with only one parent, were victims of child abuse, had relatives who served time in prison, were not married, had low levels of education, were unemployed, and were at the poverty level before entering jail or prison.[38] Although there is no agreement over the relationship between crime and various socioeconomic factors, we will need to adopt a broad approach to fighting crime that addresses the environment as well as the individual. Much like our previous chapter on welfare, an approach that reflects a melding of both liberal and conservative perspectives could provide the basis for a stronger crime policy than we have developed in the past.

As the 1990s proceed, the states are attempting to develop new approaches to deterring criminal behavior that include "back-door, front-door, and capacity enhancement strategies."[39] Back-door strategies include several methods for releasing offenders from prisons before they have served their full sentence, such as early release or parole. Front-door strategies include trying to keep minor offenders out of prison in the first place by directing them into alternative programs, such as "boot camps" or "shock incarceration." In these boot camps, first-time felony offenders are given the option of serving their prison term or undergoing three to four months in a shock incarceration center that resembles a marine boot camp. Capacity enhancement refers to construction of new prison facilities, although these prisons may be privately financed (e.g., "prisons for profit") or financed by the state government.[40] No matter which strategy is ultimately adopted, we can expect to witness continued innovation in crime policy.

NOTES

1. Richard D. Lamm and Richard A. Caldwell, *Hard Choices* (Denver, CO: Center for Public Policy and Contemporary Issues, 1991), p. 8.
2. Bureau of Justice Statistics, *Report to the Nation on Crime and Justice* (Washington, D.C.: U.S. Government Printing Office, 1988), p. 2.
3. Ibid.
4. Bureau of Justice Statistics, *Criminal Victimization in the United States: 1973–92 Trends* (Washington, D.C.: U.S. Government Printing Office, July 1994), pp. iii, 1–5, 14–15; Bureau of Justice Statistics, *Sourcebook of Criminal Justice Statistics—1993* (Washington, D.C.: U.S. Government Printing Office, 1994), pp. 248–249.
5. Bureau of Justice Statistics, *Sourcebook,* pp. 154–155, 165.
6. Bureau of Justice Statistics, *Sourcebook of Criminal Justice Statistics—1992* (Washington, D.C.: U.S. Government Printing Office, 1993), p. 183.
7. Thomas R. Dye, *Politics in States and Communities,* 7th ed. (Englewood Cliffs, NJ: Prentice-Hall, 1991), p. 249.
8. Bureau of Justice Statistics, *Sourcebook of Criminal Justice Statistics—1990* (Washington, D.C.: U.S. Government Printing Office, 1991), Tables 1-1 and 1-13.
9. Ann O'M. Bowman and Richard C. Kearney, *State and Local Government* (Boston: Houghton Mifflin, 1993), p. 480.
10. Bureau of Justice Statistics, *Sourcebook—1993,* p. 666.
11. Bureau of Justice Statistics, *Report to the Nation,* p. 116.
12. Ibid.
13. Edward Banfield, *The Unheavenly City Revisited* (Boston: Little, Brown, 1974).
14. Dye, *Politics in States and Communities,* p. 250.
15. Ibid., pp. 250–251; Bureau of Justice Statistics, *Criminal Victimization,* pp. 14–15.
16. James Q. Wilson and Richard J. Herrnstein, *Crime and Human Nature* (New York: Simon and Schuster, 1985), Chapter 2; it is also interesting to note that Richard Herrnstein and Charles Murray argue in *The Bell Curve* (New York: Free Press, 1994) that crime and IQ are linked such that crimes tend to be committed by those with below-average IQs. There would appear to be some inconsistency between the two views by Herrnstein.
17. Ibid., p. 77.
18. Richard Cloward and Lloyd Olin, *Delinquency and Opportunity* (New York: Free Press, 1960), pp. 7–23.
19. Ibid., pp. 22–23.

20. Vivian E. Watts, "Federal Anti-Crime Efforts: The Fallout on State and Local Governments," *Intergovernmental Perspective* 18 (Winter 1992), pp. 35–38.

21. John Harrigan, *Politics and Policy in States and Communities* (New York: HarperCollins, 1994), p. 332.

22. Ibid.

23. Gordon Tullock, "Does Punishment Deter Crime," *The Public Interest* 36 (Summer 1974), pp. 103–111.

24. James Austin and Barry Krisberg, "Incarceration in the United States: The Extent and Future of the Problem," *Annals of the American Academy of Political and Social Science* 478 (March 1985), pp. 15–30.

25. Scott H. Decker and Carol W. Kohfeld, "Certainty, Severity, and the Probability of Crime: A Logistic Analysis," *Policy Studies Journal* 19 (Fall 1990), pp. 2–21.

26. Ibid., p. 2.

27. Gordon Whitaker and Charles D. Phillips, eds., *Evaluating the Performance of Criminal Justice Agencies* (Newbury Park, CA: Sage Publications, 1983), pp. 211–235.

28. Tullock, "Does Punishment Deter Crime," pp. 103–111.

29. Harrigan, Politics and Policy, p. 337.

30. Robert Martinson, "What Works?" Questions and Answers About Prison Reform," *The Public Interest* 35 (Spring, 1974), p. 25.

31. Dye, *Politics in States and Communities,* p. 254.

32. Martinson, "What Works?" 35 pp. 22–54.

33. Dye, *Politics in States and Communities,* p. 254.

34. William A. Schultze, *State and Local Politics: A Political Economy Approach* (St. Paul: West Publishing, 1988), p. 304.

35. Herbert Jacob, *The Frustration of Policy: Responses to Crime by American Cities* (Boston: Little, Brown, 1984).

36. See *1993 CQ Almanac* (Washington, D.C.: Congressional Quarterly Press, 1993), p. 294.

37. Bureau of Justice Statistics, *Report to the Nation,* p. 50.

38. Ibid., pp. 48–49.

39. Bowman and Kearney, *State and Local Government,* pp. 495–501.

40. Ibid., pp. 496–499.

ENVIRONMENTAL POLICY

"Yet the conservation movement raised a fundamental question in American life: . . . How can the technical requirements of an increasingly complex society be adjusted to the need for the expression of partial and limited aims?"

SAMUEL P. HAYS

"Our political institutions, predicated almost totally on growth and abundance, appear to be no match for the gathering forces of ecological scarcity."

WILLIAM OPHULS

"Appreciating the scale of social and economic changes likely in the next fifty or one hundred years, one can easily be overwhelmed by the magnitude of the task. . . . A vital alternative is to accept Camus' simple moral vision—one does what one can, no more and no less—and one trusts that enough of one's fellow humans will do the same."

ROBERT C. PAEHKLE

For several reasons, the 1990s are a particularly exciting time to examine environmental politics and policy. First, the 1980s were a period of implementation of federal environmental policies enacted during the previous two decades: the Clean Air Act Amendments of 1970, the Federal Water Pollution Control Act Amendments of 1972, the Resource Conservation and Recovery Act of 1976, the Safe Drinking Water Act of 1974, the Surface Mining Control and Reclamation Act of 1977, the Comprehensive Environmental Response, Compensation and Liability Act of 1980, the Hazardous and Solid Waste Amendments of 1984, and the Superfund Amendments and Reauthorization Act of 1986.[1] Like the 1980s, the decade of the 1990s will be an "implementation era" in environmental policy, as well as in other areas of public policy.

Second, intergovernmental relations have recently taken on greater significance than ever before. During the 1980s, the doctrine of **new federalism** stressed devolution of authority from the federal level to the state and local levels in many areas of public policy. As part of the legacy of the Reagan and Bush presidencies, states and local communities are taking on many responsibilities for protecting the environment that were previously the province of the federal government. Indeed, the head of Vermont's environmental agency, Jonathan Lash, has said that the most important innovations in environmental protection are now occurring at the state level,[2] and many others agree with this assessment.

Finally, the states themselves have undergone a number of important transformations in terms of their institutional capacities for implementing federal programs. For example, the states have improved their revenue systems, strengthened their governor's office, professionalized their legislatures, reformed their courts, and consolidated their bureaucracies.[3] Presumably, states are no longer the "weak link" in the intergovernmental system of the United States. These enormous changes of the past two decades are so far-reaching as to constitute a "definite break with the past."[4] Scholars over the next decade will likely be engaged in the study of intergovernmental relations (and especially federal-state relations) as they affect the formulation, implementation, and impact of public policies.[5] These future investigators are likely to be concerned with the extent to which the fifty American states are providing leadership in the environmental area or conversely, the extent to which they are effectively implementing federal laws dealing with pollution.

This chapter reviews the evolution of environmental politics and policy in the United States. Before discussing the present state of environmental politics and policy, it is instructive to review briefly the history of environmental politics and policy in the United States from 1890 to 1990. Next, we review the current status of environmental policy and politics in the 1990s. Finally, we discuss the future of environmental politics and policy in the American states.

THE EVOLUTION OF ENVIRONMENTAL POLITICS AND POLICY

The history of environmental politics and policy may be roughly divided into four periods. These four periods are the **conservation–efficiency movement** from about 1890 to 1920; the **conservation–preservation movement** from about 1920 to 1960; the **environmental movement** from about 1960 to 1990; and the contemporary period of **participatory environmentalism** starting in the 1990s.[6] However, we can identify earlier attempts to protect the environment as well. For example, during the first part of the nineteenth century, the federal government took a number of actions to preserve good mast timber for ships, and President John Quincy Adams' administration even went so far as to establish a program of sustained-yield operations on forest reservations in 1827.[7] However, not much effort was given for environmental protection until some time after the Civil War. With the exception of the John Quincy Adams administration, no other political administration from Washington to Buchanan revealed any concept of natural resources that showed foresight in planning for the nation's future needs.[8] Essentially, the years between 1865 and 1890 may be characterized as a period of resource exploitation by a rising industry, during which time natural resources were subordinated to the political objectives of industrial development, removing Indians from their native lands for resettlement, homestead settlement, and the promotion of free enterprise.[9] During the reconstruction era after the Civil War, rebuilding the South and developing the American West required the use of resources rather than their conservation.

Nevertheless, by the late 1800s, serious efforts to protect the nation's natural resources began.

The Conservation–Efficiency Movement, 1890–1920

The years from 1890 until 1920 saw some of the nation's most bitter conservation battles as Republicans and Democrats began to take firm positions on the environment. The essence of the conservation movement was rational planning to promote efficient development and use of all natural resources.[10] According to historian Samuel P. Hays, "the modern American conservation movement grew out of the firsthand experience of federal administrators and political leaders with problems of Western economic growth, especially Western water development."[11] Later, federal forestry officials joined hydrographers and campaigned for more rational and efficient use of timber resources. During the 1890s, the organized forestry movement in the United States shifted its emphasis from saving trees to promoting sustained-yield forest management.[12] By 1891, action was taken to set aside "forest reserves" within the federal domain and to authorize selective cutting and marketing of timber in 1897.[13]

A number of individuals, including W. J. McGee, Gifford Pinchot, John Wesley Powell, Frederick Newell, and George Maxwell were concerned about natural resources and were employed by the federal government in the late 1800s, many of them for the U.S. Geological Survey. Together, they formulated four basic doctrines for what later became the creed of the conservation movement. These doctrines were: (1) conservation is not the locking up of resources; it is their development and wise use; (2) conservation is the greatest good for the greatest number for the longest time; (3) the federal public lands belong to all the people; and (4) comprehensive, multiple-purpose river basin planning and development should be utilized with respect to the nation's water resources.[14]

Gifford Pinchot became an important link between the intellectual and scientific founders of the conservation movement and President Theodore Roosevelt, a Republican. Indeed, the Roosevelt administration is more noteworthy for the drive and support it gave the conservation movement than it is for the initiation of new policies or legislative enactments. A new spirit of law enforcement pervaded the departments and was dramatized to the country at large by the influence of Gifford Pinchot and his role as adviser to President Roosevelt.[15] Under Pinchot's guidance, the Roosevelt administration greatly enlarged the area of the national forests from 41 national reserves to 159.[16] Pinchot, who studied forest management in France and Germany, completely reorganized the Forest Service and infused it with a new spirit of public responsibility.[17]

The period of 1908 to 1920 saw numerous conflicts over conservation policy. For example, much of the Western livestock industry depended for its forage on the "open range" owned by the federal government but free for anyone to use. Soon the public domain became stocked with more animals than the range could support. Chaos, anarchy, violence, and destruction were typical of the times. Range wars soon developed between Western cattlemen and sheep operators, and

at times, between these groups and farmers as all struggled for control of the public grazing lands.[18]

Nevertheless, the deepest significance of the conservation movement, according to Samuel Hays, "lay in its political implications: how should resource decisions
be made and by whom?" Should conflicts be resolved through partisan politics, by
compromise among various interest groups, or through the courts?[19] To the conservationists, politics was an anathema; instead, scientific experts, using technical
and scientific methods, should decide all matters of development and use of natural resources together with the allocation of funds.[20] The crux of the gospel of
efficiency, then, "lay in a rational and scientific method of making basic technological decisions through a single, central authority."[21] The inevitable tension that
developed between those grassroots interests and the technocratic elites of this
conservation-efficiency era raised a question that was to be addressed by future
conservationists—how can large-scale economic development be effective and at
the same time fulfill the desire for significant grassroots participation?

The Conservation-Preservation Movement, 1920–1960

The second form of conservationism, the preservationist movement, was very
similar to the efficiency movement, except that this movement was more concerned with *habitat* than sustenance.[22] That is, this preservationist movement
developed largely under the pressures of increased leisure and affluence and the
growth of outdooor recreation. It drew its support from the upper middle class
and also had much support from hunting and fishing groups drawn from the
working classes. Although conflicts occurred over natural resource policy, they
were largely confined to struggles between those who favored "multiple use" of
public lands and those who favored "pure preservation."[23] Although the earlier
movement was often characterized by conflicts between extractive industries in
the West and manufacturing industries in the East, the preservationist movement
often included capitalist sponsors, such as Laurence Rockefeller, who facilitated
the preservation of major tracts of land surrounding the hotels that he built.[24]

Beginning in 1920, water power, coal, flood control, and even wildlife were
given special attention in the major party platforms. Much of the emphasis on
natural resources was shifted from conservation of public lands to programs of
conservation under private ownership.[25] Another major difference between
these two movements was that conservation-efficiency concerns resided with
corporations and state agencies, whereas conservation-preservationist concerns
resided in local and especially national organizations, such as the Sierra Club and
the National Wildlife Federation.

The period from 1921 to 1950 took on a different look because much of the federal legislation for natural resources became associated with broad social and economic objectives, such as the Agricultural Adjustment Act of 1938, which was passed
to control agricultural production. The legislative history of environmental and natural resource issues suggests that Democrats attained a much better voting record than
their Republican counterparts between 1921 and 1950.[26] By the 1960s, however, the

movement began to change dramatically as environmental concern was broadened to include many new groups that had previously been inactive on this issue.

The Environmental Movement, 1960–1990

One prominent scholar of environmental politics argues that the conservation movement was an effort of the part of leaders in science, technology, and government to bring about more efficient development of natural resources, whereas the environmental movement was a product of a fundamental change in public values in the United States that stressed the quality of the human environment.[27] The environmental movement, in contrast to the conservation movement, is more typically viewed as a grassroots or bottom-up phenomenon in which environmental objectives arose out of deep-seated changes in values about the use of nature. Conservation, on the other hand, is viewed as a top-down phenomenon in which technical and political leaders were stirred toward action. Essentially, the environmental movement integrated the habitat and sustenance concerns of the efficiency and preservation movements, but it also covered a broader set of ecosystem concerns.[28] There were new concerns about social welfare issues, growth management, and production expansion decision making.

The environmental movement can also be characterized by the breadth of its constituency, as well as its political strategies. For example, the environmental movement used lobbying, litigation, the media, electoral politics, and even civil disobedience in contrast to the more modest mechanisms used by the conservationists, such as technical negotiations, corporate sponsors, and pressure groups.[29] Finally, the base of support for the environmental movement was made up of a larger sector of the public, including the middle and working classes. Table 13-1 illustrates these four periods in environmental history.

TABLE 13–1 The Evolution of Environmentalism, 1890–1990

	1890–1920	1920–1960	1960–1990	1990–present
Scope of the issues	Preservation issues	Conservation issues	Second-generation issues	Third-generation issues
Dominant policy	Efficient use of resources	Multiple use of resources	Pollution abatement	Pollution prevention
Patterns of participation	Elite-dominated	Subgovernments	Pluralism	Advocacy coalitions
Policy cycle stage	Pre-problem stage	Agenda-setting stage	Policy formulation	Policy implementation
Level of action	National government	National government	National, state, and local governments	State and local governments
Dominant concern	Environmental science	Technology development	Economics and politics	Philosophy and environmental ethics
Techniques of power	Technical negotiations	Corporate pressure	Middle-class politics	Participatory democracy

Several observations emerge from the above discussion. First, we see how the environmental movement has steadily broadened its base of support over the one hundred years from 1890 to 1990. Specifically, it has moved from being largely an elitist concern, involving scientific and government experts, to one with broad-based support including middle-class and even working-class supporters. This broader base of public support has been joined by national environmental groups, such as the Sierra Club, Natural Resources Defense Council, Friends of the Earth, Green Peace, and Earth First! This tendency toward "opening up" this issue toward greater and more representative participation is also illustrated by the extant literature that seeks to explain the formulation or implementation of environmental policy. Initially, this literature stressed subgovernments as a major explanation for environmental policymaking.[30] More recently, the literature suggests that advocacy coalitions, composed of interests from all three levels of government and the private sector, are now involved in environmental policymaking.[31] Clearly, this suggests a change in the scope of citizen involvement over the past hundred years.

A number of other changes have taken place in environmental policy and politics over just the past thirty years. For example, we have changed how we evaluate the severity of the environmental problem. Specifically, we have evolved from a primary concern over natural resource issues to environmental issues, or from first-generation problems (e.g., public lands, water rights, park management) to second-generation problems (e.g., toxic waste, groundwater protection, chemical plant explosions) to third-generation problems (e.g., global warming, thinning of the ozone layer, deforestation, acid rain). Along with this change, we have shifted our concern from purely localized issues involving air and water pollution in communities to the realization that an effective response to these second- and third-generation problems "requires diverse actions by individuals and institutions at all levels of society."[32]

Moreover, public opinion on this topic has changed dramatically over the past thirty years. Initially, public opinion in the late 1960s and early 1970s reached a high level of support, but it was judged to be "soft support," meaning that it would dissolve in the face of concerns over economic development (or jobs over the environment). In the late 1980s, on the other hand, public opinion is said to be both strong and salient.[33] The American public indicates that it wants stringent environmental protection regulations, and it is willing to pay for it in new taxes.

Finally, we have witnessed the growing involvement of states and cities and grassroots organizations in environmental management. After the advent of new federalism in the 1970s and 1980s, states and communities are increasingly being asked to assume more of their environmental responsibilities that were previously handled by the federal government. Yet not all the states are able to muster the economic and institutional wherewithal to meet their new responsibilities.[34] Indeed, the states vary greatly in their capacities to assume environmental management in the 1990s. That is a subject to which we now turn.

ENVIRONMENTAL POLICY AND POLITICS IN THE 1990s: A NEW FEDERALISM?

Two dramatic developments affected the states during the decades of the 1970s and the 1980s. First, as noted above, the Nixon, Reagan, and Bush administrations returned power and authority to the states and cities under new federalism. The new federalism, beginning with the State and Local Fiscal Assistance Act of 1972 (and accelerated by President Reagan in 1981), mandated a greatly expanded role for state governments. Among other things, states would become less subject to fiscal control by the federal government. Initially, the new federalism involved a number of short-term inducements, such as programmatic flexibility, elimination of de facto dual planning requirements for categorical grant applications, and increased consultation with state and local decision makers prior to the initiation of "direct development" activities.[35] By 1981, however, the objectives of President Reagan's new federalism were to *decentralize* and *defund* federal environmental protection activities. Seen most favorably, the Reagan administration thought that the states were now in a position (due largely to their enhanced institutional capacity) to assume greater responsibilities than ever before. States and cities would simply make difficult choices about what programs they wanted to retain (and thus replace the federal cuts with their own-source funds) and which ones they wanted to terminate. In this sense, public pressures would thus force state decision makers to take responsive actions that reflected localized policy preferences.

Critics, on the other hand, argued that the administration used the shift of responsibilities to the states, at least in the environmental area, for another reason—as a way to eliminate particular functions altogether.[36] Although there is some evidence that the states have indeed strengthened their institutional capacity to deal with contemporary public policy problems, it can still be questioned whether state administrators can assume substantially greater program responsibilities on such short notice.[37] Some policies are less amenable to an effective switch in jurisdictional authority than are others because of "spillover effects" or "negative externalities," which preclude the development of a site-specific policy approach that is geographically self-contained. Nor is there convincing evidence that all states are prepared politically, economically, and/or administratively to adopt a more autonomous role in the management of some federal programs.[38]

The second dramatic development that affected the states during the last two decades was a transformation of their institutional capabilities.[39] As noted above, the states revised their constitutions, professionalized their legislatures, strengthened their governor's offices, reorganized their executive branches, reformed their courts, increased their revenues through tax diversification, and provided greater opportunities for citizen participation in state government through "open meeting laws," as well as other reforms.[40] Of course, not all the fifty American states adopted these reforms. The available evidence suggests that some of the states were more active in adopting these institutional reforms than were others.[41] This suggests that not all the states are able to effectively assume their new environmental responsibilities under the new federalism of the 1990s. In the next section, we explore the behavior of the states in the environmental area during the new federalism of the 1970s and 1980s.

The States' Response to New Federalism, 1970–1995

So much attention has been focused on activities of the federal government that many important developments at the state level have been given less attention than they deserve. Some states exhibit striking examples of innovative activity, whereas others are more conventional and less active. In fact, studies suggest a great deal of diversity in responses by the states to the challenges posed by the new federalism of the 1970s and 1980s. A number of researchers in think tanks and university settings have studied innovative state actions and the extent of state environmental policy implementation. Some of the more impressive state activities are discussed here.

Environmental Policy Innovations

The Institute for Southern Studies has collected recent information on innovative environmental and natural resource policies. This information, published in the 1991–1992 *Green Index*, began as an assessment of environmental conditions and policies in the fifty states. The "Green Policy Initiatives" ranking is based on the status of fifty state environmental policies that are considered to be "innovative" as far as policy formulation is concerned. Table 13-2 presents these data.

The *Green Index* is a set of 256 indicators that measure and rank each state's environmental health and overall commitment to environmental protection. The final *Green Index* score is the sum of the state's ranks for all 256 indicators with each indicator carrying equal weight. These data, collected mostly in 1989, suggest that Oregon, Maine, Vermont, California, Minnesota, and Massachusetts are the most heavily committed to the environment, whereas Texas, Mississippi, Arkansas, Louisiana, and Alabama are some of the least committed.[42] Innovative state actions include a groundwater discharge permit system in Arizona; statewide recycling mandates in some states; Proposition 65 in California on toxic use reduction; and source reduction programs in twenty-seven states since 1987.[43] In addition, a number of states (for example, New York, Connecticut, New Jersey, Maine, Massachusetts, New Hampshire, Rhode Island, and Vermont) have announced restrictions on the amount of gasoline vapor that may be emitted by automobiles.[44] In another regional effort, Virginia, Maryland, Pennsylvania, and the District of Columbia are cooperating to clean up the badly polluted Chesapeake Bay.[45] New Jersey has imposed new environmental taxes and fees and set up revolving loan funds. Variations in state groundwater quality protection programs suggest that some states such as Arizona have been quite innovative, whereas other states such as Texas have been much less so.[46]

TABLE 13–2 The Best and Worst States in Environmental Management

State	Final Green Index (256 Indicators)	Green Policy Initiatives (50 State Policies)
1. Oregon	1	2
2. Maine	2	5
3. Vermont	3	12
4. California	4	1
5. Minnesota	5	7
6. Massachusetts	6	9
7. Rhode Island	7	10
8. New York	8	8
9. Washington	9	14
10. Wisconsin	10	6
11. Connecticut	11	4
12. Hawaii	12	24
13. Maryland	13	15
14. New Jersey	14	3
15. New Hampshire	15	20
16. Colorado	16	26
17. Michigan	17	11
18. Florida	18	13
19. Idaho	19	36
20. Iowa	20	16
21. Montana	21	31
22. Nevada	22	43
23. North Carolina	23	18
24. Delaware	24	25
25. North Dakota	25	37
26. Pennsylvania	26	21
27. South Dakota	27	48
28. New Mexico	28	38
29. Nebraska	29	30
30. Missouri	30	23
31. Illinois	31	17
32. Virginia	32	22
33. Utah	33	41
34. Alaska	34	47
35. Arizona	35	39
36. South Carolina	36	32
37. Ohio	37	19
38. Wyoming	38	44
39. Georgia	39	29
40. Oklahoma	40	42
41. Kentucky	41	33
42. Kansas	42	28
43. Indiana	43	27
44. West Virginia	44	45
45. Tennessee	45	40
46. Texas	46	35
47. Mississippi	47	46
48. Arkansas	48	50
49. Louisiana	49	34
50. Alabama	50	49

Source: Bob Hall and Mary Lee Kerr, *1991–1992 Green Index* (Washington, D. C.: Island Press, 1991), p. 3. Reprinted with permission.

During the 1990s, more innovative actions by the states are likely as they attempt to deal with environmental problems. Some states, however, have been far less active in changing their environmental policies during the past decade. This latter category of states is a cause of concern regarding their willingness and ability to deal with the diversity of environmental threats in the 1990s.

State Commitments and Environmental Management

As noted earlier, the states vary substantially in their commitment to environmental protection policies and in their ability, economically and institutionally, to carry out strong environmental protection programs. In addition to the *Green Index*, the Fund for Renewable Energy and the Environment (FREE) has provided another source of data on what the states have done to protect the environment.[47] Since 1987, FREE has conducted an annual study that is nonfiscal in nature and reports an assessment of where the states stand on key environmental issues such as air pollution reduction, soil conservation, solid waste and recycling, hazardous-waste management, groundwater protection, and renewable energy and conservation. According to these data, Massachusetts, Wisconsin, California, and New Jersey are the most active states, and Arkansas, Mississippi, West Virginia, and Wyoming are the least active. In FREE's most recent study, other states in the top ten are Oregon, Minnesota, Iowa, Florida, Maryland, and Connecticut.[48] Both the *Green Index* and FREE identify essentially the same states as the most environmentally concerned over time.

States' institutional capabilities to protect the environment vary as well as their commitment to environmental protection. In 1988, in 1990, and again in 1992, the Council of State Governments studied the fifty states' institutions for environmental management, their expenditures for environmental and natural resource programs, and the numbers of state government employees with environmental or natural resource responsibilities.[49] These data suggest some potential problems in the states' ability to manage the environment effectively, no matter how progressive or innovative they may be. Some environmental problems, such as toxic waste, cannot be effectively managed without enormous sums of money and highly trained staff. Yet these data, and interviews with environmental personnel at both federal and state levels, suggest that the states suffer from inadequate fiscal resources, inadequate numbers of staff, inexperienced staff, staff turnover, and other problems that will adversely affect these states' abilities to implement federal directives in the 1990s.[50]

Environmental Policy Implementation

Mere enactment of a policy does not guarantee that the policy will be put into effect. Effective implementation of environmental policies is essential, and it varies from state to state.[51] For example, implementation may be achieved by delegation of authority from the federal government to the states to manage their environmental programs after they have met federal guidelines. A number of scholars have studied the extent to which various states have assumed responsibility to run environmental programs, and thereby increased the speed of implementation.[52] Between 1972 and 1988, some states accepted primary responsibility for enforcing national environmental standards within their boundaries. States that scored highest in this regard included California, Michigan, Minnesota, New York, Washington, and Wisconsin.[53]

In addition, environmental policy implementation may be indicated by the amount of money spent on state environmental programs. The U.S. Department of Commerce collected data on environmental quality control expenditures from 1969 to 1980.[54] These data show that California, Delaware, Maryland, Massachusetts, New Hampshire, Ohio, Rhode Island, and Vermont had the highest per capita expenditures, whereas Mississippi, Oklahoma, South Carolina, Texas, Utah, and Virginia had the lowest. Unfortunately, due to budgetary cutbacks in 1981, this data collection effort was halted. Without continuous data from 1981 to the present, assessing the impact of new federalism on state environmental spending is difficult.

Nevertheless, recent efforts by the Institute for Southern Studies and the Council of State Governments have provided new data on state environmental protection expenditures that will help to fill the vacuum created by the elimination of the Department of Commerce data. Table 13-3 presents data on state expenditures for environmental protection in 1988, the most recent data available. These recent data indicate that California, New Jersey, Florida, Illinois, Pennsylvania, Washington, Massachusetts, New York, Michigan, and Louisiana now lead the nation in total environmental expenditures. Note, however, that the top ten rankings shift significantly when spending per capita is considered or when expenditures are measured as a percentage of the total state budget, which is perhaps the best indicator of the priority of environmental protection activities within a state.[55] The states of Wyoming, Montana, Idaho, Alaska, New Jersey, Oregon, Louisiana, Washington, and California lead the nation in spending as a percentage of a state's total budget, whereas New York, Texas, Ohio, Oklahoma, and Indiana spend the least as a percentage of total spending.

In sum, the evidence indicates that some states exhibit innovative and responsible behavior in implementing environmental policy by setting up appropriate environmental institutions, staffing them with capable personnel, and spending the necessary resources. Other states, however, are largely unresponsive to environmental needs. They fail to provide the necessary resources, staff, or innovative policies; thus it is doubtful that their environmental quality is improving.[56] This fact has led to a growing sense of frustration (perhaps even outrage) among the American public over the ability of government, at any level, to provide for responsible management of environmental pollution. Representative democracy, as practiced over the past thirty years, is under more scrutiny than ever before.[57] Studies of citizens involved in environmental disasters, such as those at Love Canal and Three Mile Island, suggest that these individuals have come to believe

TABLE 13–3 State Spending on Environmental Protection, 1988

State	Total in $1,000	Per Capita	% Total State Budget
1. Alabama	$64,907	$15.73	1.02%
2. Alaska	131,684	256.69	4.00
3. Arizona	46,613	13.45	.96
4. Arkansas	44,189	18.24	1.15
5. California	1,486,124	52.76	2.60
6. Colorado	76,150	23.15	1.65
7. Connecticut	61,996	19.13	.77
8. Delaware	33,170	50.26	1.80
9. Florida	465,591	37.62	2.51
10. Georgia	93,344	14.58	1.07
11. Hawaii	27,832	25.46	.85
12. Idaho	61,442	61.50	4.22
13. Illinois	392,844	34.03	2.26
14. Indiana	52,776	9.46	.68
15. Iowa	88,065	31.07	1.44
16. Kansas	47,817	19.23	1.23
17. Kentucky	120,289	32.33	1.64
18. Louisiana	193,836	43.85	2.64
19. Maine	39,332	32.61	1.88
20. Maryland	150,091	32.32	1.60
21. Massachusetts	237,936	40.53	1.56
22. Michigan	221,425	23.81	1.42
23. Minnesota	126,236	29.32	1.46
24. Mississippi	54,154	20.61	1.40
25. Missouri	119,907	23.33	1.73
26. Montana	69,560	86.52	4.29
27. Nebraska	27,988	17.48	1.29
28. Nevada	36,487	34.42	2.57
29. New Hampshire	33,588	30.62	2.41
30. New Jersey	523,874	67.86	3.61
31. New Mexico	44,782	29.66	1.48
32. New York	236,484	13.21	.59
33. North Carolina	96,943	14.85	1.00
34. North Dakota	32,524	49.06	2.32
35. Ohio	125,669	11.56	.65
36. Oklahoma	40,869	12.52	.79
37. Oregon	186,438	68.02	3.03
38. Pennsylvania	288,766	24.01	1.49
39. Rhode Island	35,879	36.06	1.86
40. South Carolina	71,124	20.36	1.21
41. South Dakota	21,264	29.74	1.85
42. Tennessee	81,180	16.50	1.34
43. Texas	113,797	6.78	.60
44. Utah	51,419	30.41	1.80
45. Vermont	20,222	36.37	1.94
46. Virginia	152,149	25.38	1.47
47. Washington	246,873	53.45	2.63
48. West Virginia	56,189	29.82	1.68
49. Wisconsin	167,779	34.54	1.70
50. Wyoming	128,051	271.87	7.73

Source: Bob Hall and Mary Lee Kerr, *1991–1992 Green Index* (Washington, D.C.: Island Press, 1991), p.148. Reprinted with permission.

that the social contract between themselves and elected individuals has been broken and that it is now up to them to take responsive actions to protect the environment.[58] This observation is further supported by recent actions in California.
Many citizens in this state believe that it is necessary to go directly to the voters
through the initiative and referendum process, because the California legislature
is so beholden to special interests that legislative remedies are impossible.[59]

Thus, to some observers, the events of the past thirty years suggest a failure of
respresentative democracy and a corresponding rise in the use of direct democracy by citizens in various states.[60] At the very least, over the past thirty years, we
have witnessed "adversary democracy" (in which there seems to be winners and
losers in every environmental policy debate), a growing frustration with conventional politics, and environmental gridlock. Given this situation, what is the
future of state environmental management? Are there scenarios that we have not
yet considered? What is the most likely scenario? These are the questions to
which we now turn.

THE FUTURE OF ENVIRONMENTAL POLITICS AND POLICY

Although attempting to predict the future is always risky, it is nevertheless useful
to focus on the variation in state capabilities in an effort to predict state environmental management in the near-term future of the 1990s. This is especially
appropriate because of the current decentralization of federal environmental programs under the new federalism. Moreover, President Bill Clinton has said nothing to indicate whether he will reverse the flow of responsibility to the states and
cities during his administration. Nor has he said whether the states will receive
more money to fund their programs. His 1992 campaign pledge not to raise taxes
for the middle class suggests that the states will be left to their own resources to
carry out their environmental responsibilities. Thus, if we assume that the trend
toward decentralization of environmental programs will continue in the 1990s,
then it seems safe to predict that environmental management will be governed
by two fundamental considerations that are *internal* to the states themselves. The
first consideration is concerned with the question of *state government capability*,
and the second consideration is concerned with *state commitment to environmental
protection*.

It was previously believed that state governments lacked the expertise available to national governments, that they tended toward parochialism, that they
were unwilling or unable to raise revenue to meet service demands, and that they
were dominated by a conservative business-oriented elite. The institutional
reforms of the 1970s and 1980s were thought to have changed all this.
Proponents of decentralization, on the other hand, now argue that state governments are in closer touch with problems to which proposed rules will be applied,
that state governments are more flexible and innovative than the federal government, and that states are more able to fashion responses that are appropriate to

their individual conditions and preferences.[61] Based on our earlier discussion, however, we know that not all the states have taken initiatives to revitalize their institutional structures.

We also know from our above discussion of the variation in state responsiveness to environmental pollution that some of the states are more committed to environmental protection than are others.[62] We notice that the same states (e.g., California, Massachusetts, New Jersey, New York, Oregon, and Wisconsin) appear to be the most innovative and the most likely to have implemented federal environmental policies in the 1970s and the 1980s. Thus, given the great diversity that characterizes states' commitment to environmental protection and their institutional capabilities, it seems reasonable to suggest that states' responses to new federalism will vary considerably from one state context to another. What would seem to be appropriate is a typology that differentiates states in terms of the likely effects of new federalism. A state's response to new federalism will depend on two different, but nevertheless complementary, dimensions: (1) the degree of state commitment to environmental protection activities, and (2) the degree of state institutional capacity.[63] Based on this typology, four scenarios can be used to describe the most probable states' response to the new federalism in the 1990s.

The Progressives

The first group of states are those with a high commitment to environmental protection coupled with strong institutional capabilities. These include California, Florida, Maryland, Massachusetts, Michigan, New Jersey, New York, Oregon, Washington, and Wisconsin. In these states substantial improvements in the quality of the environment and in the implementation of federal environmental legislation are expected. As these states move ahead with regard to environmental quality, they may adopt policies that are independent of federal mandates. Environmental conditions will likely get better, not worse.

California, for example, considers the natural environment a very important issue. For almost three decades "air pollution bills have been winning approval in Sacramento, well ahead of the national government."[64] For states such as California, the major issue will be the extent to which the private and public sectors can reach a consensus on the strong environmental policies that these states will likely pursue. Significant tensions may arise in the course of these deliberations.

The Strugglers

A second category of states includes those with a strong commitment to environmental protection but with limited institutional capacities. These include Colorado, Connecticut, Delaware, Hawaii, Idaho, Iowa, Maine, Minnesota, Montana, Nevada, New Hampshire, North Carolina, North Dakota, Rhode Island, and Vermont. These states are willing, but often structurally unable, to implement federal environmental programs effectively. They have the will but not the resources (fiscally and institutionally) to pursue aggressive environmental protection policies. Progress probably will be made in these states, but it will be slower and possibly less innovative than in the progressive states. The "strugglers" will do the best they can within the constraints imposed on them. The major issues in these states will revolve around finding the means to implement aggressive environmental protection policies. Much of the debate will focus on issues associated with tax increases as these states seek to increase their resource base for environmental protection.

Vermont, for example, is staunchly protective of its environmental assets, but historically has been described as a "low service, high unemployment, communal" state.[65] That is, it has kept the costs of government low and has preferred a decentralized, "town-meeting" approach to its problems as opposed to the development of strong state-level institutions that are necessary for effective environmental policy.

The Delayers

The third group of states are those with a strong institutional capacity but with a limited commitment to environmental protection. These include Alabama, Alaska, Arkansas, Georgia, Illinois, Louisiana, Missouri, Ohio, Oklahoma, Pennsylvania, South Carolina, Tennessee, Texas, Virginia, and West Virginia. They will probably maintain the status quo with respect to the environment and move very slowly in implementing federal legislation. Whatever progress is made will be painstakingly slow.[66]

States that are dominated by the energy industry, such as Louisiana, Oklahoma, Texas, and West Virginia, comprise this group. West Virginia, for example, has been characterized as "still struggling," which means that it has few if any areas of exceptional program management, save for welfare policy.[67] It is a state that depends heavily on the federal government for intergovernmental aid and one that has not been able to build up its political institutions in a way that would sustain innovative environmental policies.[68] The major issue in these states will be apathetic state bureaucracies that seem unwilling to respond effectively to state environmental crises.

The Regressives

States with weak institutional capacities as well as a limited commitment to environmental protection include Arizona, Indiana, Kansas, Kentucky, Mississippi, Nebraska, New Mexico, South Dakota, Utah, and Wyoming. For these states decentralization of environmental programs will likely be a disaster. They may fail to implement federal laws in this area, and they are unlikely to take independent actions. The quality of life may deteriorate so much that large numbers of the population may move to other states (especially the more progressive ones). Dirty industries may continue to move into these states, making them even more un-attractive to the inhabitants. These states will continue to promote economic development at the expense of environmental quality. At some point a catastrophe may turn the states in this category around, but at present they seem to be captured by an obsessive optimism that prevents their taking necessary precautions against further damage to the environment.

Mississippi, for example, has been described by Neal Pierce and Jerry Hagstrom as a state in which the federal cutbacks in the early 1980s made the "road ahead bleaker than anytime since the Great Depression."[69] All too often, Mississippi is singled out as the state that lags behind all the other Southern states in the area of environmental protection. The "Mississippi syndrome," as it is called, means a state that cannot, or will not, move ahead in the implementation of its programs to protect the environment.

SUMMARY

In this brief review of environmental policy under the doctrine of new federalism, we have described changes in federal-state relations and reforms of state institutions. We also have examined environmental policy innovations in the states (including their commitment to and capacity for environmental policy-making). Implementation in the states is discussed, and we have suggested four possible classifications of the states in the 1990s: progressives, strugglers, delayers, and regressives. These scenarios range from extremely optimistic (the progressives) to extremely pessimistic (the regressives) with regard to the effectiveness with which states will address environmental problems. The scenarios assume no major changes in state commitments or institutional capabilities, but public opinion, recent tendencies toward participatory democracy, and attention by the media could cause some legislators to adopt very different strategies if conditions become intolerable.

The policy implications of this discussion are significant. If we find that federal-level factors are crucial influences on state environmental management, then the argument for centralization of environmental management would once again acquire enhanced credibility. That is, if federal inducements (such as federal legislation and intergovernmental aid) are necessary conditions for successful state environmental management, then a policy of decentralization probably will not work effectively for all states. On the other hand, if state-level conditions strongly influence state environmental management, then arguments about decentralization of environmental management would acquire even more credibility. Or decentralization may work well in some states (for example, the innovative states), but poorly in others (for example, the regressive states). Thus, "selective decentralization," a policy in which some programs are decentralized for some states and other programs for other states are not, may be a more appropriate strategy.[70]

In any case policymakers need to reconsider intergovernmental relations as they affect state environmental management. The federal government may or may not be the most appropriate governmental institution to tackle environmental pollution, but the fifty states are not equally able to muster the necessary resources to deal with environmental problems in the 1990s. Novel approaches will thus be required and are particularly appropriate in an era of "regulatory federalism," which will likely characterize the 1990s.

NOTES

1. Advisory Commission on Intergovernmental Relations, *Regulatory Federalism: Policy, Process, Impact and Reform* (Washington, D.C.: ACIR, 1984).
2. Philip Shabecoff, "The Environment as Local Jurisdiction," *New York Times,* 22 January 1989.
3. Ann O'M. Bowman and Richard C. Kearney, *The Resurgence of the States* (Englewood Cliffs, NJ: Prentice-Hall, 1986).
4. Ibid.
5. J. Edwin Benton and David R. Morgan, *Intergovernmental Relations and Public Policy* (Westport, CT: Greenwood Press, 1986); see also James P. Lester and Emmett N. Lombard, "The Comparative Analysis of State Environmental Policy," *Natural Resources Journal* 30, no. 2 (Spring 1990), pp. 301–319.
6. Not all scholars are in agreement as to the exact dates of these movements, but these dates are generally acceptable as benchmarks for each movement. See Samuel P. Hays, *Conservation and the Gospel of Efficiency* (Cambridge: Harvard University Press, 1959); Alan Schnaiberg, "The Environmental Movement: Roots and Transformations," in *The Environment: From Surplus to Scarcity,* ed. Alan Schnaiberg, (New York: Oxford University Press, 1980); and Henry P. Caulfield, "The Conservation and Environmental Movements: An Historical Analysis," in *Environmental Politics and Policy: Theories and Evidence,* ed. James P. Lester (Durham: Duke University Press, 1989).
7. Ernest A. Engelbert, "Political Parties and Natural Resources Policies: An Historical Evaluation," *Natural Resources Journal* 1 (November 1961), p. 226.
8. Ibid., p. 233.
9. Ibid., p. 227.
10. Hays, *Conservation* p. 2.
11. Ibid., p. 5.
12. Ibid., p. 28.
13. Caulfield, "The Conservation and Environmental Movements," p. 16.
14. Ibid., pp. 20–21.
15. Engelbert, "Political Parties," p. 245.
16. Hays, *Conservation,* p. 47.
17. Ibid., pp. 28–46.
18. Ibid., p. 53.
19. Ibid., p. 271.
20. Ibid.
21. Ibid.
22. Engelbert, "Political Parties," p. 380.
23. Schnaiberg, "Environmental Movement," p. 386.

24. Ibid.
25. Engelbert, "Political Parties," p. 240.
26. Ibid., p. 244.
27. *Conservation,* p. 13.
28. Schnaiberg, "Environmental Movement," p. 382.
29. Ibid., p. 383.
30. Phillip O. Foss, *The Politics of Grass* (Seattle: University of Washington Press, 1960).
31. Paul A. Sabatier and Hank Jenkins-Smith, "A Symposium of Public Policy Change and Policy-Oriented Learning," *Policy Sciences* 21 (1988), pp. 123–278.
32. John Carroll, ed., *Environmental Diplomacy: The Management and Resolution of Transfrontier Environmental Problems* (Cambridge: Cambridge University Press, 1988); and Norman Vig and Michael Kraft, *Environmental Policy in the 1990s* (Washington, D.C.: Congressional Quarterly Press, 1990), p. 4.
33. Robert C. Mitchell, "Public Opinion and the Green Lobby: Poised for the 1990s," in Vig and Kraft, *Environmental Policy,* pp. 81–99; and Riley Dunlap, "Public Opinion and Environmental Policy," in Lester, ed., *Environmental Politics and Policy,* pp. 87–134.
34. James P. Lester, "Federalism and Environmental Policy," *Publius* 16 (Winter 1986); Charles E. Davis and James P. Lester, "Decentralizing Federal Environmental Policy: A Research Note," *Western Political Quarterly* 40 (September 1987); and Lester and Lombard, "Comparative Analysis," pp. 301–319.
35. These points are dealt with at length in some of the newer texts in intergovernmental relations. Consult, for example, Deil S. Wright, *Understanding Intergovernmental Relations,* 2d ed. (Monterey, CA: Brooks-Cole, 1982); Parris N. Glendening and Mavis Mann Reeves, *Pragmatic Federalism,* 2d ed. (Pacific Palisades, CA: Palisades Publishers, 1984); Laurence J. O'Toole, Jr., ed., *American Intergovernmental Relations* (Washington, D.C.: Congressional Quarterly Press, 1985); David C. Nice, *Federalism: The Politics of Intergovernmental Relations* (New York: St. Martin's Press, 1987); and Thomas J. Anton, *American Federalism and Public Policy* (Philadelphia, PA: Temple University Press, 1989). See also Lester and Davis and Lester, "Decentralizing Federal Environmental Policy," "Federalism and Environmental Policy," pp. 555–565.
36. J. Clarence Davies, "Environmental Institutions and the Reagan Administration," in *Environmental Policy in the 1980s: Reagan's New Agenda,* ed. Norman J. Vig and Michael E. Kraft, (Washington, D.C.: Congressional Quarterly Press, 1984), p. 150.
37. Bowman and Kearney, *Resurgence of the States;* see also, Parris N. Glendening, "The States in the Fiscal Federal System," (paper presented at the annual meeting of the American Political Science Association, Washington, D.C., August 1984); and Advisory Commission on Intergovernmental Relations, *The Question of State Government Capability* (Washington, D.C.: U.S. Government Printing Office, 1985).
38. James P. Lester, "Federalism and State Environmental Policy," in *Environmental Politics and Policy: Theories and Evidence,* 2d ed., ed. James P. Lester (Durham, NC: Duke University Press, 1995).
39. See Advisory Commission on Intergovernmental Relations, *State Government Capability*; and Advisory Commission on Intergovernmental Relations, *The Transformation in American Politics* (Washington, D.C.: U.S. Government Printing Office, 1986).
40. See also Bowman and Kearney, *Resurgence of the States.*
41. See Ann O'M. Bowman and Richard C. Kearney, "Dimensions of State Government Capability," *Western Political Quarterly* 41 (June 1988), pp. 341–362.

42. Bob Hall and Mary Lee Kerr, *1991–1992 Green Index* (Washington, D.C.: Island Press, 1991), pp. 3–5.

43. U.S. Environmental Protection Agency, *Pollution Prevention News* (Washington, D.C.: Office of Pollution Prevention and Toxics, 1992), p. 10.

44. The Council of State Governments, *Innovations in Environment and Natural Resources* (Lexington, KY: Council of State Governments, 1986).

45. Philip Shabecoff, "The Environment as Local Jurisdiction," *New York Times,* 22 January 1989, p. E9.

46. James L. Regens and Margaret A. Reams, "State Strategies for Regulating Groundwater Quality," *Social Science Quarterly* 69 (September 1988), pp. 53–59.

47. Scott Ridley, *The State of the States: 1987* (Washington, D.C.: Fund for Renewable Energy and the Environment, 1987). Similar reports were issued for 1988 and 1989.

48. Mark Obmascik, "Survey Places Colorado 26th in Environmental Efforts," *Denver Post,* 1 March 1989, p. A1.

49. R. Steven Brown and Edward Garner, *Resource Guide to State Environmental Management* (Lexington, KY: Council of State Governments, 1988), pp. 2–96.

50. Interviews with staff at the U.S. Environmental Protection Agency, Office of Solid Waste, State Programs Branch, July 1987.

51. For excellent discussions of the variation in state environmental policy implementation, see William Lowry, *The Dimensions of Federalism* (Durham, NC: Duke University Press, 1992) and Evan Ringquist, *Environmental Protection at the State Level* (Armonk, NY: M. E. Sharpe, 1993).

52. Pinky S. Wassenberg, "Implementation of Intergovernmental Regulatory Programs: A Cost-Benefit Perspective," in *Intergovernmental Relations and Public Policy,* ed. Edwin Benton and David R. Morgan (Westport, CT: Greenwood Press, 1986), pp. 123–137; Patricia M. Crotty, "The New Federalism Game: Primacy Implementation of Environmental Policy," *Publius* 17 (Spring 1987), pp. 57–63; James P. Lester, "Superfund Implementation: Exploring Environmental Gridlock," *Environmental Impact Assessment Review* 8 (June 1988), pp. 159–174; and James P. Lester and Ann O'M. Bowman, "Implementing Environmental Policy in a Federal System: A Test of the Sabatier-Mazmanian Model," *Polity* 21 (Summer 1989), pp. 731–753.

53. Crotty, "New Federalism Game," pp. 53–55; and Deborah H. Jessup, *Guide to State Environmental Programs* (Washington, D.C.: Bureau of National Affairs, 1989).

54. U.S. Department of Commerce, Bureau of the Census, *Environmental Quality Control* (Washington, D.C.: U.S. Government Printing Office, 1982).

55. Hall and Kerr, *1991–1992 Green Index,* p. 148.

56. For an excellent discussion of the impact of environmental protection policies on pollution abatement, see Evan J. Ringquist, "Evaluating Environmental Policy Outcomes," in *Environmental Politics and Policy: Theories and Evidence,* 2d ed., ed. James P. Lester (Durham, NC: Duke University Press, 1995).

57. Theodore Lowi, *The End of Liberalism* (New York: W. W. Norton, 1969); Charles H. Stoddard, *Looking Forward* (New York: Macmillan, 1982); and Trudi Miller, "Normative Political Science," *Policy Studies Review* 9 (1990), pp. 232–246.

58. Adeline G. Levine, *Love Canal: Science, Politics and People* (Lexington, MA: Lexington Books, 1982); and Raymond Goldsteen and John Schorr, *Demanding Democracy After Three Mile Island* (Gainesville: University of Florida Press, 1991).

59. Robert Reinhold, "Politics of the Environment: California Will Test the Waters," *New York Times,* 27 April 1990, p. A1.

60. Miller, "Normative Political Science"; John Mark Johnson, "Citizens Initiate Ballot Measures," *Environment* 32 (September 1990), pp. 4–45; and Goldsteen and Schorr, *Demanding Democracy.*

61. See Jeffrey Henig, *Public Policy and Federalism* (New York: St. Martin's Press, 1985); and John Scholz, "State Regulatory Reform and Federal Regulation," *Policy Studies Review* 1 (1981), pp. 347–359.

62. Paul E. Peterson, Barry Rabe, and Kenneth K. Wong, *When Federalism Works* (Washington, D.C.: Brookings Institution, 1986).

63. See Lester, "Federalism and State Environmental Policy."

64. Neal Pierce and Jerry Hagstrom, *The Book of America: Inside the Fifty States Today* (New York: Warner Books, 1984), p. 766.

65. Ibid., p. 199.

66. Donald G. Schueler, "Southern Exposure," *Sierra* 77 (November–December 1992), pp. 44–49.

67. Pierce and Hagstrom, *Book of America,* p. 345.

68. Ibid., pp. 338–347.

69. Ibid., p. 456.

70. Peterson, Rabe, and Wong, *When Federalism Works.*

PART FOUR

CONCLUSIONS

UTILIZING POLICY ANALYSIS

"In principle, everyone is for analysis; in practice, there is no certainty that it will be incorporated into the real-world decision process."

JAMES SCHLESINGER

A newcomer to the analysis of public policy might assume that once a policy analysis has been carried out and the findings have been reported to the decision makers, the analysis would be used in designing new policies or in changing old ones. However, in most cases nothing at all seems to happen after the analysis is delivered to those who commissioned the study in the first place. One might then assume that the policy analysis was not utilized by the decision maker because it was flawed. In fact, the quality of the methodology used in the policy analysis has very little to do with the actual use of that analysis. Many other factors influence the utilization of policy analysis, most of which are beyond the control of the analyst.

This chapter discusses the factors that influence utilization of policy analysis by the consumers of that analysis, usually governmental decision makers. If we can understand why analysis is not used, as well as the factors that influence utilization, then we can perhaps increase the use of policy analysis in the future.

USING POLICY ANALYSIS

The study of the utilization of policy analysis is "concerned with understanding and improving the utilization of scientific and professional knowledge in settings of public policy and professional practice".[1] It has benefited from periodic reviews of research, and some of this research has examined the effects of factors that influence the utilization of research by decision makers.[2] Because much of contemporary public policy research is directed toward discovering ways to improve policy outcomes in substantive issue areas such as the ones covered in this book, it is important to understand the knowledge utilization process. This includes developing both an understanding of the degree to which research findings are utilized by policymakers and the circumstances under which use typically occurs.

As we noted in Chapter 1, there has been a tremendous growth in policy analysis over the previous decade, yet early utilization research suggests that governmental decision makers make little direct use of this research.[3] Recent studies are somewhat more optimistic about the utilization of policy analyses by decision makers.[4]

Research findings are inconsistent for a number of reasons, many of which stem from conceptual and methodological problems identified by Downs and Mohr and others.[5] Moreover, knowledge utilization research is still in its infancy, and a well-defined framework does not yet exist that attempts to explain the full range of conditions under which policy analysis is useful. In this chapter, we synthesize and critique research on knowledge utilization as well as present a conceptual framework for future testing at the level of federal, state, or local government policymaking. We define what is meant by the utilization of policy analysis and discuss recent efforts at synthesizing this research. Second, we review some of the predictors of knowledge utilization. Finally, we offer some summary observations and discuss the implications of the framework for knowledge utilization by state decision makers or others.

DEFINING KNOWLEDGE UTILIZATION: PREVIOUS RESEARCH

Most of the literature examining knowledge utilization by political decision makers has been concerned with answering the question, What are the characteristics of social science research studies that make them most "useful" for decision making? According to Weiss and Bucavalas, "useful" involves: (1) whether or not the content makes an intrinsic contribution to the work of an agency; and (2) whether or not officials say they would be likely to take that research into account in decision making.[6] Among the several meanings of utilization employed by researchers, Weiss identifies the knowledge-driven model, the problem-solving model, and the enlightenment model.[7] Bulmer identifies the empiricist model, the engineering model, and the enlightenment model.[8] In the empiricist model, the task of the researcher is to produce facts that, when fed into the policy process, will enable policymakers to reach the best decisions on the basis of information available. It posits a one-way, linear relationship between the researcher and the policymaker. That is, the researcher produces policy-relevant information and the decision makers use it in reaching their decisions. Thus, the engineering model sees the social scientist as a technician who provides the evidence and conclusions to help solve a concrete problem. Therefore, the task of the basic researcher is to develop and test a logical list of hypotheses explaining use and to communicate their findings directly to policymakers. The enlightenment model also seeks specific answers to policy problems, but its emphasis is on creating the intellectual conditions for problem solving.[9]

To a large extent, the research utilization literature has adopted the two-communities theory, which suggests that direct use of policy research by decision makers is unlikely because of the competing worldviews and belief systems of policy researchers and policymakers.[10] The usual recommendation for increasing the use of policy research by policymakers is that both communities should undertake changes such that communication and interaction between the two groups is more likely. Specifically, (1) users of knowledge must become better consumers of knowledge by being more open to research and looking for applications to policy problems; and (2) researchers must become more assertive and/or more sensitive in their dissemination of knowledge.[11]

Although we recognize that both producers and users of policy analysis must become more sensitive to the concerns of each other, it is useful at this point to understand the criticisms directed at this area of policy analysis. Some of those criticisms are described below.

Some Criticisms of Previous Research

Empirical research on knowledge utilization has been the subject of much criticism by the research community. At least three main criticisms are directed toward this literature. First, previous research on knowledge utilization has relied on survey questionnaires or case studies with unknown or unreported reliability and validity.[12] We cannot be sure that the information reported on the surveys by decision makers accurately reflects the reasons for nonuse of policy analysis. Second, knowledge use has not been adequately defined. We still lack a mutually agreed on definition of knowledge use. Finally, empirical support for claims that particular classes of factors affect the utilization of knowledge in decisive ways has not been consistent.[13] Much more research will be needed to confirm that specific sets of variables are crucial to knowledge use by decision makers.

This latter criticism stems from the fact that researchers do not agree about the set of variables existing in the literature to predict knowledge use by decision makers.[14] In many cases, these models are merely a "checklist" of variables presumed to influence knowledge utilization, rather than a formal heuristic device. Moreover, there has been little rigorous research on the ability of these models to predict knowledge use.[15] Finally, these models have been developed largely in response to the two-communities perspective on knowledge utilization, in which attention is directed toward bridging the gap between knowledge producers and knowledge consumers. Thus, these models attempt to identify variables that can be manipulated by either of these two sets of actors in such a way that knowledge transfer is facilitated.

However, most of the previous models fail to take into account the context or external political environment that affects both producers and consumers of knowledge. That is, modifications in both the policymaker community and the researcher community still leave use open to impact by a number of variables and, as a consequence, a large portion of the explanation for knowledge use by decision makers may have gone unexamined. Researchers have thus ignored the comparative importance of competing sets of explanatory factors by focusing primarily on two sets of variables that relate either to the analysis itself or the users of that analysis. More attention must be given to the political environment within which analysis takes place.

Recently, a number of scholars have begun to stress the political and policy context within which both policymakers and researchers conduct their business as a key variable affecting knowledge utilization.[16] Moreover, several recent research efforts have resulted in the accumulation of a greater number of empirical variables in their findings that are helpful in developing a more comprehensive framework for examining the determinants of utilization of policy analysis by decision makers. More specifically, these studies have identified obstacles to the more complete use of policy analyses in making public policy. As we noted briefly in Chapter 8, these obstacles may be categorized into three groups of factors: (1) **contextual factors**, or factors having to do with the political environment within which the policy analysis takes place; (2) **technical factors**, or factors having to do with the methodology employed in the policy analysis; and (3) **human factors,** or factors having to do with the psychological makeup of the users of the policy analysis.

These studies provide us with a wider understanding of the range of factors that presumably affect use, and they permit us to develop a more comprehensive model of knowledge utilization. This model may help us to predict better the conditions under which policy analysis will or will not be used.

KNOWLEDGE UTILIZATION: A CONCEPTUAL FRAMEWORK

Knowledge utilization is a function of (1) inducements and constraints provided to or imposed on the user from the **context** within which analysis takes place; (2) the **analysis** itself; and (3) the decision makers' own **predispositions** toward policy analysis (see Figure 14-1).[17] A model of knowledge utilization must also recognize the interdependence of each of these three categories of factors on utilization of policy analysis. Figure 14-1 illustrates the model of knowledge utilization used in this discussion. In examining the components of the model in Figure 14-1, we need to distinguish between conceptual and instrumental uses of knowledge. Generally, conceptual use refers to changes in the way the users think about problems, and instrumental use refers to changes in actual behavior, especially changes that are rele-

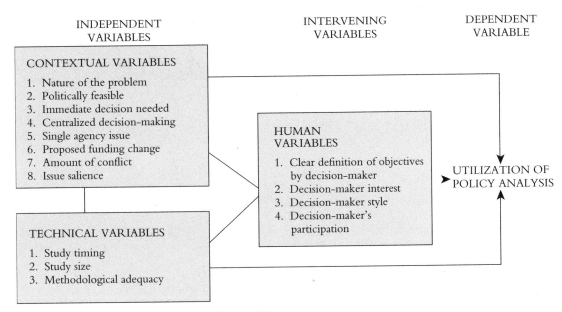

FIGURE 14-1   The Knowledge Utilization Process

Source: Reprinted from James P. Lester and Leah J. Wilds, "The Utilization of Public Policy Analysis: A Conceptual Framework," *Evaluation and Program Planning* 13, no. 3 (1990), p. 316, Copyright 1990, with kind permission from Elsevier Science Ltd, The Boulevard, Langford Lane, Kidlington OX5 1GB, UK.

vant to decision making.[18] A useful approach to understanding knowledge utilization is to "see it as the flow of information to decision-makers in which levels of utilization are conceived as stages in which each is a link in the chain of utilization."[19] Table 14-1 presents such a continuum.

Contextual Inducements and Constraints

The first set of predictor variables is concerned with the policy and political environment within which policy analysis is undertaken. The nature of the problem obviously affects utilization, because some problems are more intractable than are others. Many problem types, such as the effects of low-level radiation on human health, are subject to widely different interpretations by equally reputable scientists.[20] Highly intractable problems that are subject to diverse and conflicting interpretations tend to make utilization of knowledge much more difficult than problems for which there may be more definitive solutions. Second, the political feasibility of any policy alternative (no matter how convincing the argument) will affect the ultimate use of a policy solution. Third, the immediacy of the need for a decision will affect use because urgency creates a greater demand for analysis than the absence of urgency. In addition, centralized decision making lends itself to utilization of policy analysis as well as a proposed funding change. Finally, the amount of conflict involved in the policy issue as well as its salience to decision makers will affect utilization.[21]

TABLE 14-1   Seven Standards of Utilization

1. Reception
   Utilization takes place when policy-makers or advisors receive policy relevant information. When the communication comes to rest in the "in-basket," so that the data "reach" the policy-maker rather than remain on an analyst's desk or in the files of a distant consultant firm, utilization is complete.

2. Cognition
   The policy-maker must read, digest, and understand the studies. When he has done so, utilization has occurred.

3. Reference
   If frame of reference is the criterion, then utilization somehow must change the way the policy-maker sees the world. If information changes his preferences, or his understanding of the probabilities or magnitudes of impacts he fears or desires, utilization is a reality.

4. Effort
   To make a real difference, information must influence the actions of policy-makers. If they fight for adoption of a study's recommendations, we know a real effort was made even if political forces or other events block it.

5. Adoption
   What is essential is not whether policy-relevant information is an input to the policy process . . . but whether it goes on to influence policy outcomes. Policy results, not inputs, are the proper standard.

6. Implementation
   Policy adoption is critical but, if adopted policy never becomes practice, information has no chance to affect action. Adoption without implementation is a hollow victory.

7. Impact
   A policy may be implemented but fail to have the desired effects. Hence it may be (and is) argued that only when policy stimulated by information yields tangible benefits to the citizen has utilization taken place.

Source: Jack Knott and Aaron Wildavsky, "If Dissemination Is the Solution, What Is the Problem," *Knowledge: Creation, Diffusion, Utilization* 1 (1980), p. 539, copyright © 1980 by Sage Publications, Inc. Reprinted by permission of Sage Publications, Inc.

Technical Inducements and Constraints

The model also suggests that characteristics of the analysis itself will affect utilization. Specifically, the quality of the policy analysis itself will affect use. For example, such considerations as a study's timing, size, and methodological adequacy will affect usage. These are the only variables under the direct control of the analyst, yet they are only a few of the kinds of variables that might affect use.

User Attitudes as Inducements and Constraints

Finally, the model suggests that characteristics of the recipient of the policy analysis will ultimately affect utilization. For example, if the decision maker has a clear definition of objectives to be pursued by the policy analysts, then the chances of utilization are enhanced. Also, the greater the interest and participation by the decision maker in the subject and scope of the policy analysis, the better the chances of utilization. In addition, a decision maker's style has been shown to be related to knowledge utilization.[22]

The findings cited above suggest a basic applicability of this framework to an explanation of utilization of policy analysis by decision makers. In the remainder of this chapter, we discuss some implications of this framework and an agenda for future work in this area.

SOME SUMMARY OBSERVATIONS AND IMPLICATIONS FOR FUTURE RESEARCH

In this chapter we have reviewed some of the literature on knowledge utilization in an effort to develop a more comprehensive model for explaining such behavior. The model suggests that utilization of policy analyses by decision makers is affected by three categories of variables: (1) contextual inducements and constraints, (2) technical inducements and constraints, and (3) human (user) inducements and constraints.

The most obvious implication of the framework is that variables other than those related to the "two communities" need to be considered in future attempts to explain knowledge utilization by decision makers. Previous approaches have been, for the most part, limited to variables related to the producers of knowledge (i.e., the policy analyst or the analysis itself) or the consumers of knowledge (i.e., the decision makers). In doing so, other important conditions, such as the political context within which analysis takes place, may have been neglected as far as understanding the determinants of utilization.

A second major implication of the framework is that most of the variables affecting knowledge utilization are outside of the control of the policy analyst. Thus, it is no surprise that much of the early research found knowledge utilization to be limited. Some of the variables (e.g., methodological or technical) can be controlled by the analyst, and thus manipulation of these variables by the analyst may enhance future use. Indeed, some of the variables identified in the framework are subject to manipulation, whereas others are not. If future research finds that some of the contextual and user variables in the framework are important to knowledge utilization, and they can be manipulated, this may also suggest a means of increasing knowledge use by decision makers.

Nevertheless, a number of questions need to be answered about research on the utilization of policy analysis by decision makers. First, we need to know which category of variables has the most influence on utilization. Are contextual variables more important than technical or human variables? Second, we need to discover which variables in the framework are most important in determining utilization. Which individual variables are most important in the framework? Which variables are unimportant? Are important variables left out of the model? Third, we need to identify the relationships between and among these variables. That is, what are the interactive effects (if any) of these variables on utilization? Finally, as Beyer and Trice suggest, "researchers should employ methods that discriminate between partial and complete use by collecting data on a range of utilizing behaviors; they will then be able to investigate factors associated with greater or less utilization and with different patterns of incomplete utilization."[23] It would be useful to explore the determinants of use in each of these various stages of knowledge use. That is, are contextual factors more important in the impact stage or in the implementation stage? Are technical factors more important in the reception stage or in the impact stage? Finally, are human factors more important in the cognition stage or in the implementation stage? These kinds of questions have not yet been answered by research on knowledge use.

In the future, researchers will need to examine the utilization of policy analysis by federal, state, and local government decision makers in several functional areas including agriculture, alcohol and drug abuse, child labor, corrections, economic development, environmental protection, higher education, highway safety, mass transportation, public utility regulation, public welfare, telecommunications, and vocation education. In conducting this research, analysts will need to address three different sets of questions: (1) What are the sources of information for these decision makers? Do the sources vary by type of decision maker? (2) Do these decision makers use policy analyses in reaching policy decisions in these functional areas? If so, is this usage primarily conceptual or instrumental? Do some types of decision makers (or functional areas) utilize policy analyses more so than others? And finally, (3) what are the determinants of knowledge utilization? Do these determinants vary by type of decision maker? Future research in the utilization of policy analysis will need to answer these questions as well as to further refine the model of knowledge utilization presented here.[24]

NOTES

1. Willian N. Dunn, Burkhart Holzner, and Gerald Zaltman, "Knowledge Utilization," in *The International Encyclopedia of Education,* ed. T. Husen and T. N. Postlethwaite (Oxford: Pergamon Press, 1985).

2. See, for example, Michael Huberman, "Steps Toward an Integrated Model of Research Utilization," *Knowledge: Creation, Diffusion, Utilization* 8 (1987), pp. 586–611.

3. See, for example, Carol H. Weiss, "Knowledge Creep and Decision Accretion," *Knowledge: Creation, Diffusion, Utilization* 1 (1980), pp. 381–404.

4. David Whiteman, "The Fate of Policy Analysis in Congressional Decision-Making: Three Types of Use in Committees," *Western Political Quarterly* 38 (June 1985), pp. 294–311; and David Webber, "Legislators' Use of Policy Information," *American Behavioral Scientist* 30 (July-August 1987), pp. 612–631.

5. C. W. Downs and L. B. Mohr, "Conceptual Issues in the Study of Innovation," *Administrative Science Quarterly* 21 (December 1976), pp. 700–713; and Paul A. Sabatier, "The Acquisition and Utilization of Technical Information by Administrative Agencies," *Administrative Science Quarterly* 23 (September 1978), pp. 396–417.

6. See Carol H. Weiss and Michael Bucavalas, "The Challenge of Social Research to Decision-Making," in *Using Social Research in Public Policy-Making,* ed. Carol H. Weiss (Lexington, MA: Lexington Books, 1977).

7. Weiss, "Knowledge Creep."
8. Martin Bulmer, *The Uses of Social Research: Social Investigation in Public Policy-Making* (Boston: Allen and Unwin, 1982).
9. Ibid.
10. Nathan Caplan, "The Two-Communities Theory and Knowledge Utilization," *American Behavioral Scientist* 22 (January–February 1979), pp. 459–470.
11. Edward M. Glaser, "Knowledge Transfer and Institutional Change," *Professional Psychology* 4 (November 1973), pp. 434–444.
12. Sabatier, "Acquisition and Utilization."
13. Dunn, Holzner, and Zaltman, "Knowledge Utilization."
14. There have been, however, a number of attempts to develop analytical frameworks of the variables purported to affect the utilization of knowledge by decision makers. See, for example, Paul A. Sabatier, "The Acquisition and Utilization of Technical Information by Administrative Agencies," *Administrative Science Quarterly* 23 (1978), pp. 396–417.
15. Jeffrey Bedell et al., "An Empirical Evaluation of a Model of Knowledge Utilization," *Evaluation Review* 9 (April 1985), pp. 109–126.
16. Sabatier, "Acquisition and Utilization"; Whiteman, "Fate of Policy Analysis"; and Webber, "Legislators' Use of Policy Information."
17. See James P. Lester and Leah J. Wilds, "The Utilization of Public Policy Analysis: A Conceptual Framework," *Evaluation and Program Planning* 13, no. 3 (1990), pp. 313–319.
18. Dunn, Holzner, and Zaltman, "Knowledge Utilization."
19. Jack Knott and Aaron Wildavsky, "If Dissemination Is the Solution, What Is the Problem," *Knowledge: Creation, Diffusion, Utilization* 1 (1980), pp. 537–578.
20. William W. Lowrance, *Of Acceptable Risk* (Los Altos, CA: William Kaufman, 1976).
21. Whiteman, "Fate of Policy Analysis."
22. Webber, "Legislators' Use of Policy Information."
23. Janice M. Beyer and Harrison M. Trice, "The Utilization Process: A Conceptual Framework and Synthesis of Empirical Findings," *Administrative Science Quarterly* 27 (December 1982), pp. 591–622.
24. See James P. Lester, "The Utilization of Policy Analysis by State Agency Officials," *Knowledge: Creation, Diffusion, Utilization* 14 (March 1993), pp. 267–290.

CHAPTER FIFTEEN

TAKING STOCK: THE EVOLUTION OF POLICY STUDIES

"All is ready if our minds be so."
SHAKESPEARE

We have examined the evolution of both research on the policy process and public policy in the areas of education, welfare, crime, and the environment. By tracing both the evolutionary development of the study of public policy and the evolutionary development of selected public policies, we hope to convey the amount of intellectual growth and development that has taken place over the past two or three decades. Too often, students fail to understand how early conceptual developments pave the way for later ones. Our understanding of the policy process is constantly evolving as policy scholars develop new conceptual tools to increase their understanding. Similarly, we continue to learn more about the substance of policy and try to develop solutions that remedy pressing public policy problems in education, welfare, crime, and the environment. In addition, students need to understand that the analysis of policy problems has helped us to better understand the policy process. For example, research on environmental policy and politics has added a great deal to our understanding of public policy implementation and change.[1]

In this chapter, we summarize the major points discussed in the preceding chapters and present an agenda for future research on the policy cycle.

THE EVOLUTION OF POLICY STUDIES, 1950–1995

From 1950 to 1995 we have observed a number of changes in policy studies. These changes involve what is studied, how we approach the study of public policy, and the methods used in our analyses. Table 15-1 illustrates the evolution of policy studies during this time.

In the 1950s and the early 1960s, the focus of policy studies tended to be on the problem of **policy formulation,** in which various analysts attempted to explain why policies were formulated, using such explanatory models as the elitist, pluralist, and subgovernment models. Later, scholars developed alternative models to explain policy formulation, such as the rational and incremental models. The primary method used during this time was the **case study,** a detailed explanation of all the factors that influenced the formulation of public policy. The dominant approach was largely qualitative or **prebehavioral;** rigorous statistical analysis was not yet used. Evidence was drawn largely from detailed descriptions or anecdotal evidence.

Beginning in the mid-1960s, policy scholars began to use **quantitative statistical techniques** to assess the influence of various factors on policy formulation. Their new approach reflected **behavioralism (positivism)** or the view that public policy could be studied scientifically, that hypotheses could be formulated about these phenomena and then tested through rigorous statistical analysis. During this time period, policy scholars began to examine other aspects of the policy cycle, including **policy implementation, agenda setting, policy evaluation,** and **policy termination.** Clearly, this period in the history of policy studies witnessed tremendous growth in the field.

Finally, the most recent period in the history of policy studies, from 1990 to the present, suggests another spurt of growth and evolutionary development. In this period, research continued on **policy implementation,** and **agenda setting,** as scholars sought to refine and extend earlier research as well as to develop the concept of **policy change.** Methods and approaches have also changed. A challenge to the positivist paradigm has occurred in the form of **postpositivism,** in which it is argued that many policy phenomena cannot be studied with scientific methods and rigorous statistical techniques. Postpositivist scholars argue instead that

TABLE 15–1 The Evolution of Policy Studies, 1950–1995

	1950s	1960s–1970s	1980s–1990s
Phase of policy cycle addressed	Policy formulation	Policy implementation Agenda setting Policy evaluation Policy termination	Policy change
Dominant approach	Prebehavioral	Behavioral (Positivism)	Postpositivism
Method of analysis	Case studies	Quantitative techniques	Mixed methods

concepts such as policy implementation require more intuitive approaches. This criticism of quantitative methods and the advocacy of more qualitative techniques have brought about a healthy reconciliation. Policy scholars now rely on **mixed methods,** or a combination of quantitative and qualitative techniques, in their analysis of public policy.

In summary, the evolution of the policy studies subfield since 1950 reflects a healthy development. We know much more about the policy cycle and we are willing to study it from more diverse perspectives and methods than ever before.

THE EVOLUTION OF RESEARCH ON THE POLICY CYCLE

Research on the policy process inevitably evolves through four stages of development.

Stage 1: Concept development.   The first stage in the development of our understanding of the policy cycle is the introduction of the concept itself. Scholars must first understand what we mean by such terms as *agenda setting* or *policy implementation.* After these researchers have developed the meaning of the concept, further research can move our understanding to the next stage.

Stage 2: Model building.   The next stage in the research process is the development of models to guide research inquiries. Usually after a number of case studies of a particular phenomenon have been published, another scholar will undertake a review and synthesis of those case studies with a view toward identifying the critical variables thought to affect the behavior they are attempting to explain. This will usually result in an analytical framework that categorizes these explanatory variables and tries to make some sense out of them in an organized way. This effort usually results in a new model of a particular phase of the policy cycle. After this, researchers move to the next stage, model testing.

Stage 3: Model testing.   For the model testing stage, still other scholars (or sometimes the authors of the model themselves) will undertake an empirical test of the model. To do this, they identify specific hypotheses stemming from the model, develop measures of each aspect of the model and its hypotheses, and then test the model in a particular substantive area and (it is hoped) across time. Essentially, this part of the research process is concerned with an attempt to refute the model's hypotheses by way of rigorous statistical tests.

Stage 4: Synthesis and revision.   Finally, after much testing of the models by several investigators, other scholars are likely to revise the existing model on the basis of their own findings, to develop an entirely new version of the model, or chart a new course, which then moves the research agenda back to stage three. Such efforts are important because they can facilitate an increased understanding of the concept and its empirical determinants by sensitizing us to new sources of data and hypotheses, thus uncovering a more complete explanation than what was previously available.

In summary, our understanding of each stage of the policy cycle has advanced over the last twenty-five years, largely by moving through each of the four research stages. By examining various aspects of the policy cycle against this framework, we may see which stages are more fully developed than others and identify the next step in theory building for agenda setting, policy formulation, policy implementation, policy evaluation, policy termination, or policy change.

Table 15-2 presents a summary of the current status of research in each stage of the policy cycle. Clearly, much remains to be done in the areas of agenda setting, policy implementation, policy termination, and policy change. For example, in agenda setting, we need to see research progress to the next stage of model testing. Almost no tests of the Kingdon model of agenda setting have been completed and published. The recent work of Baumgartner and Jones has yet to be tested systematically by scholars other than the authors. With regard to policy implementation, we still do not have third-generation implementation studies. That is, we do not have studies that are genuinely comparative (across time, across units of analysis, and across policy types).[2] In policy termination, we still do not have a model of the process of policy termination that has been systematically tested.[3] What is especially needed in this area is a careful review and synthesis of the extant research with a view toward building a model of policy, program, or organizational termination. Finally, Paul Sabatier and his associates are in the process of testing their model of policy change; however, it would be useful if competing models of policy change were developed by other scholars and if testing of the Sabatier model of policy change were done by scholars other than the authors of the original model. Moreover, the models of policy change discussed in Chapter 9 and advanced by Schlesinger or Amenta and Skocpol have yet to be systematically tested.

TABLE 15–2   Current Status of Research on the Policy Cycle

Stage of Policy Cycle	Concept Development	Model Building	Model Testing	Synthesis and Revision
1. Agenda setting	★	★	Present	Future
2. Policy formulation	★	★	★	Present
3. Policy implementation	★	★	★	Present
4. Policy evaluation	★	★	★	Present
5. Policy termination	★	Present	Future	Future
6. Policy change	★	★	Present	Future

★ = Research already completed.

The future of research on the policy cycle is an exciting one, and we are confident that these areas will be addressed in the future. In addition, an area of potential interest is "how all of the extant theoretical work fits together."[4] The various bodies of theory in public policy include positivist theory, postpositivist theory, micro theory, and macro theory. Traditional policy analysis is largely composed of positivist, macro theory (e.g., models of policy formulation or implementation), whereas the postpositivists challenge us to arrive at policy prescriptions through normative and interpretive approaches. The challenge ahead is to try to find ways to integrate these various approaches into a better understanding of the policy process and substantive outcomes. There is no need for positivists and postpositivists to engage in a fruitless debate over which methods to use in policy analysis. Both approaches are useful, and together they can provide the basis for theoretical breakthroughs in policy analysis.

THE EVOLUTION OF PUBLIC POLICY

As discussed in Chapters 10 through 13, substantive public policy itself pursues an evolutionary path as well as research on the policy process. We discussed changes in educational, welfare, crime, and environmental policy over time. In Chapter 9, several alternative theories of policy change were presented to help account for the changes in substantive policies over time. Let us briefly review each of these alternative explanations.

The Cyclical Thesis

The cyclical thesis, offered by Arthur Schlesinger, argues that there is a continuing shift in national involvement between public purpose and private interest.[5] More specifically, he argues that American politics follows a certain rhythm in which it follows a fairly regular cyclical alternation between conservatism and liberalism in our national moods. There are swings back and forth between eras when the national commitment is to private interest as the best means of meeting our national problems and eras when the national commitment is to public purpose. At roughly thirty-year intervals, Schlesinger argues, the nation turns to reform and affirmative government as the best way of dealing with our troubles. According to Schlesinger, then, a major proposition about the evolution of American public policy over the past hundred years would suggest the following:

. **Proposition 1:** The evolution of public policy follows a fairly predictable pattern in which a period of private remedies (and minimal governmental intervention) will be followed by a period of significant governmental intervention and reform. A period of liberalism will be followed by a period of conservatism before the entire cycle repeats itself. This process occurs about every thirty years.

The Evolutionary or Policy-Learning Thesis

A second explanation comes from recent work by Paul A. Sabatier.[6] He has recently developed a conceptual framework of the policy process that views policy change as a function of three sets of factors: (1) the interaction of competing advocacy coalitions within a policy subsystem/community; (2) changes external to the subsystem; and (3) the effects of stable system parameters. The framework has at least three basic premises. First, understanding the process of policy change—and the role of policy learning therein—requires a time perspective of a decade or more. This is so we can observe a more complete policy cycle (i.e., from policy formation to implementation to evaluation and change). Second, the most useful way to think about policy change over such a time span is through a focus on policy subsystems, which are composed of advocacy coalitions (i.e., the interaction of actors from different institutions interested in a policy area). Third, public policies can be conceptualized in the same manner as belief systems (i.e., sets of value priorities and causal assumptions about how to realize them).[7] Basically, policy change is viewed as the product of both (1) changes in systemwide events, such as socioeconomic perturbations or outputs from other subsystems, and (2) the striving of competing advocacy coalitions within the subsystem to realize their core beliefs over time as they seek to increase their resource bases, to respond to opportunities provided by external events, and to learn more about the policy problem(s) of interest to them.[8] Thus, the evolution of public policy is explained by an extended period of policy change in which governmental actors repeatedly revised policy on the basis of policy learning brought on by events external to subsystem politics. More specifically:

Proposition 2a: Policy-oriented learning across belief systems is most likely when there is an intermediate level of informed conflict between the two. This requires that (a) each have the technical resources to engage in such a debate and that (b) the conflict be between secondary aspects of one belief system and core elements of the other or, alternatively, between important secondary aspects of the two belief systems.

Proposition 2b: Policy-oriented learning across belief systems is most likely when there exists a forum that is (a) prestigious enough to force professionals from different coalitions to participate and (b) dominated by professional norms.

The Backlash or Zigzag Thesis

A final explanation of changes in public policy over time comes from the work of Edwin Amenta and Theda Skocpol.[9] They argue that there is an erratic pattern in the history of American public policies characterized by a "zigzag effect" or a stimulus and response (or backlash). It is not so much a shift from liberal to conservative as from policy that first benefits one group, then another as a backlash to the first group. The concept of class struggle or competing societal coalitions comes to mind as a useful way to explain the above shifts. The following proposition is derived from their argument:

Proposition 3: The evolution of public policy from 1890 to 1990 is best explained by a zigzag pattern in which the public policies of one era provide the stimulus for a reaction in the next era. Thus, policies undergo drastic changes as a reaction to a previous policy; for example, policies that favor one group (e.g., citizen interests) in one era are replaced by policies that favor other groups (e.g., the corporate sector) in the next era.

A COMPARISON OF MODELS OF POLICY CHANGE

In concluding this chapter, we examine patterns in the evolution of American public policies in education, welfare, crime, and the environment. Specifically, we are interested in examining the relevance of alternative explanations of policy change over time: the cyclical thesis, the policy-learning thesis, and the backlash thesis. In Table 15-3, we suggest that each of these perspectives helps to explain the evolution of these four types of public policy.

Educational Policy Change

A review of educational policy from 1960 to 1990 suggests that the cyclical thesis best explains the evolution of this type of policy. Specifically, in the 1960s and the 1970s, emphasis was placed on compensatory education in an attempt to address resource shortages among poverty-impacted schools. The logic of liberalism guided this policy as the learning environment was considered to be deficient. An attempt was made to address environmental shortages by redistributing expenditures for education.

In the more conservative 1980s, the emphasis was placed on the individual, rather than the environment, as the cause for poor performance. The back-to-basics movement was a more conservative attempt to address learning problems by emphasizing standards, minimum competency testing, and the like.

Finally, in the 1990s, the educational environment is once again the condition to be remedied. This reflects the liberals' logic that it is the learning environment,

TABLE 15-3 Patterns of Policy Evolution Over Time

Policy Area	Pattern
1. Educational policy	1. Cyclical thesis
2. Welfare policy	2. Backlash thesis
3. Crime policy	3. Backlash thesis
4. Environmental policy	4. Policy-learning thesis

not the individual, that causes poor performance. In this instance, the environment is characterized by cultural hegemony, or a bias toward Western culture and institutions that prevents women and persons of color from gaining a sense of their own culture.

Thus, this area of public policy would seem to reflect Schlesinger's thesis that there is a recurring cycle of liberalism and conservatism every thirty years or so.

Welfare Policy Change

The history of U.S. welfare policy suggests that the backlash thesis best explains the evolution of this type of policy. Originally, our welfare policies reflected a more conservative, austere policy that put very little emphasis on societal responsibilities for the poor. This approach was reflected in the Elizabethan Poor Laws of 1601, which became the basis of U.S. welfare policy until the Great Depression in the 1930s. With the Depression, a reaction to this austere policy produced the beginnings of the welfare state in the United States in which society had a responsibility to the poor. This reaction to the earlier welfare policies lasted through the 1960s until a conservative backlash developed in the 1980s. By the 1980s, some came to believe that our welfare policies had created welfare dependency, in which our policies themselves created and sustained poverty. To a large extent, this turn in welfare policy better reflects the backlash thesis than the cyclical thesis, because the evolution of welfare policy does not seem to follow the thirty-year cycle that Schlesinger describes.

Crime Policy Change

Our crime policies are very much like our welfare policies in that there seems to be a conservative backlash against the more liberal, rehabilitation strategies that were pursued in the 1960s and 1970s. Today, incarceration (and deterrence) seems to be the preferred crime policy, along with get-tough policies including determinant sentencing, longer sentences, and greater attention to increasing the certainty that criminals will be caught and prosecuted. This change in policy seems to be more likely a reaction to the liberal policies that were pursued in the 1960s and 1970s, rather than a cycle as Schlesinger describes in his cyclical thesis.

Environmental Policy Change

In this area of public policy, unlike the other three areas, we seemed to have experienced some degree of policy learning, as evidenced by the emphasis on pollution prevention and cross-media pollution management. This area of public policy cannot be characterized by thirty-year cycles of liberalism and conservatism. Nor can it be characterized by a backlash from one type of policy to another. Rather, we seem to have learned from our past policies in this area and seem to be evolving toward much better designed environmental policies. To some extent, this evolutionary approach may be a result of our better understanding of this problem. We know what causes pollution and thus can better design policies to remedy it; unlike problems of poor student performance, poverty, or crime, we can better diagnose this problem and learn from past mistakes. In the areas of student performance, poverty, and crime, we still do not understand the root causes of these problems. Thus, our "solutions" tend to reflect public moods of liberalism or conservatism or a backlash from one approach to another.

SUMMARY

The previous chapters have discussed the nature of public policy, the evolution of public policy and policy studies, several phases of the policy cycle, and several substantive policy areas. As a final comment, we return to the point of departure of our discussion, that the student should be aware how our understanding of the policy process, as well as substantive policy, has evolved over time. Moreover, we can better appreciate how knowledge develops and the extent to which it may inform our policy choices. As policy scholars better understand the policy process, as well as problems such as poor educational performance, poverty, crime, and environmental pollution, perhaps we can design better substantive policies to remedy these public problems.

The study of public policy involves an understanding of the public policy process, the methods policy scientists used to study this process, and the substance of policy in areas of interest. All three areas interact with one another and are crucial to the ability to improve our system's performance in remedying public problems. Moreover, we can better understand where we are today by looking backward to where we have been. An understanding of historical context is fundamental to designing more effective policies in the future.

Finally, all of us are involved in the policy process whether we choose to be or not. Therefore, we must gain an appreciation of public policy, its challenges, and its opportunities. For whether we find ourselves located in the governmental bureaucracy, in policy institutes, in colleges or universities, or in the voting booth, all of us are policy analysts.

NOTES

1. See the work by Daniel Mazmanian and Paul Sabatier, *Implementation and Public Policy* (Glenview, IL: Scott, Foresman/Little, Brown, 1983); and Paul Sabatier and Hank Jenkins-Smith, eds., *Policy Change and Learning: An Advocacy Coalition Approach* (Boulder: WestviewPress, 1993).
2. For a manual on how to do third-generation implementation research, see Malcolm Goggin, Ann Bowman, James Lester, and Laurence O'Toole, *Implementation Theory and Practice: Toward a Third Generation* (New York: HarperCollins, 1990).

3. See Janet E. Frantz, "Reviving and Revising a Termination Model," *Policy Sciences* 25 (May 1992), pp. 175–189 for the most recent addition to this literature.

4. See Daniel C. McCool, *Public Policy Theories, Models, and Concepts: An Anthology* (Englewood Cliffs, NJ: Prentice-Hall, 1995), pp. 404–406.

5. See Arthur Schlesinger, Jr., *The Cycles of American History* (Boston: Houghton Mifflin, 1986); and his "America's Political Cycle Turns Again," *Wall Street Journal,* 10 December 1987. See also Walter Dean Burnham, *Critical Elections and the Mainsprings of American Politics* (New York: W. W. Norton, 1970). A more sophisticated version of the cycles model is presented in Samuel P. Huntington, *American Politics: The Promise of Disharmony* (Cambridge, MA: Belknap/Harvard University Press, 1981).

6. See Paul A. Sabatier, "Knowledge, Policy-Oriented Learning and Policy Change: An Advocacy Coalition Framework," *Knowledge: Creation, Utilization, Diffusion* 3, no. 4 (June 1987), pp. 649–692.

7. Paul A. Sabatier, "An Advocacy Coalition Framework of Policy Change and the Role of Policy-Oriented Learning Therein," *Policy Sciences* 21 (1988), pp. 129–168.

8. Ibid.

9. See Edwin Amenta and Theda Skocpol, "Taking Exception: Explaining the Distinctiveness of American Public Policies in the Last Century," in *The Comparative History of Public Policy,* ed. Francis G. Castles et al. (New York: Oxford University Press, 1989).

INDEX